THE LOST
MASTERS

THE LOST MASTERS

Grace and Disgrace in '68

CURT SAMPSON

ATRIA BOOKS

NEW YORK LONDON TORONTO SYDNEY

ATRIA BOOKS
1230 Avenue of the Americas
New York, NY 10020

Copyright © 2005 by Curt Sampson

Library of Congress Cataloging-in-Publication Data

Sampson, Curt.
The lost Masters / Curt Sampson.—1st Atria Books hardcover ed.
p. cm.
Includes index.
ISBN 978-0-7432-7423-4 (alk. paper)
1. Masters Golf Tournament (1968) I. Title.

GV970.3.M37S36   2005
796.352'66—dc22   2004062021

First Atria Books hardcover edition March 2005

1   3   5   7   9   10   8   6   4   2

ATRIA BOOKS is a trademark of Simon & Schuster, Inc.

Manufactured in the United States of America

For information regarding special discounts for bulk purchases,
please contact Simon & Schuster Special Sales at 1-800-456-6798 or
business@simonandschuster.com.

IN MEMORY OF LEO BECKMAN

CONTENTS

THE GOAT SONG

We live not only our own lives, but whether we know it or not, also the life of our time.

—LAURENS VAN DER POST, IN A MEMOIR
OF HIS RELATIONSHIP WITH CARL JUNG

Early April, 1968: "So, who's gonna win the Masters?"

"Jack," I said gravely. "Maybe Weiskopf."

The members were always asking us who we liked in the big events, or what was Gary Player really like, or what kind of ball did Nicklaus use, because we were hooked up. Once or twice each summer, a dozen or so teen-aged caddies from our club worked the Tour events in Cleveland and Akron. "Tell Arnold Palmer to put more fabric in his pants," a member said to me on the eve of a Cleveland Open, and he wasn't joking. He pinched the cloth covering his thigh. "Forty dollars I paid, and look!"

Caddie and player were paired by lottery—probably rigged lotteries, judging by the number of times the son of the president of the host club got Arnie. Usually we were assigned to Bill Parker or Warner Tyree or Charles Houts or someone equally niggardly and anonymous, but big bags came our way from time to time. My friend Rich once got Bruce Devlin, a great player and a generous man, who gave him a substantial tip: cash, a dozen Dots, and a black Spalding four wood. Pride and reluctance mixed in Rich when he showed us the club, as if he diminished his prize by giving us unworthy slobs a peek. Another friend, named Dan, looped for the mysterious and talented Bert Yancey, whom the papers referred to as "the sweet-swinging West Point drop-out." Yancey paid well but hardly said a word in their six days together, except to give this experienced caddie a tutorial in how to caddie. We were fascinated by the cool beauty of Yancey's swing and by the fact that he'd finished third in his first Masters in '67, one of the best-ever debuts at Augusta National.

We loved the Masters above all other tournaments, even the ones we worked. We caddied early Masters weekend if at all. After intense study of the sports page we watched the clock, waiting for the heaven of the CBS television broadcast. CBS gave us great announcers with wonderful voices—Pat Summerall, Frank Gleiber, Ray Scott, John Derr—no instructor/commentator offering the nerd's-eye view, only one or two former players who butchered the language, and hardly any commercials. And for the lucky few who could afford the hardware, color. Green grass, blue sky, black caddies, the green jacket.

In '68, we looked forward to the big deal at Augusta National even more than usual. Casual fans and diehards all desperately wanted what in the end that Masters could not provide: escape. Escape from the worst year in our lives, escape from the most divisive, discordant 365 days since the Civil War. But this Masters would conclude in shock and disbelief, two commodities we already had too much of.

As American society unraveled like a ball of yarn in 1968, with parents losing children in a war, is it a stretch to say this mere golf tournament rose to the level of tragedy? Perhaps the answer lies in the word itself, which derives from the Greek *tragos*, a male goat, and *oide*, song. Literally, then, tragedy is the song of the goat. The Masters of '68 produced two goats. One unfortunate was so like a favorite uncle everyone felt they knew him. The day he suffered so was his birthday, sharpening his anguish and our feeling for him. His face fell, his body slumped, and the nice man cried. He got all the sympathy. The other player was a goat in the scapegoat sense of the word, one who takes the blame for others. He got all the shit.

The perspiring arts produced another shocker six months later, and two more goats.

In the summer Olympics in Mexico City, Americans finished first and third in the two-hundred-meter run, a much-desired moment of pride for the live TV audience in the United States. But then the athletes turned their moment on the stair-step medal winners' podium into a Statement. It was *so* 1968. While a tape of the Star Spangled Banner played in the cool night air, San Jose State teammates Tommie Smith, the gold medalist, and John Carlos, who won the bronze, closed their eyes, bowed their heads, and stuck gloved fists into the air—to remind us of the oppression of black men and women in the United States, they said later.

The gesture backfired. Smith and Carlos were immediately booted from the team by the United States Olympic Committee and banned from the Olympic Village. Although they thought of themselves as brave idealists, the sprinters were excoriated as disloyal bums, and hearts hardened against their cause.

The effect of the mess at the Masters took a much longer time to reveal itself.

In the hundred days before the '68 Masters, world events clicked in random but repetitive two-bullet bursts, like staccato fire from an M-16.

In late December, at Cam Ranh Bay in South Vietnam, President Lyndon Johnson urged soldiers to ignore the war protests back home. Two days later, police arrested 546 war protestors in New York City, including Dr. Benjamin Spock, author of best-selling books on how to bring up babies, and poet Allen Ginsberg.

January: recognizing a dazed, impotent giant, North Korea seized the USS *Pueblo*, its commander Lloyd M. Bucher, and its crew of eighty-two. Eight days later. North Vietnam attacked one hundred cities in the south, from Saigon to the Highlands. The Tet Offensive achieved a public-relations victory for the North, if not a military one, in that it showed that the Viet Cong could carry the fight throughout the divided country.

On February 1, former vice-president Richard "Peace With Honor" Nixon declared his candidacy for president. A week later, former Alabama governor George "Segregation Forever" Wallace also threw his hat in the big ring.

March 16: Charlie Company, under Lieutenant William Calley, massacred most of the village of My Lai; of the 347 dead, many were women and children. Fifteen days later, President Lyndon Johnson announced the beginning of the end of the bombing of North Vietnam. At the end of his speech, LBJ added a shocker. "I shall not seek, nor will I accept, the nomination of my party as your president."

April 4: As he and his aides prepared to go out to dinner, Dr. Martin Luther King, Jr., leaned over the railing of the second-story balcony of the Lorraine Motel on Mulberry Street, cheap lodging in a bad neighborhood, in Memphis. Jesse Jackson was introducing him to Ben Branch, who was standing below, at street level. Branch was the leader of the Breadbasket Band, which would be entertaining at the rally that evening in support of the striking Memphis garbagemen. Smiling, Dr. King asked the musician to play "Take My Hand, Precious Lord" and to "play it real pretty." His last words. The group heard a muffled but startling thud, like a firecracker exploding under a pillow. The sniper's bullet ripped off Dr. King's necktie and threw him backward. Blood poured from a gaping wound in his neck.

And here Augusta, Georgia, appeared as a faint, three-part footnote in the history of this crazy time.

Eleven days before his death, King had stood behind the pulpit at the Beulah Grove Baptist Church in Augusta and addressed a crowd that spilled out onto Poplar Road. "I couldn't get in," recalls William Howard, who'd left his 3:30-to-midnight job in the psychiatric ward at the VA hospital early, but not early enough. "There was a loudspeaker, but I couldn't hardly hear him, either."

"This country has lost its sense of direction, its sense of purpose," Dr. King told the six hundred people who'd jammed into the tiny church. "For we cannot fight an immoral war in Vietnam, where many of our young men are dying, and at the same time finance the war on poverty."

By linking the civil-rights and antiwar movements, King had ratcheted up the tension around his every public utterance and action. Increasingly, the protest marches he led were degenerating into riots. Editorial writers who had proclaimed the 1963 Nobel Peace Prize winner an unalloyed hero now called him unpatriotic, and out of his depth, and worse. Did his opposition to the war cause his death?

King had become so controversial and his safety so difficult to guarantee that it had taken a lot of effort to find a place for him to speak in Augusta. He tried the black Baptist churches first. Tabernacle? No. Thankful? No. Springfield? Sorry. The City of Augusta's Bell Auditorium? No. Paine College? No. Finally he got an affirmative from Beulah Grove, which sat between the red-brick sprawl of a housing project and the equally sprawling Tulip Cup factory.

After his sermon, and after shaking a few hundred hands, King checked into the Uptowner Hotel ("Dine in Our Delightful Camellia Room," read their print ad. "Relax in Our Sans Souci Lounge.") The Uptowner was downtown; Augusta's core city was much more the center of things then than now, and some of its hotels and restaurants advertised that they were FULLY AIR-CONDITIONED. In the morning, King flew out as he'd come in, in a twin-engine prop plane. Ten days later, he died on the concrete balcony outside his room at the Lorraine Motel.

And various inner cities burned. Fire lit the night sky and thirty-one people died in the worst racial rioting in U.S. history. Washington, D.C., looked like it did the night the British overran it in the War of 1812. Combat troops ringed the White House and a machine gun poised on a tripod outside the Capitol Building. Boston was one city that was not torched, thanks in large part to Augusta's most prominent citizen.

On the day after Dr. King's death, soul singer James Brown, the Hardest Working Man in Show Business and a native and resident of Augusta, was scheduled to play the Boston Garden. Brown had a new hit—"I Got the Feelin' "—to go with a dozen others, such as "In a Cold Sweat" and "It's a Man's Man's Man's World," and he expected an audience of fourteen or fifteen thousand. But Mayor Kevin White asked him to cancel the show to keep people off the street. Then someone came up with an idea: broadcast the concert live on TV. Mayor White guaranteed the gate, so Brown allowed WGBH, the local public station, to roll in its cameras and lights. "Let's not do anything to dishonor Dr. King," Brown said between songs in the nearly empty theater, the spotlight glowing off his blue-black pompadour. "Stay home. You kids, especially." Roxbury, Boston's mostly black neighborhood, remained eerily quiet.

President Johnson declared Sunday, April 7—Palm Sunday—a national day of mourning for Dr. King. On Monday, Coretta Scott King, Martin's widow, led a silent march through Memphis, and fifteen thousand marched with her. At the memorial service in Atlanta at Ebenezer Baptist, King's home church, twenty-three U.S. senators attended, as did Bobby Kennedy and five other presidential aspirants, Jacqueline Kennedy, Sammy Davis, Jr., Jackie Robinson, and Harry Belafonte. About one hundred thousand people mourned in person and about 120 million watched on TV.

On Thursday, April 11, Congress passed the 1968 Civil Rights Act that prohibited racial discrimination in the sale or rental of housing.

And the Masters began. Augusta inched its way into the national consciousness a third time, more emphatically.

It was only a golf tournament, just a little story played out against a larger context. But the '68 Masters became something else—a morality play, a rumination on fairness, and a demonstration of panic and grace by men under pressure. It was also an event disturbing and strange enough to elbow aside King, Vietnam, and the presidential race for a while. The leading men were not Palmer or Nicklaus, rivals who were then the very definition of professional golf. Instead, three actors from the chorus stepped forward.

The winner received thirty telegrams the day after the tournament—"not all of them nice," his wife said, a bit puzzled. The new champion eventually received about five hundred pieces of hate mail, all of which he saved, for some reason. Now they're in a cardboard box in his barn, food for mice. "I'd like to put you and that bastard Sonny Liston in concrete and drop you both in the Atlantic Ocean," wrote one of his unwanted correspondents. "I hope you burn in hell for all eternity," wrote another. A heckler at one of his first post-Masters tournaments offered a particularly brutal comment in a loud voice. The new champion didn't react, but Gardner Dickinson, his playing partner, could not abide such rudeness, and strode angrily into the crowd and rebuked the man. Snide comments floated over the gallery ropes all year.

They booed the defending champion when he returned to Augusta in 1969, a sound as shocking as catcalls in church. The scorned man pretended not to notice, but he couldn't pretend he didn't care.

THE LOST
MASTERS

CHAPTER ONE

MR. JONES

Golf is not fair. Neither is birth.

—JACK BURKE, JR.

Mr. Jones waited for his company.

He sat in a light green cloth-covered chair in a tiny room on the second floor of a big house on Tuxedo Road in Druid Hills, Atlanta's wealthiest neighborhood. Over his pajamas he wore a bathrobe of dark silk, a garment long enough to cover his swollen, useless legs and billowy enough to hide the plastic tube of a catheter and its collection bag. Across the arms of the chair rested a bean-shaped hospital tray, made of a shiny metal. On the tray someone had placed five cigarettes in holders, a bulky silver lighter, and two cups with straws, one containing water, the other, bourbon. He didn't touch any of it.

The next few hours would relieve the pain and thinking about pain that consumed most of his day. He had a withering disease of the spinal cord no one knew much about. Each day syringomyelia consumed a little more of him, until he couldn't walk, couldn't grasp, couldn't even pee. In his waking rigor mortis, Jones's torso and limbs atrophied and his hands curled into

1

claws that twisted inward toward his forearms. His agony could be masked a bit by codeine or whiskey but it never really left. He was sixty-six and had been slowly dying for twenty years. He didn't have much time left.

It was the first week of May 1968. Jones had returned from Augusta two weeks earlier, where he'd attended both the best and the worst Masters ever. The best because of its fantastic finish and the worst because of, well, that's a long story. He'd been ill during the week with something like flu, an almost intolerable addition to his usual burden. He had decided—with help (or pushing, depending on who's telling the story) from Masters and Augusta National cofounder Cliff Roberts—to forgo his traditional interview of the winner for television. Influenza or not, the TV thing might have been scotched anyway, since Jones looked like hell and, worse, often drooled when he spoke.

All tournament week Jones lay in bed or sat by a curtained window in his house by the tenth tee, swallowing antibiotics and watching the passing parade. Small groups came by to chat, including Herbert Warren Wind, a man with elephant ears and a lyrical pen who wrote golf essays for *The New Yorker*. Wind listened, rapt, as Jones talked happily about the superiority of very hard and fast golf surfaces, in particular the Old Course at St. Andrews, and a match he had there with Cyril Tolley in 1927. "I could listen to Jones all day," Wind would write. But he couldn't, because Jones couldn't talk very long. Fatigue rolled in like fog and the visits ended. He would never see most of these friends again. None of them knew but all might have suspected that this would be the last Masters for Bobby Jones.

Once he'd been a hero big enough to close down lower Manhattan. After winning the first two legs of the Grand Slam in July 1930, Jones looked up from the rear deck of a black convertible into a snowstorm of ticker tape, his hair parted down the center as if by a laser beam, his manner modest, though not entirely happy, and a look about him much older than his twenty-eight years. The motorcade passed beneath the office window of Charles de Clifford Roberts, a broker of stocks and a student of wealth and power. The attentive veteran of World War I and Wall Street had been friends with Jones for several years and had found out what the man of the hour really wanted: privacy in combination with a place to play golf. Only two years later, Augusta National opened, delivering both.

Augusta National arrived with a wondrous network of rich and powerful new friends, many of whom—especially Roberts—wanted to increase Jones's wealth. They succeeded with all of it. The club became a kind of heaven on earth for the power elite; the club's annual Masters Tournament soon stood with the World Series as an event; and Jones did well enough with his investment in an Atlanta member's company—Coca-Cola—to reside in a Venetian Gothic mansion grand enough to have a name: Whitehall.

But God is a comedian playing to an audience that's afraid to laugh. Just when the middle-aged Jones should have been enjoying things most, with his three children grown and his fortune secure, that seven-syllable disease invaded his body. Jones did not complain in public or talk much about his illness with his peers or the press. Those who knew him were awed by the courage he showed in the things he didn't say.

But now, after twenty years of compounding misery, Jones had had just about enough. "My life day and night is about as nearly miserable as one could imagine," he would write to Dr. H. Houston Merritt at Columbia-Presbyterian Medical Center on September 10, 1968. "I am sixty-six years old. I have wasted away to a bare skeleton and keep going only with the aid of three or four devoted people. I have chronic asthmatic bronchitis, a low blood pressure, and for several years have been wearing a permanent catheter because of a slight prostate enlargement."

Two days later, Jones wrote another note, this one to his own doctor, Ralph Murphy: "I have a very real horror of spending my final years lying paralyzed or in twisted agony. Any other way out, no matter how quickly it comes, would be better. I am sure you will agree." He wanted to die.

But he didn't die. Until the day in 1970 when he absolutely couldn't, he still went to his law office, still played his role as golf's gray eminence. He signed his dictated letters by gripping a tennis ball punctured with a pen, unembarrassed that the outsized letters of his "Bob" wandered like a child's first attempt at cursive. His mind was still sharp, those who knew him say, but his stamina was obviously shot to hell. In the eleventh hour of the '68 Masters, with the world waiting (at least some of it) outside his door, he'd been called on to make a momentous decision.

Had he been up to it? Which had been stronger in him, his intellect or his disease?

Now, in the gentle May evening, at his home in Atlanta, Jones waited in his little room at the top of the stairs. He listened for the doorbell's three-part chime.

Out in the street, a college student named John Lambert slowed his car at the wrought-iron fence and turned right, into the Joneses' driveway. He'd left the Sigma Chi house at Georgia Tech ten minutes before and had driven carefully for his first day on an odd job. His route took him from the fraternity house on Techwood Road north to Hemphill, to Northside Drive, then over the expressway, past Bobby Jones Municipal Golf Course, right on West Paces Ferry, left on Tuxedo. He paused for a moment as he got out of the car, looking at the nice-enough-to-live-in garage/maintenance building to the right, at the two-story white stone mansion with its porte cochere to the left, and at the flagstick and immaculate putting green in the front yard. With gracefully trimmed shrubs accenting tall white columns, the house looked as though it belonged to a Renaissance count. Lambert hadn't realized the Joneses were so wealthy.

A nurse led him up a winding marble staircase. A door opened at the top of the stairs and out of it came billows of smoke and Mrs. Mary Jones, a statuesque woman with short dark hair and Lauren Bacall's voice. "It's nice to meet you, John," she said in a two-pack-a-day contralto. "We're so glad you're here." She'd been treated for cancer of the larynx a few years earlier.

Mrs. Jones took the college boy across the carpeted hall to meet Mr. Jones, a gaunt, twisted figure in a dimly lit eight-by-twelve-foot room. He greeted the young man warmly and invited him to sit but to turn on the TV first. Jones bent his head down to the tray and took one of the holdered cigarettes in his mouth. Then he punched the button on the heavy silver lighter with his right thumb and lit the tip of the cigarette to show his guest that he was not quite helpless.

For most of the next three years, from 1968 to 1971, Lambert visited the dying golf hero two, three, or four evenings a week, one of several brothers of Sigma Chi who sat with Jones for a couple of hours every night. The job required a polite but unintimidated young man with conversational skill and physical strength. "In '67 or early '68 Mr. Jones had an operation to relieve the pressure in his sinus cavity and that seemed to be pretty much the end," Lambert explains. "He lost the strength to get from a chair to his wheelchair or to get from the wheelchair to bed. That's why he needed big guys, athletes. You'd pick him up under the armpits to move him. He wasn't heavy, of course, but he was deadweight, and you'd have your arms extended." Lambert played a year of basketball for Tech. He stood six-one and weighed 205.

The college kids and the dying hero would chat about Tech

football and basketball. Jones still loved the place; he'd been a Sigma Chi himself and a mechanical engineering major there sixty-something years before. Mostly, they watched television. But never the news; the news during the Vietnam era was invariably bad and Jones wanted above all to laugh. Once he almost fell out of his chair chortling at *The Bill Cosby Show,* as the star picked up a date in a garbage dump truck and then activated the dump when trying to turn on the windshield wipers. "You know what time it is, John?" Jones would ask Lambert on Wednesday nights. "It's Al Mundy time." And he'd grin, exposing tobacco-browned teeth and a remarkable determination to fight despair. Alexander Mundy didn't seem to be much of a weapon in his battle. In *It Takes a Thief,* Mundy—played by the ultra-suave Robert Wagner—was a former second-story man now stealing for the government. ABC ran sixty-six episodes of the series and sixty-six times Wagner kissed the girl, recovered the microfilm, and wore a tuxedo.

Night after night, Jones would sip and smoke and hope for a laugh. Then a sturdy college kid would pick him up and put him in his wheelchair, roll him to his bedroom, lift him again, and put him into bed. Lambert stepped on the catheter once, which must have been painful, but the old man didn't make a sound. Another time, the maid's TV caught fire, but Jones's son Robert T. III was there. He picked up his father, cradling him in his arms like a baby, and carried him out into the front yard. Other than that, the evening ritual never varied. The visits began at 7:00 P.M. and were as short as two hours or as long as three—it depended on Mr. Jones's strength and what was on the tube.

"We all knew who he was—Bobby Jones was a household name in Atlanta, like Coca-Cola," Lambert says. "We knew he founded Augusta National and the Masters, that he won the Grand Slam. But we never asked too many questions. Mary had cautioned us about talking about the past. And no pictures. 'He doesn't want anyone to see what he looks like,' she told us."

On those warm nights in the spring of 1968 Lambert wondered what had really happened at the just-completed Masters, but of course, he dare not ask. And Mr. Jones never volunteered. There were no laughs in that subject.

Three weeks before, Hoyt had docked Jones's yacht–like Cadillac Fleetwood under the canopy outside the front door. Hoyt—no one ever used his first name, George—had for years worked as the family's servant and driver. Weekdays, he shaved and dressed Mr. Jones and drove him to work at the law office on Poplar Street in downtown Atlanta. He'd been a janitor at the gym at Emory University, and had recruited the first college kid to come sit with his boss, a swimmer named Jack Schroeder. Now the black man loaded luggage and Mr. and Mrs. Jones into the big blue car and drove it slowly out of Atlanta's mansion district, dense with trees with new leaves and blooming shrubs of red, white, and pink. In ten minutes the waxed Caddy glided onto Interstate 20, heading east, toward Augusta. The car thumped gently over the seams in the concrete.

Swords, Siloam, Norwood . . . the little East Georgia towns stood as still as hitchhikers as the big car rushed past. What kept Jones from telling Hoyt to exit up in Mesena and just turn the damn car around? Jones carried on because he loved the Masters as a parent loves a child and he knew the end was near. Besides, Augusta in April was as close to a gentleman's paradise as anyone could hope—the scents of springtime flowers in bloom, the sounds and smell of bourbon poured over ice, reunion with dear friends, and an air on Sunday as electric as a heavyweight title fight. That was Masters fever. Jones wanted to catch it one more time.

Actual competitors felt the fever all the more acutely, of

course. The 1965 PGA champion, Dave Marr, commented famously that he began to choke the moment he drove up Magnolia Drive, Augusta National's driveway, and that he felt as if he wouldn't get to heaven if he didn't play well. A redheaded law student from the University of Virginia felt the same anxiety.

The dreaming man is a haunted man, so they say, and Marvin McCrary "Vinny" Giles's dreams would not stop. For weeks before the tournament, he tossed and turned at night and kept to himself during the day. Such behavior was completely outside the norm for Giles, who was normally cheerful to the point of goofiness. He was twenty-two, married, and a hell of a golfer, having merited an invitation to the '68 Masters because of his runner-up finish in the 1967 U.S. Amateur. His number-one goal in golf since the first time he picked up a club had been to compete at Augusta National, but at night it seemed to him that the day would never come.

During the day, he fondled the little square of paper he'd wanted so long.

The Board of Governors
of the
Augusta National Golf Club
cordially invites you to participate in the
Nineteen Hundred and Sixty-Eight
Masters Tournament
to be held at
Augusta, Georgia
the eleventh, twelfth, thirteenth and fourteenth of April
Robert Tyre Jones, Jr.
President
RSVP

"My plan had been to drive to Augusta after my classes on Saturday morning," Giles recalls. "But when I woke up on Thursday morning, I said to my wife, 'I don't think I can wait.' "

So a full week before the competition was to start, Giles packed his black '65 Mustang with clubs and clothes and kissed his wife, Key, goodbye. Deep shadows crisscrossed Magnolia Lane when he pulled into Augusta National's driveway. At about that time, Martin Luther King fell bleeding with a hole in his neck, sending the nation into shock and violence. "He died that week?" Giles says now. "Until you told me, I didn't know."

Vinny bunked in the attic at the club, in a little five-bed dormitory called the Crow's Nest. All amateur participants were invited to stay there for a token charge. "It was really spartan then," Giles says. "They didn't even have doors on the rooms, just curtains." The room's main feature was overhead, a four-sided cupola. At daybreak, Giles got out of bed and climbed the twelve steps to the top of the Nest, the morning sunlight illuminating the hair on his naked legs. Observing the world through a window in the little dome made it easy to pretend it was a hundred years ago. Those men mowing and raking the golf course would have been slaves tending the indigo plants that once grew on this august patch of Georgia. Modernity lurked two miles to the north, as cars droned past on Interstate 20, but Giles could not see or hear them.

I-20 and the rest of the interstate highway system had been the brainchild and perhaps the greatest legacy of an Augusta National member. As he toured conquered Germany, General Dwight Eisenhower had been greatly impressed with Hitler's broad four-lane autobahns. Such highways would simplify the evacuation of major cities in case of nuclear attack, a point President Eisenhower made when selling the idea to Congress. The American autobahn transformed the landscape and the culture, speeding up the lives of people in a thousand different professions, including the original kings of the road, touring golf professionals.

Flying would come later. In the sixties, for most of the players most of the time, the end of one tournament meant a long drive to the next one. The straight lines and engineered blandness of the interstate highway system made contemplation almost unavoidable between Jacksonville and Greensboro, Greensboro and Augusta, Augusta and Dallas, Dallas and Houston, and Houston and New Orleans. But more chances to think were unwelcome in a game in which the noise in your head was really the only thing that prevented the perfect execution of every shot. Thinking led to ambiguity, which led to doubt, sometimes even to fear. Thinking was the enemy.

Popular culture romanticized car travel—especially *Route 66*, an early sixties TV show about two young guys and their Corvette convertible. The road was the destination, as various books and songs and films told us, and rootlessness was cool. But the reality for the touring pro on a never-ending loop between distant Holiday Inns was that too much time in a Buick could just about drive you crazy.

At least they got nowhere fast; back then you could go eighty legally on some stretches of interstate. The golf pro's cars had long wheelbases, bench seats, and big engines that burned a lot of thirty-four-cents-a-gallon gas; five years before the Arab oil embargo, no one talked mpg. Their vehicles were made in Detroit and didn't always have seat belts or air conditioners. No recorded music—bulky eight-track tape players didn't become available in cars until the early seventies, and, of course, no cell phones. So the long-haul drivers twirled the dials on the radio. The Beatles were still in business; "Lady Madonna" was their hit. Black stations across the country played a new song—an anthem, really—performed by Augusta, Georgia's own James Brown: "Say It Loud—I'm Black and I'm Proud." The four most popular songs in April 1968 were wistful—"The Dock of the Bay" by Otis Redding and "Cry Like a Baby" by the Box Tops—or so sweet they could induce coma: "Young Girl" by Gary Puckett and the Union Gap, and Bobby Goldsboro's cloying "Honey." When the music and commercials stopped at the top of the hour the news gave the latest body count from the war in Vietnam.

The golfers gripped their steering wheels and listened to Goldsboro's whiney composition for the hundredth time and, inevitably, they thought about money, not "Honey." On his drive to Augusta, Don January chewed on the 73 he shot in the final round of the Greater Greensboro Open, an expensive finish to a tournament he'd begun with rounds of 68-67-66. He finished tied for eighth and won $3,895.84, when a mere 70 would have given him a tie for second and about $10,000. "That was about a four- or five-hour drive," January recalls. "I didn't dwell on it. At times like that, you just had to regroup and forget it. If you let something like that stick in your craw, you'd go nuts." Only Palmer and a few others made significant endorsement money; tournament winnings were vital to everyone else.

While the Jones party rolled east, January's was one of a score of cars with clubs in the trunk approaching Augusta from the north. About a third of the seventy-six golfers who'd made the cut at the Greater Greensboro Open owned invitations to the Masters. The drive from Greensboro to Augusta took a tolerable amount of time, and the Carolinas looked gorgeous in April sunshine. But the golfers were tired. And they were late—twice the GGO had come to a complete halt. When rain washed out the Friday round, the best game in town became watching National Guard troops march through the drizzle into downtown Greensboro. The mayor, hoping to prevent a riot following the sniper murder of Dr. King in Memphis on Thursday, imposed a 7:00 P.M. curfew and a temporary ban on liquor sales. The golf resumed on Saturday—Billy Casper shot 67 and led by two—but President Johnson declared Sunday a national day of mourning and the tournament shut down again. Julius Boros, a relaxed man, went bass fishing. Casper, a religious man, spoke at a worship service at a Church of Jesus Christ of Latter-Day Saints. And Palmer, a driven man, got into his jet, flew to Augusta, and played a practice round. He shot 68 and jetted back to Greensboro.

The prelude finally concluded at dawn on Monday, thirty-six holes on a soggy golf course. Casper won and Palmer finished tied for fifth, good omens for taciturn Billy, the most boring great player in golf history, and for Arnie, the most exciting. Tommy Bolt observed a little cruelly that Casper was the only guy who played the tour for twenty-five years and never made a friend. Palmer, on the other hand, had thousands of best friends. Off the course he had an about-to-burst-out-laughing manner that suggested you and he were in on the same joke. In competition, he cared so passionately about the outcome of each of his shots that spectators became participants in his drama, not just observers. Casper treated his golf like a day at the office, refusing to emote. "I was trying to be like Hogan," he said. "A lot of us were."

In a day or two they would all stand together. The confluence of Arnie, Vinny Giles, and Bobby Jones symbolized the magnetic pull of the Masters, the only event that attempted a reunion of champions from earlier eras within a big-time competition. Add the magnolia-lined driveway, southern hospitality, spring in east Georgia, flawless tournament administration, and a golf course as thrilling as a roller-coaster ride, and you had a thing pleasing in all its proportions.

Except that in 1968, nothing flowed smoothly, everything

was an argument, and no one gave an inch. This Masters would be like a soap opera on Telemundo, an overwrought thing with tears and passion and close-up reaction shots of each of the leading men after each crazy twist in the plot. The drama played out against a background of war—not just Vietnam, but a vicious little fight for the control of professional golf. Fed up with being a mere adjunct to the parent organization (the PGA of America), and sensing that money could be made, the tour players had threatened secession. Lawyers were hired. Feelings ran high. The media sided with the club pros. Some, like Gardner Dickinson, were firebrands for severing the union, some were opposed, and to the frank disappointment of both sides, Palmer sat on the fence. He proposed a compromise that went nowhere.

Anyway, Arnie had his own conflict. He wouldn't admit it, but he'd been recently deposed as the best player in the world by a farctate blond from Ohio. He did not like it. The new best player had a logo, a yellow bear in profile. "Why do you have a pig on your chest?" Arnie would ask when he saw it on someone's shirt, and then he might excuse himself to "go take a Nicklaus."

Nicklaus's big problem was not acknowledging his big problem. He was blameless compared to the chest-thumping dumbasses who now populate a lot of spectator sports, but he and they had the same blind spot: they were entertainers who didn't care enough about what people thought of them. Jack played golf like a god, but his too-tight clothes on his too-heavy body made him look like a sausage with arms. "Nicklaus looks like a good golfer," Snead said. "A couple of good golfers." While many of the other fellas were allowing their hair to grow away from 1955, Jack kept his locks short and immobilized with Vitalis.

He took too long to do what he did. With eyebrows knit, and standing over putts like a bird waiting for a worm, Big Jack played the calculating technician to Palmer's inspirational, improvisational hero. "The race is not always to the swift," wrote Jim Murray in the *Los Angeles Times*. "Just look at Jack Nicklaus."

All of this took the best player in golf downmarket. During the '68 Masters, Jack Nicklaus Autograph Model golf balls were available at area Firestone Tire dealers, three for a buck thirty-three; pro shop brands like Wilson Staff, Dot, and Maxfli cost $1.25 each. You could get an entire set of Jack Nicklaus clubs, with a bag, for $99.95.

Jack's greatest sin wasn't too much fat or not enough hair, however, it was beating Arnie in Augusta, the epicenter of his popularity. Palmer won the Masters in '58, '60, '62, and '64. Nicklaus barged in with far less popular wins in '63, '65 and '66. After one of these victories, probably the '66, a spectator from Augusta remembers being stuck for almost an hour in traffic outside the club on Washington Road. He decided to bail out at a McDonald's. And there in one of the three-deep lines stood Jack and Barbara Nicklaus and their three children. No one approached him with congratulations or a request for an autograph. If it had been Palmer ordering Happy Meals and Big Macs, they'd have had a riot.

In this era of bad feeling, pros from Europe, South Africa, New Zealand, and Australia competed for the first time on the U.S. tour in significant numbers. Bruce Devlin, for example, moved to Florida in '68 after six years of grueling commutes from his home near Sydney. His next-door neighbor in Pompano Beach, Bert Yancey, seemed pleasant enough, but Devlin found that some of his new peers "just had a red ass for anybody who wasn't from the United States. 'This is our tour' they said." Which American pros welcomed him least? "Dickinson," Devlin says. "Dan Sikes. Bob Goalby."

Independently, incredibly, English professional Tony Jacklin names the same three names. "Goalby was a hard case," Jacklin says. "I played a round of golf with him at the Tournament of Champions and he didn't say a word to me. Gardner was bloody awful, mean-spirited. And Dan Sikes. . . . They resented you, like you were stealing their money. An unpleasant experience, being around those guys. Thank God that group was the end of it."

Professional golfers not from the United States were called "foreign," a term Devlin particularly disliked. But nothing seemed to bother the two best "internationals" (the modern term). Gary Player, in fact, was more likely to do the bothering than to let anything or anyone put him off his game. A five-foot-seven-inch pro from South Africa, Player possessed a Hogan-like work ethic and a somewhat off-putting intensity. So great was his enthusiasm for Gary Player that early in his career he had trouble getting anyone to play a practice round with him. In an older man, his demeanor might be described as extreme heartiness; in a thirty-three-year-old it looked like something else. Perhaps his unswerving, occasionally laughable positivism was a shield—against bigger, stronger, opponents—or to ward off his poor boy's perpetual insecurity. And another thing: Unlike any other player on the tour, Player was under attack. As the most visible South African in the United States, and probably the world, he was targeted by antiapartheid demonstrators. One of them would scream as Player putted from a foot in the 1969 PGA Championship. He missed and lost by one—and somehow kept his positive attitude.

Depending on the week, Player was the second-, third-, or fourth-best player in the world, behind Jack, but in there with Palmer and Casper. Although he hadn't won a tournament in the United States in three years, that win had been in the U.S. Open.

The most recent major-winner of the internationals was

Roberto Ricardo De Vicenzo, the British Open champion of 1967. Although he'd been playing in the United States since 1947, he didn't play here much, so American fans were only dimly aware of his accomplishments. Just as much as Player, who likes to talk about the twelve million airplane miles he's flown, the man from Buenos Aires played everywhere on the globe they have a golf course. He'd eventually win one hundred relatively important international tournaments, including four on the U.S. tour. Counting all his Uruguay Opens, his career win total swells to an astounding 257, the most ever. In that sense, at least, he was the best player in the world. But he was getting old—forty-four—and his best days were behind him.

Everything about him was big—talent, strength, personality, nose, feet, and hands. Freddie Bennett, the Augusta National caddie master, liked De Vicenzo as a person but did not look forward to seeing him in April. His handshake was excruciating and he liked to shake hands every day. "A huge man, strong," says Bennett. "Man's hands were so big it gave you a headache.

"But people would con him. I heard he won a tournament and he gave all the money away."

Perhaps Roberto shook hands so hard because he felt so much love for his fellow man. His warmth and humanity couldn't be missed by golf galleries around the world or, more impressive, by his fellow competitors. "The greatest guy I ever met in my life," says Bob Rosburg, whose grim competitive demeanor was the opposite of De Vicenzo's sunny approach.

"A real gentleman," says Doug Ford. "A delight," says Jacklin. "An inspiring man. I remember playing with Roberto at Augusta in '71 or '72. I had hurried all day and it had cost me. He always called me 'Boy.' When we walk off the eighteenth green, he says, 'Boy, I'm glad I'm not you. You can't win before you play. You have to be like the boxer. Always be ready to duck.'

"When I won the U.S. Open [in '70], he says, 'Now, boy, just be nice to people and you'll make millions.' "

De Vicenzo's muscular wrists and mitts helped make him one of the longest hitters in golf, despite a rather punchy, truncated swing. But his hands didn't look that good on a putter. On the greens, with his big-headed Ray Cook mallet, he always seemed to be guessing; the great putters—like Palmer, Nicklaus, Bob Charles, and Casper—looked as though they knew. If you can't putt, you can't do squat at Augusta National no matter how well you hit it. Roberto was a case in point. They'd been inviting him to the Masters since 1950, but a tie for tenth in '67 had been his high-water mark.

A more likely foreign contender was the enigmatic George Knudson of Canada. He had won two consecutive tournaments in the desert in the winter and he ranked second on the money list with $50,655. A wraithlike figure, he liked to drink and he liked to be alone, usually a bad combination, but here he was with a better first quarter than almost anyone else in the game. The other guys didn't know what to think of him. "In Phoenix, I saw him on Saturday night, in the hotel bar," recalls Miller Barber. "I was going out to dinner. I came back a couple of hours later and he hadn't moved." Barber remembers that incident from February 1968 because Knudson was at that moment leading the Phoenix Open and the next day he would win it. Another story had Knudson waking up on a locker room bench the following week, at the Tucson Open on Sunday morning, in his Saturday clothes. True or not, he won Tucson, too.

Knudson was not the only man holding a cocktail. "We drank," says January. "Compared to the current tour, we drank heavily. Not that everyone was getting loop-legged, but some guys would have a beer just to hold 'em until they could get to the bar for a whiskey."

January shakes his head when he recalls the time he tried to keep up with Hogan and Cary Middlecoff as they drank postround martinis. Dan Sikes also set a fast pace in the nineteenth hole, January says. Doug Sanders and Raymond Floyd, the '68 tour's top two all-arounders, shared their thoughts on escaping pressure with *Golf World UK* in a 1972 story entitled "SEX . . . is it out-of-bounds?" "Let's put it this way," said Sanders, who loved to claim he spilled more booze than the other fellows drank. "I play better when I am relaxed and sex makes me relaxed. That's why I like late starting times, so I don't have to get up too early . . . I can relax a little more."

Floyd, a husky pro from Fort Bragg, North Carolina, whose tight pants looked all the tighter because they had no hip pockets, described his ideal tournament preparation: "A few drinks the evening before the practice rounds, and if one is available, a chick. I am an insomniac and do not like to sleep before nearly dawn. But when the tournament begins I make sure I get to bed by one."

A woman walks into a bar and sees, no joke, Ford, Art Wall, and Goalby. "So this gal comes up to Bob and says, 'I'm trying to get away from Gay Brewer,' " Ford recalls. "So we all go up to my room. Then there's a knock on the door—Brewer. So everybody runs into Frank Stranahan's room." Stranahan, a weightlifting and fitness devotee, looked at this giggling group and said, 'Jesus Christ, is this the way you guys train?' "

Golf, booze, sex . . . and drugs? The times, they were a-changin'. "A long time ago, a college friend came to a tournament and we went to dinner," Nicklaus recalled for *Golf Digest*. "He asked me if it was OK to smoke. I said, 'Of course.' He said 'No, Jack, you don't understand. I don't mean smoke what I always used to smoke.' " The Bear joined his friend in the fun, but never again, because by eight o'clock he was ready to hibernate.

In this happy atmosphere, Lonesome George doesn't look so bad. He could obviously handle his drink.

Knudson was mysterious, with his dark glasses, his solitude, and his eerie channeling of Ben Hogan, but Bert Yancey was a riddle. That he had suffered a "nervous breakdown" in his fourth and last year at West Point was no secret on the tour. But why would a kid from Florida who loved golf go to a school so rigorous, so strict, and so cold? And what the hell was a nervous breakdown anyway? How could you play golf as coolly as Yancey did and still be so nervous that you broke down? Maybe he just didn't want to be a first lieutenant on the ground in the next foreign war. But Yancey provided no answers. He seemed uninterested in being one of the boys, most of whom treated him like a contagion. His intellect and his disease isolated him.

Some years later, CBS approached Yancey about doing a movie of his life. He had other things on his mind. But one thing more than most: the Masters.

Although the weight of his preoccupations made relationships difficult, Bert Yancey had friends. He had a special bond, in fact, with the leading money winner ($67,085) going into the Masters, Tom Weiskopf, who had an obvious problem of his own. In its Masters preview, *Sports Illustrated* described the monkey on Tommy's back as "an almost psychotic temper," a harsh assessment but probably true. Weiskopf mixed high expectations with a low tolerance for adversity, but he had so much game he often won or came close in spite of himself. There were self-esteem issues, too. Like Nicklaus, Tom was from Ohio and had gone to Ohio State, and he hit it a mile. Everyone compared him to Jack, expected him to approach Jack's accomplishment, but the monkey wouldn't let him do it. "He couldn't drive the ball better than I could, nor could he hit his long, middle, or short irons as well," Weiskopf recalled in 1991. But: "He putted better . . . I didn't have Jack's concentration. I couldn't form a game plan and stick to it the way he could. He had tremendous patience. I was too emotional."

Five weeks before the Masters, at Doral, Weiskopf bogeyed four of the final five holes, allowing Dickinson to win by one. When asked to explain, he talked about the gallery marshals. "It was the worst [job] I've ever seen and you can quote me," he said. "When I was about to hit my second on eighteen the cameras were going and they sounded like machine guns. . . . I'll never play here again . . . worst galleries I ever saw."

With a thin frame stretched over seventy-five inches and perfect posture, the twenty-six-year-old Weiskopf looked good in fashionably loud clothes; he could wear yellow plaid pants and still exude a vaguely military bearing. He had his hair then, two fistfuls of light brown and blond steel wool, which stood up in a breeze. But what went on in that hatless *weiss kopf* (German for white head)? His *kopf* seemed to contain so much trouble and so little peace.

"Tom was wonderful to be around," says Jacklin, "except when he was angry."

"I was sitting with [club manager] Phil Wahl in his office when Tommy just bursts in," recalls Frank Christian, Augusta National's official photographer. "Don't remember the year. All he says is, 'I'll pay for the goddamn door,' and then he's gone." In time, Wahl and Christian discovered that Weiskopf had just torn the locker-room door off its hinges in anger over an inappropriate autograph request.

Terrible Tommy's opposite in appearance and public personality may have been a short, swarthy, gum-chewing ex-Marine from Dallas playing in his first Masters. Between the gum and a constant stream of funny but nervous chit-chat, Lee Trevino's jaws never stopped moving. He'd done absolutely nothing in golf until June 1967, when he finished a shocking fifth in the U.S. Open, winning $6,000 and an invitation to Augusta in '68. Large scuba goggles obscured his face in the fourth round; they did that in dusty West Texas and he'd gotten used to it. He'd committed to play in the Cleveland Open the week after his breakthrough at the Open, but Trevino was dying to get back to his thirty-dollar-a-week job as the professional at Horizon Hills CC in El Paso to start a party with his new fortune. So he intentionally drove out of bounds at the end of his second round to keep from making the cut. An odd sight, that, the Mexican-American in his cheap high-water pants aiming for the woods, instead of the fairway, on the seventeenth hole at Aurora Country Club.

He didn't fit in. No one else dressed like him, looked like him, or hit a ball like him. Surely the college boys on the tour could not fathom the poverty of his childhood. His father split early, leaving Lee, his mother, and his grandfather, a gravedigger, in a drafty shack one hundred yards from a now-defunct golf course in northeast Dallas called Glen Lakes Country Club. Little Lee played the course over and over with the son of the greenkeeper. He thinks he met his father once, when he was very young, but he's not sure.

"I saw where he lived," recalls January, another Dallasite. "It was a *hut*. Dirt floors." The four-room hut huddled between a pond and an outhouse. No electricity. Mary Kay Ash, the founder of the cosmetics company, would eventually buy the lot where Grandpa's shack once stood and build a somewhat grander edifice.

Lee quit school in eighth grade and worked at jobs that continued his exposure to golf—he swung a pick and shovel as part of the construction crew building the Columbian Country Club in North Dallas, and he helped maintain and run a combination pitch-and-putt and par-three course. His game really came together during his four years in the Marines, but no post golf course could prepare him for the white-glove atmosphere at Augusta National.

After three rounds in the '68 Masters, Trevino would be within two shots of the lead. After four rounds, well, that's another story.

The players vs. the PGA, Arnie vs. Jack, Jack vs. Arnie's gallery, homeboys vs. foreigners, Tom vs. his temper, Lee vs. the powers that be—professional golf mirrored the anger in the land. Meanwhile, inevitably, columnists wrote their first-ever negative words about the Masters. Usually the task in the standard preview story was finding a new way to describe azaleas. But recent civil-rights legislation and the emergence of black athletes in other sports caused writers and editors to ask whether something wasn't amiss. Why had a black man never been invited to compete in the Masters? A pretty good black golfer named Charlie Sifford had won the Hartford Open in '67. Why wasn't he in the field?

"The Masters golf tournament is as white as the Ku Klux Klan," wrote Jim Murray in 1969, when another Masters began without a black player. "Everybody in it can ride in the front of the bus."

Augusta National had once been a plantation, so those who accused the club of racism did so with the confidence of logic. Just look at this place, they said, look how far it hasn't come. While the country integrated, slowly, often angrily, every caddie, waiter, and locker-room attendant at the National was black and solemnly or cheerfully deferential. Every member of the host club and every tournament player—white.

But the truth of the situation was not as black-and-white as the crusaders supposed. For one thing, Sifford's win in '67 didn't result in an invitation because tournament winners didn't automatically qualify for the Masters until 1972. From 1961 through 1967, a dozen white golfers had won on the tour and not been invited. Dave Hill won twice in '61 but did not receive the wedding invitation–like card from Augusta National. Could the club have manipulated the rules to get Charlie in the field? Of course it could. But Jones and Roberts were less opposed to having a black participant in the Masters than they were to being told what to do. If this gave the world the impression that Augusta National was clinging to the South's racist past, so be it. Cliff and Bob had a lot more invested in the institution than did its critics, and they thought a hell of a lot more of their own judgment than that of the thousands of Democrats outside the gates.

They weren't deaf or stupid or oblivious to public relations, but no more self-righteous men ever walked the earth.

"Roberts would walk into the press room, the old quonset hut, for his annual meeting with the press on Wednesday morning," recalls an old newspaperman who asked not to be named. "He always looked lost in space, like he couldn't focus through those glasses he wore.

"And he'd come in the room with five other guys trailing behind him, all of them in green jackets, and all of them CEOs but acting like Cliff's lackeys. Someone would ask 'why no blacks?' and Cliff would peer out, trying to find who had asked the question. One year he's all exasperated. 'I don't know what you mean. We had that boy from Thailand last year and he was black as the ace of spades!' "

Roberts uttered that response to the annoying and by then annual question in 1972. The dark-complected Thai in question, Sukree Onsham, an amateur, shot 77-78 in '71 and missed the cut. But what Roberts couldn't or wouldn't articulate, and what the press never picked up on, was that segregation at the Masters in the late sixties had more to do with the official dislike of Sifford than with the members' supposed dislike of blacks. Jones extended an olive branch in a letter to Sifford in 1968, promising he'd be invited if he qualified. "I for one would be particularly happy to see you realize this ambition," Jones wrote. Charlie told reporters that he felt threatened by Jones's note, not such a ridiculous reaction, for the letter's clear subtext was to urge Charlie to shut the hell up. It didn't work. As he'd been doing for several years, Sifford continued to moan loudly and repeatedly about those racist bastards at Augusta National who wouldn't have him in their lily-white tournament, exactly the behavior that guaranteed he'd never be invited.

And so the varied cast rolled into Augusta in April of '68. Some were driven, some were discouraged, and some were just happy to be there. The man who started the whole thing was dying. The smoke from guns and burning cities seemed to clear for the four-day drama but, in the end, the angry mist overtook even the Masters.

CHAPTER TWO

SNEAKING ON

Nothing happens to any man that he is not formed by nature to endure.

—MARCUS AURELIUS

Although the conflicts in professional golf in 1968 were deep and complex, one sure way to sort things out was to put Bob Goalby in charge.

And for many days and in many ways, Goalby was in charge. His peers made him the head of this committee or that, and put him out front in the player's break from the PGA of America. He made himself an arbiter—perhaps the arbiter—of things like player comportment and dress. Rookies feared him, not only because he'd tell them to get a haircut but because he played golf with a glowering intensity that was genuinely frightening.

Even after he won a U.S. Open, Lee Trevino felt Goalby disapproved of him. "He wasn't impressed," Trevino wrote in his autobiography. " 'In five years,' he told someone, 'we'll be playing benefits for that guy.' " Typical Goalby. But it was also typical, after Trevino won his second Open, for Bob to run across two fairways to shake Lee's hand. "I'm proud of you," Bob said, a tacit welcome to the club.

The fact that he was one of only a handful of touring pros tolerable to both Ben Hogan and Sam Snead didn't hurt his standing among his peers, of course, but Goalby was no politician gathering useful friends.

The small group of salt-of-the-earth pros around Snead liked to laugh and liked each other, and never played a practice round without a bet. January, Ford, Jerry Barber, Jay and Lionel Hebert, Dickinson, and Goalby were talented players who were amazed at Sam's still greater talent and amused by his weaknesses for women and money; plus you could fool him by holding back on a five iron and saying, "man, I crunched that four." Snead's boys had joined the tour in the fifties and carried an old-school sensibility uncomfortably into the garish late sixties. They had shorter haircuts than the new guys, calmer clothes, and a fresher memory of the microscopic prize money of an earlier day. They always wore coats—and often ties—to dinner.

Hogan and Snead were Washington and Jefferson to Goalby and he absorbed lessons from both. He recalls that he played exactly thirty-one rounds with the Hawk, most of them practice rounds, each of which began the same way. On the practice tee at ten-thirty in the morning, Hogan had his caddie inform the combatants that they'd been chosen. At noon, the four would leave the tee for the dining room. Hogan usually had soup. After a bathroom break, the foursome would reconvene on the first tee at one o'clock. Hogan assigned the partners, named the game, and set the bet. Hogan ran everything.

"Weiskopf comes to our table, I think this was at Augusta, and he's shifting his weight from foot to foot," Goalby recalls. "He says, 'Did you get that letter from Bert Yancey and myself? We were really hoping you'd play a practice round with us.' Hogan had this way of looking really naive. 'Oh no,' he says. 'I'm sorry. I didn't get the letter.' Weiskopf goes and Hogan says, 'I got his fucking letter. I'll play golf with who I want to play golf with.' "

A round with Snead—Goalby had hundreds of them—involved less formality, a smaller wager, and a demonstration of the most rhythmic swing in golf. Like Hogan, Sam excelled in all the little things that made a great competitor, though Goalby needed no help in that department. In fact, he could have been giving the lessons.

Despite what January calls "a short, hooky-lookin' swing" and a driver that hit a short hooky-looking shot way too often, Goalby had won seven times on the tour going into the '68 Masters. Seven wins in ten years put him firmly in golf's upper class, behind the royalty—Palmer, Nicklaus, Casper, and Player—but not too far behind. He knew how to compete, all right.

He swung at a golf ball the way a boxer swings at a body; his right uppercut of a swing produced divots as big as manhole covers. He'd been in the military and looked it. He'd been a football player and looked it. Handsome son of a bitch, too: Every year at the Los Angeles Open they bugged him to drive over to Hollywood to take a screen test until finally he did. But Robert George Goalby had no interest in being a movie star.

Television also called. Somebody at the Hughes Sports Network noticed his looks and his clear, crisp baritone. "We were using different players different weeks as guest commentators," recalls John Derr, who announced for Hughes as well as CBS. "We used Beard and Casper and a number of others. Goalby was to be the guest on the tower at seventeen in Greensboro, the last tournament before the '68 Masters.

"That was the highest tower we ever had. You got a nosebleed just going up there. Well, Bob came up for a rehearsal but then after Martin Luther King was killed we were told that there were death threats against the broadcasters. We made a pretty good target.

"So we were called in and Bob didn't get to make his debut. I'd like to say I saw a great deal of potential in him as a broadcaster, but I didn't. But we were close friends and perhaps a little closer after that."

Goalby believes Derr errs—TV didn't discover how well he modulated, he says, until a few years later, at a Western Open. About all he remembers from the week before the biggest week of his life was that the Greater Greensboro Open was "cold and miserable. Lots of pollen. I got out of there Friday night and was on the practice tee in Augusta on Saturday morning." Except that he wasn't. He forgets that weather and the King assassination discombobulated the '68 GGO and that his second and final round took place on Saturday, not Friday. Thus it had to be on Sunday, April 7, that Goalby's Buick courtesy car rolled under the arched magnolias. He'd flown in from Greensboro.

"Your man's here," caddiemaster Freddie Bennett said.

Marble Eye nodded and hustled from the caddie pen by the first fairway to the parking lot.

Augusta National had only about fifty good caddies for the seventy-four players in the Masters, so they had to bring in extras from Atlanta. Frank "Marble Eye" Stokes was one of these—he caddied at Bobby Jones's old home course, East Lake. He'd arrived in Augusta the day before, with his first cousin, James Blandenburg, another East Lake caddie. They came east in James's Riviera, which was far from new but rolled without mechanical incident during the two-hour drive. The cousins checked into a rooming house at Ninth and Walton Way, a downtown dwelling owned by Nipper, an Augusta National caddie. Then they went out to the club to talk with Freddie.

At age thirty-seven, Marble Eye—the name was a gift from an

East Lake member who'd been impressed with his calm, koala-bear look—had been a caddie more than half his life. He'd started at Chastain Park, a modest daily fee course, then moved up the ladder to elegant East Lake. "I caddied thirty-six holes on Saturday and thirty-six on Sunday, two bags at a time, $1.50 a bag," he recalls. "If you went around with ten or fifteen dollars in your pocket back then, you were just about rich." He debuted in the caddie big time when the Ryder Cup came to East Lake in October 1963, on Casper's bag. This was the first time Marble Eye laid eyes on Goalby, who had qualified for his first and, as it turned out, last Ryder Cup. Playing in the match just in front of or right behind Casper four times, Bob hammered his opponents in the U.S. versus England all-star match, with three wins, a tie, and a narrow loss in Fourballs. An Augusta National caddie named George "Fireball" Franklin—Doug Ford's man at the Masters—carried for Goalby.

When Fireball told him that he could probably get a bag at the next Masters, Marble Eye was immediately interested. Casper gave him a nice check for the Ryder Cup and his regulars at East Lake were not stingy but they didn't play much in the winter. He already supplemented his caddie pay with a regular shift as a bellhop at the 144-room Garden Hotel in downtown Atlanta. He and his wife, Doris, had two kids, Bridget and Tony, and a third, Roxanne, would arrive in '65. "Sure, Ball, I'll see you in April," Marble Eye said. He and his cousin went to Augusta for the '64 Masters.

For nothing, apparently. Bennett didn't assign him a bag. "If Freddie didn't know you, he didn't give you nothing," Marble Eye says. But then the notoriously angry Tommy "Thunder" Bolt fired his caddie after nine holes of the first round.

"Do you think you could get along with Tommy Bolt?" Freddie asked.

"Yes, sir," Marble Eye replied, and he was in the Masters.

"That Bolt was funny," the caddie recalls. "Flashy dresser. On number-seven green we're looking at a putt and he goes and asks a lady in the gallery to change the way she's sitting. 'You're distracting my caddie and me,' he says." Frank Stokes's unthreatening look and calm disposition soothed the worst temper in golf. Bolt shot 73–77 and missed the cut but he played the last twenty-seven holes in relative peace and with the same caddie. Marble Eye's reputation was made. He could handle the difficult players.

But out-of-town caddies like him got only what the Augusta National regulars left on the table. "Usually it was one of the Japanese or someone else cheap," he says. Or someone who'd had the temerity to fire one of the brotherhood in a previous Masters. Someone like Goalby, who had fired several. Three bags were open in '68, Marble Eye recalls, Goalby's and those of a couple of the penurious men from Japan. "Freddie asked me to take Goalby because he had so many problems with caddies over the years," Marble Eye says. "He almost never ended the tournament with the same man he started with. Some guys would quit and he fired two or three. Freddie thought I could make things a little bit easier for him."

It wasn't just Goalby—many, possibly most of the touring pros were dissatisfied with their bearers at the Masters. "Despite what you hear, the Augusta National caddies were not that good," Goalby says. "They could tell you a putt broke this way or that, but not by how much. They were good for members but not for the best players in the world."

John Mahaffey tells the classic story in the genre. "Which way does this break?" he asked his man during his first Masters in 1974. He had a tricky three-footer on sixteen, which the caddie studied from several angles. Then, he delivered his solemn verdict.

"Toward the hole," he said.

As annoying as incompetence for a former looper like Goalby was the exalted self-regard of the Augusta National caddies. They saw themselves as indispensable guides over dangerous ground, not mere employees. At reunions, they would talk about how a player "embarrassed" them, an unimaginable concept for most boys and men who have carried a golf bag for pay. But Marble Eye wasn't a local, and he had no chip on his shoulder. Could he and Goalby get along?

At the trunk of the car, in warm, flower-scented air, the two men sized each other up.

Goalby saw a stocky black man in a green golf cap and a white jumpsuit, the caddie's uniform at Augusta National. A thick carpet of mustache separated his nose from his mouth, a mouth that hung open in repose. His unusually large eyes expressed alertness and cooperation.

"Frank Stokes," he said. "Nice to meet you."

Stokes observed a dark-haired white man whose face and body seemed all rectangles and straight lines. He moved with an athlete's grace. The middle of the United States was in his voice.

"Bob Goalby," he said. "Frank? Is it Frank? You know anything about the golf course, Frank?"

"Yes, sir."

The caddie knew this midwesterner could really play. In '67, the year before, he'd won at San Diego and finished tenth on the money list. He owned the all-time record for consecutive birdies—eight—set at St. Pete in '61. He'd almost won the U.S. Open a few years back. But this year he was playing badly. He'd won only about four thousand dollars in '68, his worst start since 1958, his first season on the tour. And his record at the Masters didn't match his accomplishment everywhere else. They'd been inviting him to Augusta since 1960, but he'd had exactly one good round in all his seven appearances—a 69, to tie with Palmer, Player, and Bruce Crampton for the lead in the first round in 1964. That year, however, Goalby wobbled to the finish line in 75-74-77 for a tie for thirty-seventh, while Arnie shot 68-69-70 and won. In twenty-four rounds at the cathedral in the pines Goalby had shot par or better just twice. With this history, his 78-78-thanks-for-coming-Bob in 1967, and his missed cut in Greensboro, neither Bob nor Marble Eye had the slightest reason for optimism.

But Goalby was always willing to work hard on his problems.

The caddie took the boss's fire-engine-red golf bag from the trunk and hoisted it to his shoulder. Embroidered in white on the front was SPALDING and below that BOB GOALBY. Above the names, again in white, the Spalding logo stood out: the outline of a little bird perched on a golf ball to indicate that the Spalding Dot flew as if it had wings. Marble Eye walked off to the practice tee with the big bag and a matching sack for shag balls, while his man entered the antebellum clubhouse to register and get his locker assignment. Left behind in the trunk of the Buick lay a heavy iron bar, a twenty-pound symbol of Goalby's big problem in the Masters. It had to do with his hook.

Conventional wisdom held that a hook was the shot at Augusta National. Bobby Jones had looked over Alistair Mackenzie's shoulder when he laid out the course in 1931 and, as aficionados knew, Jones liked to play a high hook off the tee—thus the preponderance of left-bending holes at the National. Moreover, the only four-time winner of the tournament, Palmer, played a right-to-left spinner that was as aggressive as a cornered badger. Conventional wisdom did not, however, explain Demaret or Nicklaus—three-time champions who faded the ball. And it didn't explain Goalby. He hooked and he couldn't break an egg in the Masters. "A hook's the *worst* shot at Augusta," Goalby says.

"All the trouble's on the left. On two, five, eight, nine. On eleven, you don't want to hook. Thirteen is OK, a perfect hook is good. But if it's not perfect, you can make a high score."

Pursuant to his goal to tame his dominant right hand, which closed the club face, which caused his hook, Goalby swung the big black bar thousands of times, left-handed.

Bob and Marble Eye went right to work. A few of the caddies on the tour called him "Nuther Bag" as in "let's hit another bag of balls." Goalby swatted out the first of hundreds of practice shots to Marble Eye, who stood on the practice ground, retrieved the balls after they landed, and put them into the red bag. Then Goalby played, then practiced again until dark. "He practiced *a while*," Marble Eye says. "The only man who hit more balls that week was Nicklaus."

Sometime that day or the next, the angels sang for Goalby. Something clicked. "I started doing one thing instead of four things," he says. "I came up with a little mental gimmick." Trying to ingrain the gimmick—which was nothing more than a feeling of trying to cut the ball with his driver to make that hook go away—Bob stayed on the practice tee for hour after hour.

When his old comrades talk about Goalby, they usually mention this dedication to craft. And they say one of several certain phrases: "Greatest guy in the world off the course," "Jekyll and Hyde," and the pregnant, "I never had any trouble with him." Bob Rosburg, one of the I-never-had-any-trouble-with-hims, respected Goalby greatly as a man and understood him as a competitor. "He was probably a lot like me," Rosburg says. "He had had some enemies. He told it like it was."

"Bob is *such* a nice guy," says Irwin Smallwood, a writer for the Greensboro newspaper who covered Goalby's first win on the tour in 1958. "One of the truly authentic people in golf." "He's a doer and a good thinker," says January. "Bob leads. He had a lot to do with the success of the Senior Tour." Harold Henning, the late South African who came in the late sixties with the influx of other overseas pros, comments that "you either liked him or you *despised* him," leaving no doubt how he himself felt. Opinions varied on Bob Goalby, but no one ever accused him of being a phony—or of backing away from a fight. Certainly there was no artifice in the way he approached the game on the course or off.

Except that he sometimes took it too far. Golf does not always succumb to sheer effort and those who fail to absorb this truism can find themselves embittered or crazy or playing tennis. Back in his football days, when the opponent played dirty or talked trash, Bob, the quarterback, would call a play that allowed him or a surrogate to smash the evildoer into the Illinois ground. Retaliation in baseball was simple: Hard slides and hard tags usually did the trick. In a severe case, Goalby, the catcher, might give the pitcher a target behind the batter's chin. In basketball, you could foul to get even, and you could do it five times before they asked you to leave. Goalby once fouled out of fourteen straight games. Golf was different. It made him just as angry as any of the other games, angrier even, but offered no release. Maybe something deeper or more subtle than football spirit had its claws in Goalby. Whatever it was, golf could just boil his blood.

"We had something happen in '61 or '62," recalls Al Balding. "We laugh about it today.

"Goalby's in the bunker and I've already chipped up. He hits his sand shot, not a very good one, and I go up to mark my ball. And Bob's angry—he takes another swing—an anger swing. And just covers me with sand. I look at him and he looks at me. He doesn't say, 'I'm sorry.' And we didn't speak for the next three years. He was so intense."

Doug Ford loves to tell about the time he and Dick Mayer

were paired with Goalby at Dorado Beach, a resort in Puerto Rico. "Bob three-putts a green and he's not too happy. And just as we get to the next tee, there's a torrential rain. We're sitting there under umbrellas as it pours straight down. The rain finally stops and Bob drives it right down the middle. I notice he's walking by himself, with his head down, and he's stepping in every puddle. So I walk over to him. He's talkin' to his shoes! 'I'll fix you, you goddamn white shoes,' he says. 'I'll walk you through every damn puddle on this course.' "

Which he did. Afterward, Goalby gave his waterlogged and unlucky spikes to his caddie.

Were you considered a mean guy? asked a reporter from *Golf Digest* in 1998.

"I think I played mean, let's put it that way," Goalby replied.

But there was this: As any woman who saw him back in the day will attest, Bob Goalby was a strikingly handsome man, with a resemblance to movie star Tyrone Power or any number of actors who played cowboys. "He was dazzling," recalls the former Sarah Dillaha (pronounced dilla-hey), a TWA flight attendant who married him in 1962. "Gorgeous." Still, golf course rage distorted the pleasant geometry of his face. He always seemed to play mad or about-to-be mad. And with that dark glower and his blocklike body exuding physical power, Goalby could look downright scary.

One thing dependably reddened his neck—that hook. Nowadays, the quick, unexpected right-to-left curve ball seems a throwback to an earlier age, like goiter or the rising cost of kerosene, because modern manufacturers have dumbed down the ball so much that the merest hacker can hit it straight. But in '68, the ball still spun. Hooks had been the bane of Ben Hogan's existence until he rebuilt his swing and cured himself. Goalby never did. Not that he didn't try. Relentless practice of his deep-divot swing made him one of the best iron players in golf. If his irons were an A, his putting was usually about a B. But with the longest stick in the bag—the driver—the club with poltergeists inside whispering "fore left," Goalby was no better than a C.

"I don't know how many times he'd call from the road and say, 'You know, I've found something. If I can just keep my third toe in line with my elbow or my knee . . . ' " recalls Sarah Goalby. The breakthroughs came and went like clouds. A few days before the first round of the '68 Masters, he told his wife he'd found another one. Something or other about his hands and hips.

For such a reliably unhappy-looking competitor, Goalby was remarkably charming and cheerful after he signed his card. A great communicator, he went out of his way to understand and be understood, which caused him to pepper his conversation with "you know?" and "isn't that right? Huh? Huh?" He possessed the bearlike magnetism of Arnold Palmer and Lyndon Johnson, and had their habit of wrapping an arm around the shoulders of people he talked with, a gesture that brought him a spot of trouble many years later. He got an announcing job with NBC in 1979, not in a tower by a green, but as a "roving reporter." With Raymond Floyd's group one Sunday, Goalby wrapped his strong left arm around the intense Floyd while a cameraman ran alongside. "Great shot back there on fifteen, Raymond," the reporter said with a big grin and stuck his microphone in the vicinity of the golfer's mouth. Floyd, annoyed, said something not memorable and complained after the round about the way he'd been treated. TV and the Tour soon had an understanding that interviewers would no longer touch interviewees. It's called the Goalby Rule.

There had been another sort of Goalby rule when he was a kid in Belleville, Illinois. Whatever team Bob played on—football, basketball, or baseball—and whether it was a pick-up game or a high-school contest with referees and umpires, Bob's team always seemed to win. He played the command positions: quarterback, pitcher, catcher. Forward in basketball because he was big, six feet tall, and solid as a piano leg. "You shot the free throws with two hands, underhand," he recalls. "You shoot one-handed and they'd call you a hot dog and the coach would take you out." Golf didn't enter the picture until his junior year, when he asked the baseball coach to let him out of a Saturday practice so he could try to qualify for the state golf tournament. Coach Gunderson gathered the troops. "Goalby here wants to play golf tomorrow," he told the team. "Should we let him?" The other boys said yes—a small turning point. Bob shot 72 in Peoria and made it to the big show in Urbana, where he shot 77-74 in the first out-of-town golf tournament he ever played in. With the possible exception of tennis player Jimmy Connors, he was the best athlete Belleville ever had.

In one famous passage in *All the King's Men* author Robert Penn Warren painted a picture of another best athlete. Tom Stark, the son of the governor of an unnamed southern state. Young Tom "was fast and he was a son-of-a-bitch. He was going to be All-American quarterback on anybody's team.

If bottle and bed didn't manage to slow down too soon something inside that one hundred and eighty pounds of split-second, hair-trigger, Swiss watch beautiful mechanism which was Tom Stark, the Boss's boy, the Sophomore Thunderbolt, Daddy's Darling, who stood that night in the middle of a hotel room, with a piece of court plaster across his nose and a cocky grin on his fine, clean, boyish face—for it was fine and clean and boyish—while all the hands of Papa's pals pawed at him and beat his shoulders, while Tiny Duffy slapped him on the shoulder, and Sadie Burke, who sat a little outside the general excitement, in her own private fog of whiskey and cigarette fumes, a not entirely unambiguous expression on her handsome, riddled face, said, "Yeah, Tom, somebody was telling me you played a football game tonight."

Adoring hands also patted Goalby's shoulders. Like Tom Stark, the best high-school quarterback in Illinois ran a football "like a cross between a ballerina and a locomotive," and he threw it like Zeus hurling lightning bolts. Too many touchdowns too early made the fictional Tom insolent and unbearable, but Goalby didn't entirely believe his success or the resultant accolades, so he never became that familiar type, the athletic son of a bitch. An appealing sliver of humility punctured his skin. It was his blessing as a human being and his curse as an athlete.

Trains haunted the night outside his little house. "Noisy as hell," Goalby says. "In the summer, we'd have the windows open—we didn't have air-conditioning, you know?—and when that train came by, you'd just about jump out of bed in the middle of the night."

Today the modest house at 222 Miller Street is a box covered in aluminum siding, white with black shutters, as broken-in and comfortable looking as an old recliner. Its backyard dips steeply downward, with the concrete remnants of a dog pen peeking out of the grass at the bottom. High on that telephone pole by the driveway used to hang a homemade (by Bob) basketball goal, a gathering place for Goalby and his friends for years. The house had two bedrooms. Bob slept on a rollaway in the dining room; when his older sister Shirley went away to nursing school, Bob got her room. "The railroad track was right there, just a five- or six-mile spur for the coal cars. See that? Where that house is?" He gestures to a building on the other side of the road, the mine superintendent's house. "The mine shaft was right there. The foreman's house was always by the mine opening. That pond there is called the tipping pond. There's the pulley, see it? Grandpa worked in the mine and my dad, too, but he wouldn't even let me go in."

One of his first memories is of the day Swift, the meat-packing company, hired his father to drive one of their trucks. "I remember when he got the job, in 1935," Goalby says. "Getting a job in 1935, that was like Christmas. All the aunts and uncles came over to celebrate." Bob was six when his father started driving from Belleville, a far suburb of St. Louis, up to Springfield or Decatur in the heart of the state, and sometimes all the way to Chicago. Goalby Senior hauled quality Swift cured meats through the Land of Lincoln for thirty-nine years.

Daddy also caddied from time to time in those dark Depression days at St. Clair Country Club, which was a hundred yards and a world away from the Goalby home. Starting at age nine, Bob followed his father over the road and across the railroad track, through a gulley and past the mine shaft, to the little Shangri-la for Belleville's upper class. When World War II started, the exodus of manpower opened up a job for Bob on the grounds crew at St. Clair. They handed him a table knife and showed him what a weed looks like. "You'd cut a little V with the knife and pull the weed out," Goalby recalls. "Milk weed, you could grab it and get it out pretty good. Crabgrass was tougher." A good worker, young Bob got promoted to greens mowing and doubled his pay to fifty cents an hour.

His father had given him his first golf club, a Bobby Jones six iron with a brown-coated shaft (early steel-shafted clubs were often painted to look like the traditional wooden shafts they replaced). Golf and its possibilities did not suddenly explode in the teenaged mind of Goalby, however; the athletic sugar plums dancing in his head were of football, baseball, and basketball, games he already knew and was instinctively good at. But the vintage Spalding club and the proximity to a golf course did spark an addiction to a mildly sinful activity beloved by poor young golfers for generations: sneaking on.

Goalby discovered that a golf course at twilight, when you're not supposed to be on it, can be the loveliest place on earth. From his front yard he studied the early evening movements of the members and the grounds crew, trying to get the lay of the land. When the coast was clear, he'd slip through an opening in the trees by the tenth green. He hunted for lost balls nearly every night in the spring and summer, and he used the six iron plenty of times on those recovered Club Specials and Titleists. He got good.

"Those were the happiest times of my life," Goalby says. "On the golf course, alone, with clean clothes, and the sun slanting down. Cool green grass in the summer when everywhere else was burned out. I thought I was a member—or the pro."

He won the St. Clair Country Club caddie championship in 1942 and gambled for the first time at a nearby sand green course you could play for twenty-five cents a day, but his horizons in the other sports expanded so rapidly that golf remained just a sideline. As the Maroons' sophomore quarterback, he completed twelve of thirteen passes in one game. Twice he led Belleville to wins in the Big Game, the Thanksgiving Day match with East St. Louis. In the '47 game, he intercepted a pass and ran it back for a touchdown. He threw twenty touchdown passes that season, his senior year. His 11–5 record as a pitcher and .357 batting average attracted the interest of several major-league baseball teams. He wasn't similarly blessed as a basketball player, but fouling out of fourteen games in a row had a certain charm. When a classmate named Martha Sauer says, "He was a *very* popular young man," she understates. He was a hero in Belleville.

Goalby's athletic success allowed him to move anywhere

within the high school's caste system, even into the top stratum, the Signal Hill crowd, the sons and daughters of Belleville's most prosperous families, who resided near St. Clair Country Club. They occupied the same hill, but the Goalbys lived on the wrong side of the coal car tracks and the wrong side of the golf course.

The girls wore long skirts, short white socks, saddle oxfords, and sweaters. The boys often wore suits on Saturday night, gaudy, super-sized "zoot suits." Underage drinking was rare; smoking defined the outer limits of daring behavior. A date meant the Chatterbox, a dive on the old St. Louis Road, for dancing, soft drinks, a burger. A bigger date was a cruise on the Mississippi in the *Admiral,* which is now docked in St. Louis and lives on, predictably, as a floating casino.

"Bob was our leader," recalls Don "Smoky" Bruss, a retired farmer who played halfback and center field in those glory days. "He could do about anything he wanted to do, and not just in sports." Another teammate, Dr. Paul Martin, now a dentist but then the right fielder, says Goalby "had a determination level of ten on a scale of one to ten. If he said he was gonna do something, he'd do it."

But do what? As graduation day approached, Goalby faced an unusually large range of options. He could go to this university for baseball, that one for football, or somewhere else for both. Or he could forget about school, which he didn't like much anyway, because both the Cubs and the Cardinals offered minor-league baseball contracts—Class D, $150 a month. But doubt and self-deprecation froze him. He no longer loved the sports that had made him locally famous, and the only game that spoke to his soul seemed so uncertain that he couldn't even talk about it.

"Signing for the minors [in baseball] wasn't such a big deal in those days," Goalby says. "I knew I wasn't that good. I wasn't fast and my arm was sore and I didn't like it enough to play it every day. But if I'd told the other kids I was gonna be a golf pro, they'd laugh. Who knew how to be a golf pro? I was gonna beat Hogan and Snead? I didn't know how or why or when, but I knew I was gonna play golf."

And so began Goalby's years in the desert. After rejecting the possibility of professional baseball or golf, all that remained was the coal mine or college football. The Missouri coach came to town and made a pitch, Arkansas hosted him for a weekend in Little Rock, and half the Big Ten schools expressed interest. He chose Illinois, partly because of Belleville's proximity to the campus and partly, Goalby says, "because I'm from Illinois." He didn't last. In the late summer of '47, he found himself on a very crowded football field—more than three hundred young men tried out for the team, many of them returning servicemen, who must have felt at home in the barrackslike housing at the parade grounds. Goalby made the freshman squad and played regularly, but the thrill was gone. He quit the team and the school in the spring and went straight to one of his lesser suitors, Southern Illinois University. He played baseball—right field—and reported back to Carbondale in the fall for football. But the Salukis ran the single wing, a running offense, which didn't use Goalby's big strength, throwing the ball. He quit again.

"I wasn't doing very well in school, either," Goalby says. "A psychology professor recommended a trade school. So that's what I did."

Ranken Technical School in St. Louis taught the twenty-year-old Goalby a lot about something he already loved—cars. With all his athletic options seemingly closed, he had decided to become a mechanic—maybe first at a dealership, then hanging out his own shingle. He was living at home during this period when the forties became the fifties, when Sinatra was king and the population boomed. Going out held little interest; in fact, he skulked around a bit, in the self-conscious manner of the high-school hero not having a heroic run in the real world. "I was discouraged with myself," Goalby says. "I never thought that mechanics was what I should have been doing." He went to school at night and worked at a Phillips 66 garage/filling station in East St. Louis during the day.

"Naw, I didn't play golf then," Goalby says. "Well, a little. I'd sneak on with one club and look for balls."

He graduated from Ranken in March 1950 and went to work tuning up Imperials and Saratogas at Miller Chrysler-Plymouth in Belleville. Three months later, the United States of America instructed the twenty-one-year-old college dropout to report to Camp Breckenridge, Kentucky, on November 1. The country was at war. Sort of. That we couldn't decide what to call that thing in Korea—a war, a "conflict," or a "police action"—indicated our tragic ambivalence. After four months of basic training, 175 of the 180 young men in Goalby's company were shipped off to the "conflict." But the soldier voted Outstanding Trainee was not among them. Goalby was shocked to be separated from the group and doubly so when he was sent to Fort Benning, Georgia, for training as a tank mechanic.

"They got sent to the thirty-eighth parallel," Goalby says, emotion rising in his voice. "You know what happened at the thirty-eighth parallel—a slaughter. You talk about Vietnam—this was far worse. Everything had been downsized and disbanded after World War II. The tanks and Jeeps were junk. They didn't even have the right clothes. They sent our boys tropical-weight uniforms to wear in the middle of the winter in Korea."

After a summer near Georgia's gnat line, the Army ordered Private Goalby to report to the big U.S. base in Frankfurt, Germany. He served out the rest of his two-year hitch playing football and baseball for the Division teams, maintaining tanks, and saving his money—"I was a tightwad. I made that nineteen dollars a month last. I even saved some." He went to a golf course exactly once during this period, but he felt horribly out of place and made virtually no effort to play. He got out of the Army in December 1952, still denying or not yet knowing what he really wanted to do in life. So he repeated his football mistake. Ray Elliott, the head football coach at Illinois, took him back, gladly, and for a while things went all right. But just before the end of spring practice, an assistant coach dropped a bomb. "I've got bad news, Goalby," said coach Bob King. "You won't be eligible to play this fall." Someone had discovered that Bob had played baseball at Southern Illinois a couple of years before, and the rules then dictated that a transferring student had to sit out one season.

After that, Goalby says, "I was kinda lost. I just drifted." He bought a new car that summer with money he'd been squirreling away for years, a two-toned '53 Mercury, maroon over cream, that made it look like a convertible. In the fall, he drove back to Champaign to quarterback the scout team, a twenty-four-year-old ex-Army man whose glory had faded like a sunset. "Feeling like a jerk-off," he says. "Most of the kids were much younger than me . . . the guy who's ineligible is an outcast, anyway." After a month or two of this, he quit football for the final time.

But the university had built a golf course on flat land six miles south of town. Goalby found it. For some reason, he'd put his clubs in the trunk.

Vinny Giles awoke in the Crow's Nest and looked at the blue sky through the windows in the cupola. His first conscious thoughts were that he had a pass to play the glorious course outside his door all day, if he wanted, and an invitation to dine with Bobby Jones on Wednesday night, if golf's aging hero was up to attending the Amateur's Dinner. For a solid week, Giles lived his dream. "Birds chirpin', mowers goin', the sun's shinin'," he recalls happily. "I'm in the closest thing to heaven you can find."

Due to the late finish in Greensboro, the place was deserted, relative to the hustle of a modern pre-Masters. Giles did not recognize a lot of the people he saw, the special invitees, the members, and most of the foreign players, men named Sugimoto, Travieso, De Vicenzo, and Ching-Po. He doesn't recall whether he saw a bull of a man—Goalby—taking divot after deep divot on the practice tee for hour after hour.

Snead arrived Monday and quickly discovered that his friend Bob had found something in the dirt of the Augusta National practice tee. Doug Ford and Gene Littler joined the fourball matches, but Goalby's hook never showed up. He shot 67-68-68 and won every bet in their ten-dollar nassaus.

"Hey, boy," Goalby said to Snead on the eighteenth green each day, "fast pay makes good friends." Sam hated to be seen paying off in public, which Goalby knew, so Sam gave Bob his forty or fifty dollars by the urinal in the second floor of the clubhouse.

"Damn," Snead said. "I've never seen you play so good."

Twice before the tournament began on Thursday, CBS television announcer John Derr chatted up Goalby. Derr described the action at a particularly dramatic juncture, the fifteenth green, with a clear mellifluous voice and an actor's emotional range. He could make Palmer playing the fifteenth seem like Caesar entering Rome, if he was winning, or like a tragic figure in an opera if he was blowing a lead. In person, Derr was warm yet serious and a great storyteller. He always had tea during Masters week with Cliff Roberts, who enjoyed the gentlemanly announcer so much he gave him a plum assignment: escorting the wife of the new Masters champion from the Butler Cabin, where they did the post-tournament TV interview, to the practice green, where the formal presentation was held.

"We'd come down to Augusta from Greensboro on Tuesday," Derr recalls. "I saw Bob then and asked him how he was playing. They usually don't tell you, but he said, *'Great.'* I saw him again on Wednesday. 'How'd you do today?' I asked. He looked around. 'John,' he says, 'in my last twenty-seven holes I've made thirteen birdies.'

"Wednesday night was the social highlight of the week—the calcutta (player auction) at a private house for all the people associated with CBS and *Sports Illustrated*. Very crowded, what with all the wives, girlfriends, and assorted chippies and pick-ups. As usual, Bob Drum was the emcee. 'Time out, time out!' he says. 'Now, I'd like to remind you that there are ladies present. So the first time any of you motherfuckers use any bad language, I'm gonna throw you out on your goddamn ass.' "

Most of the bids and most of the money went for Nicklaus and Palmer. Jack sold for sixteen hundred dollars.

Knowing what he knew, Derr searched the sheet listing the entrants for Goalby's name—and couldn't find it. Another partygoer confirmed the oversight. Inspired, Derr rose and addressed the podium. "I think it's disgraceful that Jock Hutchison and Freddie McLeod will go to the first tee without a bet," he said. Hutchison, eighty-three, and McLeod, eighty-five, were honorary starters, not full competitors.

"They only play one goddamn hole," someone said.

"Nonetheless," said Derr, "I will bid five dollars on Hutchison and McLeod—and anyone else not on the list." After his bet was accepted, Derr let it slip—loudly—that Bob Goalby was another name not on the list. Despite several protests, Bill MacPhail, the calcutta's treasurer (and the president of CBS Television), ruled that Derr's wager would stand.

"I told Bob about it the next day," Derr says. "But he wasn't too happy that I'd told anyone how well he was playing."

But it didn't seem to matter much. Goalby never did anything at the Masters.

CHAPTER THREE

EL MAESTRO

GLOSSARY

hijo—son

puta—whore

Nueve de Julio—the ninth of July, Independence Day in Argentina

mate—tealike drink popular in South America

nietas—grandchildren

qué pasa—what's happening?

fumar—to smoke

fuerte—strong

copa—cup

abierto—open

escritore—writer

café—coffee

té—tea

leche—milk

cómo se dice—how do you say?

importa—important

papel de baño—toilet paper

simpático—pleasant

jugador de beisbol—baseball player

los Maestros—the Masters

On a sunny autumn day two weeks before the '68 Masters, Roberto De Vicenzo drove into Buenos Aires. The southern part of the city didn't look like much—where the wide mouth of the brown Río de la Plata met the blue Atlantic the land was swampy, commercial, and overcrowded. But in downtown B.A., broad avenues and classic architecture provided an almost cinematic setting for slim and wonderfully dressed men and women who always seemed to be taking a two-hour lunch. At night, the beautiful people danced a dance with long, gliding steps and melodramatic poses—the tango. British gold, Italian blood, and French culture created the Paris of South America, the wealthiest and proudest city—and country—on the continent. But Argentina always seemed to be suffering from self-inflicted wounds. Repeated military coups and chronic political corruption made many Argentinians cynical, even violent. By year's end a major workers' uprising in Córdoba would scent the air with revolution. But De Vicenzo wished only to show patriotism. He pointedly wore a light blue coat into town that day in '68, the same sky-blue as his country's flag.

He straightened his tie as he stood near the white stone obelisk at the end of the world's widest thoroughfare, the twenty-lane *Avenida Nueve de Julio*. Then the man next to the man with a camera waved his arm, Roberto's cue to cross the street. He walked, approximating nonchalance. But some young *hijo de puta* in an orange sweater fell in step beside him and peered into the camera as if he, too, should be in the Masters highlight film. They used the shot anyway.

"Well, we are here in Buenos Aires, looking to the city," De Vicenzo said in the voiceover. The camera showed him strolling down a busy city sidewalk, then at home, sipping *mate* from a straw, under the trees at a backyard table with his wife, Delia, and one of their cute little *nietas*. The golfer and the film crew had already shot the airport scene, in which Roberto ascended an outdoor boarding ramp marked Braniff International, pretending to begin his long journey to Augusta. "I am ready to take the plane next week to play the big toonamin. You know, I won the British Open last year and I be feeling very happy to win the Masters. And I am ready right now to go there."

Was he ever. After years of winning scores of run-of-the-mill tournaments but kicking away leads in the biggest events, he'd finally learned how to win a major. He was forty-four, almost forty-five, getting old for championship golf, but winning the Open had made him feel young again.

Young again . . .

Three and a half decades later, Roberto returned to the little course where he'd learned golf. He can't remember the last time he'd been to Miguelete. Two years? Five? Ten? He has no reason to go there anymore. Across the busy highway and a railroad track stands the compact two-story house where he grew up with the clickety-clack of a passenger train in one ear and the cries and whispers of seven siblings in the other. His mother died young, and his father had a gambling problem. How long has it been since Roberto visited his childhood home? Never. Until today, he's never gone back. Sixty years . . .

De Vicenzo drives a black Audi of recent vintage, an A-4, and pulls up to the shaggy entrance to the golf course, a gap in a brick wall like a mouth missing a tooth. A wooden gate with faded white paint halts ingress, a gate that is operated by a man with a wondrously bad toupee. They charge a few pesos to park in the golf course lot; since the devaluation, everyone in Argentina needs revenue. The gatekeeper peers into the car, affording passengers a closeup of his wandering hair hat. He straightens. "De Vicenzo," he says reverently, and lifts the gate.

A billboard above the entrance announces Miguelete's formal name, CLUB DEPORTIVO FERROCARRIL GRAL. MITRE, which means that this is the Railroad Sports Club, named for General Bartolome Mitre, a hero of the war with Paraguay in the 1860s and the first president of the Republic of Argentina. When the English built the railroads here around the turn of the century they paused every twenty kilometers or so to put up a town. And what was a town without a golf course? Miguelete is one of those. It's as flat as spilled wine but its trees have grown over the years, dividing this fairway from that. It's not so bad.

"I was born here," Roberto says. "Born in a hole on the golf course. Hole number seven, I think." He parks in the shade. It's hot in the outskirts of Buenos Aires at noon in early March, and the two dogs on the floor of the clubhouse are so splayed and inert it's as if they were dropped from the ceiling. On one of the red clay tennis courts out front, four middle-aged men play a game that's slower than golf. "You're too old to play in this heat," Roberto calls out as he walks by. "You're going to kill yourselves." The game stops. The men are excited and come to the edge of the court to talk. It's De Vicenzo! De Vicenzo is back!

Someone asks Roberto as he walks along if he can picture himself again as a six-year-old, carrying a skinny canvas bag twice around Miguelete's nine holes for one peso and change, when pesos were four to an American dollar. "No, can't remember," he says. "Everything has changed." He gestures at a spot next to the practice green. "Here there was a little *edificio*, a little building for the clubs and for the caddies to wait. All is new. *Qué pasa.*"

Liters of Isenbeck beer appear on his table in the clubhouse as friends old and new stop to say hello. *"Cómo estas, bien?"* he says to each of them. How are you, good? He eats crackers mortared with butter and sprinkled with a blizzard of salt until his steak arrives, and after the steak he recalls the time he followed his older brother Elias across the street to the golf course. The game fascinated him immediately. "I can remember hitting a ball with a tree branch, but they all say that," says De Vicenzo. He didn't use a stick for long because making a real club, especially a small one, presented no problem. Wood shafts broke and golfers threw them away; with a saw, a salvaged clubhead, and some whipping string to hold the parts together, caddies built their own. But clubs didn't interest him that much and never would. He liked the ball. He stuck a nail in a cork from a wine bottle and hit it for hours, day after day, studying the physics of the thing. Soon he could spin the cork-ball around corners or make it seem to float in the air and jump backward after landing. When his magic had won him twenty cents in bets with the railroad golfers, he had enough to go to the *cine* to see a Hollywood cowboy movie—"*bandidos* versus *policía*"—with no music and no sound, with the dialogue written in Spanish on the bottom of the screen.

To get real golf balls, *Robertito* took off his shirt and rolled up his pants legs. He was a *lagunero*, a retriever of balls drowning in Miguelete's water hazards. He'd take the balls home for cleaning and sorting, then, from his tiny front yard, he'd attempt to hit some of them over the railroad track and the Model Ts and horse carts in the busy street. It took a mighty wallop to reach the golf course, about two hundred yards with a short, hickory-shafted club, but Roberto could do it. He was a strong kid, very likable, and so adept with a golf stick. When he was ten, Mosquera, the caddiemaster, and Gardino, the pro, allowed the best golfer in the caddie pen to play the course any time he liked, not just on Mondays like the other boys.

"One Monday, I want to play golf as always, but I also have to take care of my brother, Juan Carlos," Roberto recalls. Juan Carlos was just a baby, perhaps a year and a half old. "So I took him with me. Hit the ball, put Juan Carlos on my back. Hit the ball, put Juan Carlos on my back . . ."

The family fractured in 1935, when Rosa De Vicenzo died attempting to deliver her ninth and tenth children. The twins died, too. Roberto was twelve. The remaining parent, Elias, a house painter, "was tall, with white hair, a good father," Roberto says.

"But he liked to bet on horses." And, of course, he lost more than he won. "Once he found out I caddied for a famous jockey, and he make me go ask this jockey for *el favorito*. 'Who is going to win, for my father?' I ask. 'Tell your father not to bet,' the jockey says.

"When I go to play in toonamin, my father asks me how I play. If I say 'not too good,' he says 'better you look for work. I think this golf is just for bums.' "

Both De Vicenzo's grandfathers were born in Italy, in Genoa and Sicily, part of a significant migration of Italians and Spaniards to the former colony of Spain between 1880 and 1920. Elias died of lung cancer at age fifty-three. *"Fumar mucho cigarettes,"* De Vicenzo says, in the Spanglish he uses for unilingual guests. "Black tobacco. *Muy fuerte.*" The De Vicenzo home had rattled with sound: from the street, from the railroad, and from eight kids—Jose, Antonio, Juana, Elias, Eduardo, Osvaldo, and finally, Juan Carlos. Roberto, who turned eighty in April 2003, was the fifth born. "I have six brothers," he says. "All are dead. They're sending for me but I won't go."

Later, when this party breaks up and someone inveigles him into driving to the little house on the corner, the house where he grew up, De Vicenzo will not get out of the car. His guests meet the current owners and inspect the place without him.

"A lot of people are dying now that never died before," Roberto's friend Raul Cavallini says in the warm afterglow of lunch, quoting a typically rueful old saying in Argentina. He sips from a glass of red Argentine wine, and for a moment the table is quiet. The *pock . . . pock* sound of the tennis game outside becomes audible. Then Raul and Roberto start to giggle as they take turns delivering mock funeral orations for each other. "He was a good guy BUT," they say, and they laugh until tears come. "But *que bolludo!*" What an asshole!

"It's impossible not to like this man," Cavallini says, when

Roberto slips away from the table for a moment. "And he speaks like a sage, like an old Japanese man." Until a few years ago Señor Cavallini, a white-haired cavalier, was a bank president with a large budget for promotions. He surmised, correctly, that sponsoring golf pro-ams would elevate the visibility and the status of Banco de Argentina, and that hiring De Vicenzo to participate would guarantee that people would come out to play and to watch. *Dios,* they had fun. Once one of Roberto's nervous amateur partners sliced his tee shot into a pond and prepared to put another ball in play by the water's edge. The amateur faced the green, reached his right hand over his shoulder, and dropped a new ball—which De Vicenzo stealthily intercepted before it hit the ground. He and the other players in the group tried but failed to suppress their laughter as they helped their dumbfounded partner search for his "lost" ball.

De Vicenzo was used to dealing with amateurs, having turned pro at age fifteen. He'd completed his formal education years before. *"No obligario* after sixth grade," he says. "You only go to high school if you have money." For fun, he played *futbol*—soccer—and was good at it. He aspired to work on the railroad, or perhaps as a boxer, both logical occupations for a young man with big arms and no money. But slowly, by degrees, he turned to golf. With borrowed shoes and pesos donated from the Miguelete caddies, the fifteen-year-old pro took the train into Buenos Aires to attempt to qualify for his first tournament, the Argentina Open of 1938. "How did you do, Espaghetti?" they asked when he got back (the nickname was a commentary on those muscular forearms; the equivalent cartoon character in the United States was Popeye). "Missed by one shot," Espaghetti said, not in the least discouraged. For two years he taught the worst hackers at Miguelete and worked on his own game, and then his life changed profoundly.

He hitchhiked two hundred miles to a *torneo* in Córdoba, and there the pro at Argentina's best club introduced himself. Armando Rossi had been impressed by the young man's friendly disposition and by his thunder off the tee. Rossi offered an assistant pro job at Ranelagh (ronna-la), thirty miles south of the city. Roberto accepted. Ranelagh, he discovered, was no Miguelete. He lived in a room—his own room!—in the big Tudor clubhouse. The golf course was beautiful, more a place for railroad executives than for railroad workers. Rossi fixed his too-strong grip. "You start with a good grip," Rossi told him, "and the body will follow." The teenager ingrained the lessons by hitting as many as one thousand practice balls a day. There wasn't that much else to do. Because of World War II not many people played, no one held a tournament, and there was a golf ball shortage. "You could take the cores from old balls and re-cover them," Roberto says. "Sometimes you hit these balls and the covers explode off."

In a brief interlude with Argentina's Navy, De Vicenzo was stationed at Port Belgrano, conveniently close to a golf course, which allowed him to continue to practice every day. After the war, the twenty-one-year-old Roberto married Delia, the daughter of the locker-room manager at Ranelagh, accepted the head pro job at a club in Rosario, an hour's drive north of Buenos Aires, and began to lose his hair. "At Rosario, I start to understand myself," De Vicenzo says. "I lose my time working. Waste? Yes, waste my time working." When they began to have tournaments again, he played. And he won. He won every provincial *abierto* from the *pampas* to Patagonia, in fact, then went outside Argentina and kept winning. Engravers etched his name on the silver *copas* in cocaine capitals and banana republics; in the cold, thin air of the Andes and on coastal plains where the air was so humid you had to chew it before you could breathe it. A few sponsors lost their enthusiasm and in some cases withdrew their backing, because Roberto's presence deprived their tournaments of the publicity suspense can create.

Two challengers arrived in 1945: Jimmy Demaret and Sam Snead, two of the best pros from the United States. During their four-week tour, Roberto played against the Americans twice, in the Argentina Open and in an exhibition at Ranelagh. Demaret took the *Abierto,* but in the match on his home course, Roberto won easily. "Demaret can't believe," he says. "I hit over Snead. . . . After this I start moving to all South America, U.S., Europe. Every place that have a toonamin that I could win money, I go there."

"CAFÉ, TÉ, O LECHE?" The stewardess would have to shout to be heard over the roaring drone of the two Pratt and Whitney fourteen-cylinder piston engines in the DC-3. *"Por favor, café,"* the golfer would say. The Douglas DC-3, the workhorse of world aviation, seated about thirty, and those in the window seats could see that its wings were startlingly flexible in flight. No overhead bins, no movie, and no business class where you could stretch your legs. How many cramped hours did De Vicenzo spend inside the cigar tube of a DC-3 fuselage to get to, say, the British Open? He shrugs. A long time. In those prejet days they did not fly at night, and he might have to change planes five times between Buenos Aires and London. When they reached land on the other side of the ocean, the stewardess would give the passengers frameable certificates to mark their accomplishment. A trip to Miami required stops in Lima and Panama and took three days.

The money wasn't much—"I spent twenty-five thousand dollars to win fifty thousand dollars"—but the experience compensated. He was paid in stories: stories he tells all the time, stories he just remembered, stories he can't tell. On a trip to Europe in 1950, he won the Dutch, French, and Belgian Opens and the hearts of the Dutch, French, and Belgians. Young King Baudoin of Belgium took a particular liking to the golf champion from far-away Argentina.

"You had breakfast with a king?" the members at Ranelagh asked. "What did he say?"

Roberto: He said, "pass the sugar."

Members: What did you say?

Roberto: I said, "Che King, here's the sugar."

The word *che* doesn't translate that well but it's informal and familiar, like buddy or pal. As if, "King, my man, here's the sugar."

"In Manila I think in '51, they have five thousand dollars for a hole-in-one but hole-in-one is impossible! They make flagsticks so *cómo se dice*, so thick that it would hardly let a ball in. And so bouncy, if you hit it, your ball ends up fifty yards away."

He made his first brief stab at the American golf tour in 1947. "They tell me I can learn from the American pros," De Vicenzo says, "but my second week there, *they* watch *me*." The American pros had plenty to teach him, however: "One year I play Azalea [he pronounces this Azza-lea] Open then go to Masters with Lawson Little. But he is drunk. We want to leave the hotel at nine o'clock but Lloyd Mangrum say, 'Roberto, you no go with this guy, he is drunk, he will kill you.'" Although he was as familiar with South Carolina highways as he was with the surface of the moon, Roberto drove—and stayed lost the entire night, because his snoring passenger could not be roused to navigate.

Where Roberto didn't go, the Shell Oil Company sent him. For its series of travelogue/exhibition matches filmed for TV, Shell hired De Vicenzo fourteen times, more than any other player. Cameras were not mobile in the sixties, when the series began, and videotape had not been invented, so the matches took as long as four days to record. He played Bob Rosburg in Chile;

Johnny Pott in Venezuela; Tony Lema in Greece; Tony Jacklin and Bert Yancey in Kenya; and Tom Weiskopf in Morocco. Competitive men thrown together in unfamiliar surroundings for days on end could have problems, but Roberto got along with them all—except Dan Sikes. Twice he played the golfing lawyer from Jacksonville in "Shell's Wonderful World of Golf" and twice Sikes gave him the cold shoulder and the stink eye. "I wonder, why do you look to me like this?" De Vicenzo says. He couldn't fathom how anyone could play golf mad. For Roberto, you must be pleasant to win.

His match with Sam Snead at Congressional in Washington, D.C., in 1967 also felt a bit unsettled. "We go for practice the day before they film, and he beat me easily," Roberto recalls. "We go back to hotel. He says, 'Well, Roberto, we have dinner together tonight.' When we walk into restaurant Sam says, 'I bet for dinner that I can jump and touch this door jamb with my foot.' " Although De Vicenzo was unaware of it, this was one of Snead's oldest and best tricks. After an internal debate—*what if he breaks his neck?*—Roberto accepted the wager. And Snead, at fifty-five still an incredibly limber athlete, kicked up his leg and planted the sole of his foot on the jamb eighty inches off the floor.

"Next day on the practice tee I notice that Sam is not moving so well. Maybe his jump bothered his back? He comes to me: 'Roberto, how about we split the money?' I say no—tax problems, whatever." Snead seemed miffed. De Vicenzo won.

De Vicenzo won—a combination of proper noun and verb that *escritores de deportivos* wrote hundreds of times. He won forty-two national championships of fifteen different countries. He won, he won, he won, he won. . . . While finishing first is not a character flaw or a symptom of a disease, most golf champions exhibit an almost breathtaking amount of self-interest. But here was De Vicenzo winning more often than Hogan or Snead or

Nicklaus with an almost apologetic manner. Jealousy is as common in golf as oxygen in air but Roberto won and the other guys actually liked him. Was he the unique sportsman who could succeed without having a mean, competitive streak, or did he just hide it very well? On some deep level, did he *need* to win? No, Roberto says, it was simple. It wasn't him—it was the other pros: "They taught, I practiced." But that's not strictly true—he taught a lot, while still finding time to practice and to play.

Although he states his motives clearly—"I needed money"—psychoanalyzing him is difficult. He's as aware as any pro of how much he made for this tournament or that endorsement yet he is disdainful of dollars and pesos. "He could have been a millionaire many times over if he had been interested," his banker, Cavallini, says with a sigh. In 1968, Roberto often talked about wanting thirty-five thousand dollars or so a year—no more. "This money ruins people," he says. *"No importa es.* Tiger makes millions but money for him is nothing. A piece of paper. *Papel de baño!*

"You don't (shouldn't) care for how much money play. Just play and have a good time. And a better time when you get the big check."

Whatever his motivation, De Vicenzo won wherever he went—except in the one tournament he wanted most. For any golfer not from the United States, the Open—Americans call it the British Open—was the greatest prize in the game. Roberto's Open blues began in 1948, the first year he played. He had won a tournament in Argentina sponsored by KLM (the Dutch airline) in which the first prize was a ticket to Europe, and a local club pro named John Cruickshank proposed that they travel together over the pond, so Cruickshank could visit his family in Scotland and Roberto could play in the Open at Muirfield. "I don't wanna go," Roberto says. "I don't speak English. Too far. But I go."

He shot a 28 for one of the nines in the first tournament he played in Europe—the North England Open—and won by fourteen shots. At the Open two weeks later he finished third to Henry Cotton, an amazing debut. In 1949, he was third again in the Open, as Bobby Locke won. In 1950, second to Locke. In '53, he played practice rounds with Ben Hogan, who then picked him to win. But Hogan won and Roberto finished sixth. The tantalizing near misses continued. Third in '56, third in '60, third in '64, fourth in '65. At Royal Birkdale one year, he three-putted the ninth green, then four-putted it the next day. His consistently high finishes proved his talent, but Roberto had bad racing luck in the biggest events.

"In the 1957 U.S. Open (at Inverness, in Toledo) I'm leading with nine to play," he recalls. Ten and eleven are short par fours, two of the easiest holes on the course. "On the tenth hole, Billy Joe Patton's ball mark is right in the line of my birdie putt. Back then, you are not allowed to fix ball marks. So I decide to chip but I don't hit it so good. Make bogey. On the next hole I drive in the rough and make a six. I shoot 41." Dick Mayer won.

In *los Maestros*, the Masters, nothing. This was funny, because in South America they'd started to call De Vicenzo *El Maestro*. The Master did nothing at the Masters.

Finally, in 1967, he won the Open. When De Vicenzo walked up the final fairway at Royal Liverpool, it was as if a long-standing injustice had been put right. "To a man, spectators rose to their feet and stamped them, [the sound] so thunderous that we were silenced," recalled Ben Wright, who was at that moment interviewing Jack Nicklaus for *The Financial Times*. "His victory was the most popular that I'd ever seen." Wright glanced at Jack, the defending champion and the runner-up, and saw his eyes glistening. Roberto got their hearts in their throats again at the presentation ceremony when he said he looked forward to handing the Claret Jug to an English professional the next year. At forty-four years, ninety-three days, Roberto was the oldest champion the Open ever had, and probably the most lovable.

America yawned. Who was De Vicenzo? He hadn't played in the United States enough to have an identity. Besides, Arnie owned American golf. Unless Palmer won, the British Open didn't make much of a splash.

But in a few months, De Vicenzo would be more recognizable than Ho Chi Minh, General Westmoreland, and Bobby Goldsboro. With his sudden spike of fame came an immortal linking to a man with whom he had so much in common but was so unlike, the quarterback from Illinois, Bob Goalby.

Items from the *Augusta Chronicle* in the spring of '68:

April 1: On sale at the Piggly Wiggly—Winkie Dog Food, fifteen #300 cans for $1; five pound bag of Aunt Jemima grits, 33 cents.

April 2: A moonshine still said to be the largest operating within Augusta's city limits in more than a decade was discovered and destroyed Sunday and two men were arrested. The still had a 960-gallon capacity and was producing 150 gallons a day.

April 5: Lawmen cordoned off a large area of metropolitan Augusta Thursday night as restlessness spread following the assassination of Dr. Martin Luther King. Someone threw a brick through a windshield; a bullet grazed a driver, who crashed; four people were injured, all of them white.

April 5: Pat Summerall, former end and placekicking ace of the New York Giants, will be the guest speaker today, Monday, at the 1 p.m. Kiwanis Club meeting at the Town House Hotel. . . . He will be making his debut as anchor man at the 18th hole for CBS's Masters television coverage.

April 5: A total eclipse of the moon will occur on April 12 and 13, from 11:22 p.m. to 12:12 a.m., when the orbiting moon passes through the earth's shadow. . . . The double feature at the Hilltop Drive-In includes *A Man Called Dagger* (He's Different. He's Dangerous. He's Dagger. You'll dig him) and *Wild Wild Planet* (WILD is the word for this World!) $1.25 for adults, children, free.

April 7: On this national day of mourning, a "poor people's" tribute for Dr. King is scheduled for 3:00 at Bell Auditorium.

Late in the afternoon on Monday, April 8, De Vicenzo arrived at the course and went straight to the first tee without hitting a practice ball. Dudley Martin, a reporter for the *Augusta Herald*, watched as Roberto smashed a driver and a four iron onto the back edge of the green on the par five second hole.

"No, winning the British Open hasn't made any big changes in my life," Roberto said. "I'm doing pretty much the same things I always did." Which was win golf tournaments. He'd played in five and one TV match thus far in '68, he said, and had "lost one."

"You pick the club and I'll hit it in the hole for a hole-in-one," he said to his caddie on the tee of the sixth, a downhill par three of 180 yards. The caddie handed him a six iron. "Six? Is too much. The ball will land five or six feet past the hole." When he left the shot thirty feet right of the hole, De Vicenzo said he hit it "like a grandma."

He shot one under par 35 for the nine holes and played in fifty minutes. The light was fading but the golfer and his caddie walked briskly to the tenth tee for a few more holes. How did he like his chances? the reporter asked in parting.

"Too early," Roberto said. "It's much too early to tell."

Tuesday, April 9

Marble Eye peered up into the gray sky and searched for a golf ball. Even when he couldn't see the Dot exploding off Goalby's club, a dozen things told him where to look. Mr. Bob, as he called him, was a hooker. Too quick from the top or an incomplete back-swing and he's hooking every time. Disgusted body language usually meant a hook, too. Goalby took a divot with every iron but his caddie knew when the splash of black dirt and grass was too big or too small and what that meant for the flight of the ball. He also knew the direction and strength of the wind, the club the boss was using, and how he'd hit the last one. He'd shagged thousands of balls over the years, and had developed the vision and instincts of a center fielder.

So it irked him when Goalby hit a ball off-line and he stood there pointing this way or that, as if his caddie were a blind man or a rookie.

"Hey, man, I can see out there," Marble Eye said when he came in. He emptied the red bag at the golfer's feet. "You make me look bad when you point." People were watching, and the caddies thought of themselves as performers, too. Goalby agreed to desist.

Back out on the broad, green practice fairway, Marble Eye observed a five-part tableau: a sea of smooth grass; then the practicing golfers; spectators restrained behind green and white nylon rope; the tops of ancient oak trees with new, light-green leaves; and the dark roofs of the club buildings. Everything looked like Masters past except for the crowd, which was much smaller and quieter than usual. They had buried Dr. King in Atlanta earlier that day, and a lot of people stayed home to watch on TV. Public entertainment had virtually vanished. Actor Gregory Peck had announced that the Academy Awards show would be postponed from Sunday this week until Wednesday night, and that the ball afterward was canceled. The NBA and ABA basketball playoffs took several days off, and Major League Baseball delayed its opening day, which, despite wars, it had never done. The Masters warm-up went on but in a restrained way.

From time to time one of the golfers on the tee was likely to bend forward and massage the front of his legs, because the steep hills at Augusta National caused an annual epidemic of shin splints. Nicklaus pounded out shot after shot, the power and height of his shots plainly superior to anyone else. Smokers smoked between shots. Hard-hit balls often described a slowly ascending ski-jump arc, thrilling to behold, a flight the twenty-first-century ball cannot take. The magnetic Palmer and the foppish Doug Sanders arrived with crowds attached. Marble Eye noticed that when this new guy, Trevino, swung, the ball flew very low and very straight and his club never seemed to get above his waist. The fat man was Casper, the thin lefty was Bob Charles, the very smooth swinger in a white visor was Yancey, and the complicated blur of elbows and knees was George Archer, who looked too damn tall to play golf. Goalby punished the earth with each emphatic stroke. He paused when Archer, then Casper, came over to talk. Getting a lesson, Marble Eye supposed, incorrectly.

"They talked but I didn't listen," Goalby says. "I was hitting it pretty good."

Daybreak, Robert Bass, Cigarette, Willie Peterson, Marble Eye, Carl Jackson—caddies with nicknames and caddies without watched the sky like artillery observers. In the moment of panic when they couldn't find a ball in flight, they listened for its incoming hiss, and the hair on their arms and necks stood at attention. But one man moved on the practice fairway like he had radar. In fact, he caught most of the shots his man hit *on the fly,* his left hand cushioned by a small white towel, and he did it with a Willie Mays flair. Crosshanded Henry Brown was De Vicenzo's caddie.

"*Un negro fantástico! Muy simpático!*" Roberto recalls. "*Un jugador de beisbol.* The people come out to watch him, not me." Some of the practice-tee fans did, in fact, focus on Crosshanded Henry Brown and applaud when he made a particularly good catch.

Brown played golf very well, right-handed, left-handed, and as his nickname implied, crosshanded. He drove a cab when he wasn't caddying and he was said to be illiterate. He headquartered at the Patch, a sporty but casually maintained muni over by Daniel Field, the private airport. "I played him twice in about 1967," recalls Ricky Howard, an Augusta National caddie. "He was intimidating for a little white kid. He had that big old neck. He was just so strong. And he talked some trash. He was always cocky about his ability.

"I'd have sixty-five cents in my pocket and by the end of the day, he's got fifty-five of it. Henry caddied for Lee Elder [in 1975, when Elder became the first black to play in the Masters] and the joke around here was that Lee should have carried the bag and Henry should have played."

"Henry Brown could shoot 65 for a dollar Nassau but for twenty-five dollars, he couldn't play," says Carl Jackson, who would one day win the Masters, in the caddie sense, on Ben Crenshaw's bag. "He was a really easygoing guy but a bit of a showoff. I saw him challenge the pros to a long-drive contest a couple of times. And he'd drop 'em [over the net at the end of the range] right onto Washington Road."

Daybreak—aka Bennie Hatcher—says Crosshanded Henry Brown "might have beat De Vicenzo from either side"—a dubious sentiment, but revealing of the esteem the best caddie-golfer enjoyed, a status both Roberto and Bob Goalby had had when they were kids.

Crosshanded Henry Brown lived on Pine Street, downtown, but most of the homegrown caddies lived about a mile from the club on the Hill—sometimes called the Sand Hill—an enclave of unimpressive houses, a church, a whorehouse called the Oak, a diner, and Hill's Pool Room. Chipping contests on the street medians often erupted during Masters week, lit by the moon and house lights and fueled by strong drink. Hill residents also stuck empty soup cans in the ground in their front yards for putting matches. "If you can read dirt, you can read grass," the caddies said. No less than in the spacious homes in which white Masters patrons drank a sea of gin and tried to empty the ocean of shrimp, Masters week meant a party in black Augusta. Momentarily big men in the community, with potentially fat wallets if their golfers did well, the caddies were the stars of front porches and barrooms. At the DeSoto, the Top Hat, Shoe's, and Charlie Reed's, they laughed louder than other men, told more interesting stories, and looked more attractive to women.

"On a smaller scale, we mimicked the millionaires we worked for," recalls Wesley Ellis, who in '66 succeeded the legendary Bowman Milligan as maître d' at the club. "We'd say 'Run the drink! I'm buying a round for all the poor people in here!'"

A viewer of old Masters highlight films will see caddies lying near and even on the green while their men try to hole important putts. Their recumbent postures proved that carrying a heavy golf bag up and down Augusta National's hills with a hangover for company could just about knock you out.

Augusta National's first and second members didn't leave the grounds at day's end. Jones had his cabin by the tenth tee while Cliff Roberts resided in his virtually undecorated apartment at the end of the clubhouse nearest the detached dwellings. Before his elevation to maître d'hôtel, Wesley Ellis had been a waiter at the club for two years, and for part of that time he had a specific assignment to serve Mr. Roberts. As the waiter would discover, Roberts had his ways. Like many men in their seventies (Cliff had turned seventy-four in March of '68), his dietary habits were as constant as the sunrise: cereal, pound cake, peaches, tea, white bread, white milk, chicken salad . . . and if his strip sirloin or lamb chops were medium instead of medium rare, there was hell to pay. He did not like the greeting "How are you?" because he thought it insincere. Ellis learned to boom out "Top of the evening, Mr. Roberts!" and got a "Top of the evening, Wesley!" in return. Mr. Roberts was not to be disturbed during *Gunsmoke*, the TV western starring James Arness. A. Very. Deliberate. Speaker, he filled the holes between words with long "ahhh's." "Talking with him was difficult," recalls Steve Melnyk, the ABC-TV announcer who played in the Masters five times. "He'd take so long to respond you weren't sure you were even in a conversation."

Ellis once listened to half of a telephone call between Cliff and Augusta's chief of police, regarding a planned protest by blacks outside the National's gates. He remembers three sentences:

"Well, ahhh, godammit, they're not gonna do it."

And: "If I have to get Dick Nixon, I will."

And: "I guess I told him, didn't I, Wesley?"

Wallace Gilliam took care of the king of the club for the six months Cliff was in residence between '70 and '71. "He had so many medicines and vitamins, he looked like a drugstore," Gilliam recalls. "And you didn't just tell him it looked like a nice day. Someone called out to the weather bureau so you could tell him exactly. He wanted to know how to dress and if it was going to be warm enough for him to play golf."

Ellis and Gilliam agree that despite his quirks, Cliff remained mentally sharp in his eighth decade. Although his fastidiousness had made the club and the tournament what it was, something important had escaped his notice.

But all seemed in order late that Tuesday afternoon. Roberts dressed for dinner—the annual (since 1952) gathering of past champions, hosted by the defending champion. Tradition demanded that the host, in this case Gay Brewer, would get to pick the entrée. He decided not to push the culinary limits.

"Steak," says Gay Brewer, in answer to the obvious question. "But you know, you can pick something off the menu if you don't like what the champion picks. Like Sandy Lyle with his haggis in '89. I didn't eat that. I knew what it was.

"When I won in '67, it was the last year that Hogan played and the last year that Jones showed up at the dinner. In '68, Jones was there at the club but he didn't attend. He was in his cabin—he had that bone disease."

In addition to hosting a group that included such as Gene Sarazen and Arnold Palmer, Brewer's most vivid memory of returning to Augusta National as the defending champion was a simple one. When he checked in and opened his locker, a green jacket was hanging there. On a piece of masking tape on the hanger was written BREWER.

At about the time the men who'd won the Masters were assembling, Marble Eye carried Goalby's clubs to the trunk of his car—after someone stole a putter from a bag being stored at the club, Bob decided to keep his sticks in his Buick. They set the time to meet very early the next morning and said farewell. Marble Eye walked to the caddie area near the first fairway and slipped off his sweaty white jump suit, then he and his cousin rode the Riv to Fireball's rooming house. Most of the caddies prepared for an exciting evening on the Hill or in the ghetto. Crosshanded Henry Brown returned to his home downtown. Jones, Roberts, and certain exalted members and guests remained inside golf's original gated community.

The players spread out. Where they chose to lodge indicated something important about their attitude toward the Masters. Some players—including Goalby—simply found a hotel, like any week on the tour. But a large and increasing number of the competitors treated the Masters as anything but business as usual, and they rented a house for the week. The Masters had become an event to be savored with family and friends over the charcoal grill in someone else's backyard. "The thing was, there weren't that many good restaurants in that town," Brewer says. "I always rented a house and bought groceries." Given his gregarious nature and the tremendous effort the club made to make its foreign entrants feel at home, it was no surprise that De Vicenzo spent Masters Week '68 in private lodging, or that his host was a true Augusta National insider—Cliff Roberts's secretary, Wilda Gwin. Ms. Gwin, a good-looking woman with short brown hair, also ran the tournament headquarters. Wilda and her husband, Tom, remained in their house in nearby Country Club Hills and treated Roberto as an honored guest.

Roberto came in a package with Fred Gilbert, a high-strung and extremely enthusiastic De Vicenzo fan who had worked for DuPont in Argentina. They'd met at Ranelagh. "He reminded me of Woody Pecker [Woody Woodpecker]," Roberto says. "Woody Pecker? When he make letters to me he wrote in Spanish, very bad Spanish. We have a family reunion when we get his letters so we can all laugh. . . . He was like me writing in English. Everything I write is wrong."

As usual, real writers wrote about the previous Masters on

these last few days before the next one. Head scratching was their theme; the '67 event had been aberrant, almost perverse. Nicklaus, the defending champion, shot 72–79 and missed the cut. Hogan, who some people had thought was dead, shot 66 in the third round. Only once since 1957 had someone not named Palmer, Player, or Nicklaus won in Augusta, but in '67, Kentucky boys named Gay Brewer and Bobby Nichols were one-two, and first-timer Bert Yancey led by himself for two rounds and was tied for first going into Sunday. He finished third. Yancey caused a sensation. Dave Kindred later wrote that he seemed to float around the golf course, so smooth was his swing and his walk. His hands on a putter and his putting stroke also looked not of this world; he once played nine hundred consecutive tournament holes without three-putting. His skin was very white, his face was very serious. He harbored two secrets: mental illness, and his firm intention—no, obsession—to win the Masters. Third place would not do.

Retracing Yancey's steps in '68 begins at 315 Berckmans Road, a plain Jane one-story brick house he rented every year. It's almost directly across from Gate 6 to the club, hard by the busy intersection of Berckmans and Washington Road. Two large Augusta National–worthy pines in the front yard save the place from complete blandness, but the trees have shaded and acidified the ground so much that no grass grows beneath them. Although the house appears to be too noisy and small for a big-time golfer, Yancey was apparently intrigued by the name of the owner, Mr. J. B. Masters.

If you go there today a large young woman answers the bell after a long pause and speaks to you through the storm door. She's got an unhappy kid on her hip and more inside, judging by the muffled caterwauling from within. She gives you the what-are-you-selling look. No, she's not related to J. B. Masters. No, never heard of him. Never heard of Bert Yancey. We got nothing to do with the Masters. 'Bye.

So you stand for a minute under those big pines and listen to the swish of the wind and imagine the scene here almost forty Aprils ago. Because his place was so close to the course, Yancey hosted an occasional bridge game. The card-players and kibbitzers were all foreigners, in one way or another: Tony Jacklin, Harold Henning, Tom Weiskopf, Deane Beman, Ben Wright. Their cars would have crunched this gravel and been parked under these trees . . .

"Take a look at this," Yancey said to Weiskopf in '67, probably after a card game. He slid something large from underneath his bed in the Masterses' guest room.

Mounted on a sheet of plywood were eighteen green-painted Play-Doh replicas of the greens at Augusta National, with plastic straws serving as flagsticks.

"Damn," Weiskopf said.

"The models were very well done," he recalled for *Golf World* in 2001. "Each one was about the size of a pie plate. They were painted but pliable enough that he could move the little flagsticks around. He would look at all these hypothetical situations."

Yancey had arrived early for his first Masters the year before, armed with forty-two cans of Play-Doh and pages of notes on the intricately contoured greens he'd only seen on television and film. He worked late into the night on his science project, a regular behavior for him when he was obsessing about something. Word eventually got out about his model greens and he had to explain himself. "It was a matter of putting this information in my head and doing it physically with my hands," he said.

"It became apparent that all Bert wanted to do was win the Masters," Frank Beard said. "The healthy side of the line is called a passion and the unhealthy [side] is called obsession. Palmer and Nicklaus had a passion . . . Bert's was an obsession."

He walked around each spring like a man at the grocery store who had forgotten his list, a state of mind his friends called his Masters fog, and they called him Foggy. "He always said, 'I want to win one tournament,' " recalls his tour caddie, J. D. Gardner. "The Masters was all he ever talked about."

If genius is the infinite capacity for taking pains then Albert Winsborough Yancey was born a genius. From an early age his mind attached itself like a barnacle to complicated matters such as biochemistry, engineering, mathematics, medicine, and for better or worse, golf. But so much of golf is random, and so much of the interaction between brain and mood and muscle is unknown and probably unknowable. Golf doesn't respond well to formulas. Scientists like Yancey are often drawn to the game but they're seldom happy in it.

His start in golf presented a twist on the standard caddie-to-player epic. Malcolm Yancey, the city manager of Tallahassee, Florida, would awaken his twin sons Bert and Bill on summer mornings and drop them off at city-owned Capital City Country Club on his way to work. It was cheap baby-sitting, and cheap is important when you've got ten kids. Any of the four oldest Yanceys—Mary, Francis, Malcolm, Jr., and Jim—could have predicted how their eighth- and ninth-born siblings would act in the structured environment of golf. One brother would appreciate the challenges and possibilities of this new sport while the other brother would prefer to clamber around in the creeks, searching for frogs and throwing rocks at fish. Then the purposeful one would get mad at the playful one for his lack of attention. Albert and William Yancey were as different as twins could be.

"We were not really friends," Bill says. "That was a real hole in my life."

A burly man with a full beard and a gentle voice, Bill Yancey lives in Philadelphia, where he is a professor of sociology at Temple University. "No, it wasn't that there was so much competition between us, simply because he was better than me in golf, and baseball, and in school," he says "I remember the delight I felt in seventh grade—the first year we weren't in class together. I finally had some independence."

He also had to endure a few fewer comparisons to the brilliant Bert, who while still a student at Leon High School accepted a job in the biochemistry lab at Florida State University. With the advice and encouragement of a revered older brother, Jim, Bert's golf also progressed. Jim Yancey, a golf Renaissance man, was both a respected instructor and the superintendent of high-profile golf courses such as Doral. When Jacklin won the U.S. Open in 1971, he thanked Jim Yancey publicly.

And when Bert went manic deep in the night and he just had to talk-talk-talk, he called Jim.

Bill didn't know of his brother's mania until it got out of control in the summer of '61, his last year at West Point. Bert had gone to nearby Florida State for a year, then he surprised his twin by seeking and accepting an appointment to the United States Military Academy, up the Hudson River from New York City. The weather and the culture couldn't have been a bigger change. Florida was warm and Florida State was low-key, but at often chilly West Point, talking, whistling, being late to drill or having a smudge on your shoe were offenses that were quickly punished. First years ate their meals at attention and occupied only the front two inches of their chairs. Except for one ten-week furlough at the end of the third year, a cadet never saw a girl; the penalty for a Public Display of Affection—a kiss, for example—was twenty-two demerits and forty-four hours of walking back and forth with a rifle. Cadet Dwight Eisenhower got demerits for dancing too fast at one of the mixers during the ten weeks.

"Imagine spending the four most crucial years of adult social development, 18 to 22, segregated from your culture and peers," wrote Alex Vernon, class of '89, in a story about the Point entitled "Ghost Stories" (*American Heritage,* October 2002). "Instead of learning how to get along with others according to American norms, you learn rules and regulations. . . . All interactions between people at West Point are official, public, regulated." Rigid spines and rigid academics: mathematics and its derivative, engineering, formed the basis of all instruction at the USMA. Yancey thrived in the severe atmosphere; he was in the top 2 percent of his class. Then came his senior year.

People inherit manic depression, but Bill and his oldest sister, Mary Stuart Hartmann, remain vague about antecedents in the Yancey family. Dementia may have marked father's mother and mother's sister certainly hallucinated, "but I've never convinced myself that's where Bert's disease came from," Bill says. Possibly—psychiatrists aren't so sure about this—external events can cause eruptions. If that is true, Bill is sure his twin's first manic attack can be laid at the door of Billy Graham. In the summer before his senior year, Bert had gone to one of Reverend Graham's revivals.

Perhaps that would be the place to begin the movie of his life, the movie CBS wanted to make. To get to the dramatic point quickly, the opening scene might show the evangelist on an outdoor podium at night. "You have to make a choice between two masters," Graham booms in North Carolina accents, a halo of light glowing off his backlit hair. "It's either self or Christ. You also have to choose between two destinies. Oh, yes. The Apostle Paul said, 'And you were not redeemed by silver and gold but by the blood of Christ.' " In the audience, a young man with a military haircut nods. Yancey.

In Scene Two, we see a helicopter shot of the high granite walls of West Point, a forbidding yet gorgeous complex on a hill above a river. Inside we see Yancey wearing the uniform of an upperclassman. Others who are dressed like him are upbraiding the new guys, the plebes, shouting *Brace!* in their ears, and the new men stand so rigid and straight that their shoulder blades almost touch. The camera and the sound find Yancey. "You're gonna have to make a choice between two masters," he is telling a stiff-backed young man, whose eyes betray some confusion. "It's either self or Christ." In subsequent scenes we see Yancey not sleeping, his brain on fire with mania.

After the commercial, we see a black wrought-iron gate, and VFGH above the gate in swirling Gothic letters. Valley Forge General Hospital consists of many red-brick buildings connected by a labyrinth of corridors. Inside one of these buildings, Yancey sits alone in a padded room. In other rooms he convulses in shock therapy and converses in group therapy. He takes pills and washes them down with water from a paper cup. He dresses in pajamas and a robe and he walks, slowly, and talks, slowly—a slow locomotion known as the Thorazine Shuffle, after the numbing antipsychotic drug. Pages of a calendar fall off like leaves from a tree, indicating the passage of nine months.

Somehow, the screenwriter would communicate that they didn't actually know what the hell they were doing with Yancey in the Army hospital, and that they never diagnosed his illness.

"Bert, you should find a job with a minimum of stress," a psychiatrist tells him in an exit interview. "With your aptitude in science, perhaps something in medical research?"

"I plan to play professional golf," Yancey says.

"Oh?" the doctor says, surprised. And . . . cut.

But there was no movie. Yancey failed in a first attempt at the tour and then took a club pro job in Philadelphia. For several years he pursued golf in his single-minded way, combining constant drill with deep research into the theory and history of the game. As the late Harold Henning said, "Bert was a student in everything he did."

Wednesday, April 10

In the fifties, when Bobby Jones was too ill to play golf but felt well enough to fish, a member's son named Briscoe Merry III sometimes wheeled him down the path to the pond behind the cabins. One day Mr. Jones wanted to fish but the entertaining Briscoe Merry was not immediately available. His friend Larry Jon was there, however, and he knew how to fish, and he was given the honor. Larry Jon Wilson remembers the perfect neatness of that path and its border, and the consistent thickness of its tiny stones. And he can't forget the tasteful, expensive casual clothes Jones wore, or how kind he was. The wheelchair slid easily down the path.

"This OK, Mr. Jones?"

"This is fine, Larry Jon."

The boy set the parking brake on the chair and got the cane pole ready. He baited the hook with not one but two meal worms; one of the malodorous beetle larvae might work but two worms would fight and wiggle, which was usually irresistible to the perch in the pond. The boy cast out about five yards, the bait and hook breaking the still surface of the water, then handed the pole to Mr. Jones.

Jones stared at the liquid reflections on these outings, smoking, not talking much. He'd catch a fish and feel the tug of life on the other end of a monofilament line, then hand the rig to the boy after a few moments because he didn't have the strength to bring it in. They'd catch, release, repeat. After about forty-five minutes of this, Larry Jon Wilson rolled Robert Tyre Jones Jr. back to his cabin.

Ten years later, the pond had become a hazard on Augusta National's jewel-like par three course. One afternoon a year, on the day before the Masters, thousands of people sat on its banks.

He stopped fishing when the pain outweighed the pleasure but Jones continued to move. "There's something about playing in the Masters," Frank Beard had told a writer on Tuesday. "All those green coats, all that green money, and Bobby Jones riding around." In the fifties, when golf carts were as rare as Republicans in Georgia, the club acquired a battery-powered three-wheeler with the round look of an amusement park bumper car. In it, with stern-faced Cliff behind the wheel, Jones continued to make his presence felt in a public way.

Sometimes it was great to see him, sometimes it wasn't. On Sunday during the 1959 tournament, the cart glided to a stop next to Art Wall as he stood in the thirteenth fairway. "I understand you're a very good puttah," Jones said. Wall, a very modest man, said "oh, shucks" or something like that, then went birdie-birdie-birdie-par-birdie-birdie to win by one. Five years later and one hunded yards from where he'd met Wall, Jones and Roberts parked by the twelfth tee to join the breathless throng watching Nicklaus try to catch Palmer. A dramatic moment: Jack pulled an eight iron from the bag, and seconds dripped by as he completed the numerous steps in his preshot and preswing routine. Finally, he hit. And shanked the damn thing right over his hero's head.

But in 1968, Jones had taken his last cart ride.

They closed the course at noon on Wednesday. As always, the grounds staff lowered the blades on the greens mowers from medium to marbleize, and filled cylindrical hand rollers with water. Then they cut and rolled and cut and rolled, thereby making the practice rounds a gigantic game of bait-and-switch. While the greens were being manicured to the bone, the crowds and the players retreated to the par three course. Built in 1958 and first used as the warmup before the main event in 1960, the par three was the best thing of its type in the world. Designed by George Cobb—with constant, occasionally helpful input from Cliff Roberts, who considered it his baby—the course had the indescribable appeal of a perfect miniature. Most of the holes played downhill over deeply recessed ponds, including the one Jones used to fish in. Most every invitee played, even the aged and infirm former champions who could no longer tackle the big course. Though the crowd was exceedingly small in '68, and the skies remained somber, the air carried a familiar scent of expectation, flowers, and beer. What time's your party tonight, Mike? Hey, Danny, when's Arnie play tomorrow? Say, isn't that Claude Harmon, the '48 champ? Yes, it was. And the father of Butch Harmon still had some game, at least some short game. He made the people shout as one when he made holes-in-one with his pitching wedge on holes four and five, the first and so far last player to hole out from the tee twice in the par three. Harmon, the only club pro ever to win the Masters, got crystal vases for his aces. Bob Rosburg won with a five-under 22, and Harmon tied for third with 24. In the real tournament the next day, he played nine holes in 40 and retired—arthritis in his hands—but they paid Mr. Harmon one thousand dollars just for gracing the place with his presence.

When the par three tournament adjourned, Augusta took a deep breath. Restaurants and bars filled. Scores of calcutta parties commenced. Caddies partied in their hidden, parallel society. The Academy Awards show, hosted by Bob Hope, came on TV at ten. What would win for Best Picture—*The Graduate, In the Heat of the Night,* or the superviolent *Bonnie and Clyde?* Hope told a joke—which immediately became infamous—that referred to the postponement of the ceremony from Sunday to Wednesday because of the assassination of Dr. King. "About the delay," he said. "It didn't bother me, but it's been tough on the nominees. How would you like to spend two days in a crouch?"

Augusta National hosted the twentieth annual Amateur Dinner. For a final time, Bobby Jones attended.

Hoyt hoisted him into his chair, Mrs. Mary Jones fussed over him, and off he went. When he arrived in the Trophy Room in the clubhouse, Jones told the host, Augusta National member Charles Yates, that he would not be able to address the group as he always had. Of the sixty or seventy diners, eight were actual participants in the tournament, and the rest were honorary invitees and members of golf's governing bodies, the USGA and the R and A. They ate, they listened to and gave speeches, they swiped souvenir matchbooks. Just as Yates was about to send the group out into the night, Jones struggled slowly to a more or less standing position. "I just want to say a few words," the ghost said, but his voice was so weak the audience could hardly hear him.

CHAPTER FOUR

LIKE A DUCK,
LIKE A MONKEY

*One always feels that he is running from something
without knowing exactly what or where it is.*
—BOBBY JONES, DESCRIBING TOURNAMENT PRESSURE

Wind ruffled Alfred Wright's dark hair as he strode into Augusta
National's Quonset hut press building, an elegant man entering
a dump. The lead golf writer for *Sports Illustrated* had the faintly
preppy air of his alma mater, Yale, and the kind of looks that
women liked. He'd wooed and won one of the world's certifiable
babes, the actress Joan Fontaine, the Academy Award winner for
Best Actress in 1941 for *Suspicion*. Wright brought his glamorous
third wife to Augusta one year, and Dan Jenkins, Wright's backup
in '68, had a ball talking movies with her.

"Al was a wonderful guy," says Jenkins. "Highborn but regular. He was the last guy you'd figure for a war hero but as a Navy
pilot in WW deuce he was known as 'Mad Dog' Wright, flying a
Hellcat [dive bomber] and landing it in the dark on carriers after

shooting down Japs. . . . Al learned just enough to get by as a sportswriter—because the life appealed to him."

Wright was born and raised in Los Angeles and moved in interesting circles. He knew Humphrey Bogart and Dorothy Parker and Ronald Reagan, and he played Ping-Pong with W. C. Fields. He wrote beautifully but, compared to his successor, Jenkins, slowly. Jenkins, an ex-newspaperman, could pound out a few thousand insightful words on his Olympic typewriter in a couple of hours after a tournament but Wright, who'd been with *Life* before *SI*, frequently took all night. The effort exhausted him. This would be his last Masters. He was moving back to L.A.

His account of what happened that week in Augusta would be the definitive one, mostly because *Sports Illustrated* had become *The New York Times* of sports journalism, the official account. TV created no record: It didn't save what it broadcast, and it only showed a couple of hours on Saturday and Sunday. The Masters began on Thursday.

"It was a bright sunny day with a crisp wind out of the north," wrote Wright.

Thursday, April 11

The breeze swirling in Augusta National's tall pines made it hard to select the right club, and hard to know if you'd be more comfortable with the sweater, or without.

Freddie McLeod chose a red V-neck, a white shirt, dark tie, and white socks. At 9:37, McLeod, eighty-five, the 1908 U.S. Open champion, and Jock Hutchison, eighty-three, who won the PGA Championship in 1920, tapped ceremonial tee shots into the valley in front of the first fairway, and the thirty-second Masters had begun.

Then the first real competitors, Bob Goalby and Lee Trevino, took one of the great walks in sports, downhill from the putting green through a corridor of excited, happy fans, to the first tee. It was golf's equivalent of the Notre Dame football team emerging from the stadium tunnel onto its home field, like gladiators into the Colosseum. "Dot," said Goalby. "Maxima," said Trevino—identifying their golf balls for each other to avoid confusion and a playing-the-wrong-ball penalty. A man in a green jacket gave Bob and Lee their score cards and informed them that United States Golf Association Rules would prevail, an important detail for those in the field who played on the PGA Tour, which was most of them. The two organizations—one made of gentlemen from the country club, the other, employees at the club—were uneasy in each other's presence. The cultures clashed annually at the other non-PGA event the pros played in, the U.S. Open. The USGA had recently made two rules that the tour simply ignored. In a futile effort to speed up play, they decreed continuous putting, and allowed a player to lift and clean his ball only once, before the first putt.

The chairman of the Masters Rules Committee, Isaac "Ike" Grainger, was a former USGA president, and had been friends with Jones since Bob was a teenager. He was also a member of Augusta National. The current USGA president, Hord Hardin, also belonged to the host club. Jones had won nine USGA championships in his glory days. As Doug Ford reminds, "Bobby Jones was USGA down to his underwear."

The Masters may have smelled slightly of the USGA—Old Spice battling BO from wearing a dark blue blazer on a hot day—but Bob and Cliff's tournament was its own thing, not a USGA event per se and certainly not a crass extension of the venal professional tour.

Now there were handshakes, shaking hands, cleansing breaths, silence, and the incredibly exposed feeling of Augusta

National's first tee, a treeless plateau in a sea of green. Then . . . "Fore, please. Now drivin'. Bob. Goalby!" An Augusta National member with a carrying voice and a Georgia accent introduced everyone the same way. Phil Harrison, the starter since 1948, was as much a part of the first-tee ceremony as old Freddie and Jock.

Everything and everyone looked vivid in the bright sunshine. After two days of rain, the white dogwoods and red azaleas spiked to maximum color and the fertilized fairways popped to emerald green. The crowd around the tee reached high tide when Harrison called out "Now drivin'. Onnold. Palmah!" Arnie wore cobalt blue, and where he rolled up the sleeves of his cardigan, the light picked up the sinews and seams on his ditch digger's arms. The only other player with defined muscles was Player, who wore, as usual, black. Nicklaus, the 4–1 favorite, walked to the tee feeling extraordinarily tense for reasons he couldn't explain. He stood over his tee shot in his forest green trousers and black cardigan for long moments, his blond head swiveling from ball to target two or three more times than anyone else. Observers always felt relieved when Jack finally hit, and Jack felt relieved when he birdied the first hole. Sanders paraded in purple, Yancey wore baby blue beltless slacks and matching collarless shirt, and Casper looked like a bowling trophy in three shades of gold.

As Billy demonstrated, pants were worn tighter then, and shorter; good form demanded that you show a bit of sock. Neat was the fashion byword. New fabrics such as Arnel triacetate and Fortrel polyester sounded like rocket fuel additives and were not particularly comfortable but their creases never ceased and they would not wrinkle. With no belt to loop and buckle and no buttons to button on the front of the collarless shirts, you could get dressed in twenty seconds. Although shoes made of Corfam were infernoes for the feet, they still looked like new after a hundred wearings. Hair had grown away from most scalps—influence from young people influenced by rock musicians and revolutionaries—but it was not allowed to wander. You had it formed into a helmet by a stylist, then you commanded it to remain as stiff as a driving range mat with Consort Hair Spray, if you wanted to use the brand endorsed by Boston Red Sox outfielder Carl Yastrzemski in the pages of *Sports Illustrated.*

The playful colors on the first tee contrasted with the serious expressions on the golfers' faces, because the stakes were high, as high as they get in golf. Everyone coveted the chance to return to Augusta as an honored past champion for all the Aprils left in his life. Even postmortem, a win promised the immortality of your name on the 125-pound sterling silver trophy and on souvenir drinking cups. Arnie and Jack, the two guys with their own planes, saw the Masters as even more, as the first step to an almost unimaginable level of glory. As they said many times in the sixties, you couldn't win golf's four Majors in one calendar year—the modern Grand Slam—unless you won the first one, the Masters. First place paid $20,000; since a new Volkswagen beetle cost $1,600 in '68, and VW's equivalent car goes for about $17,000 today, we can impute a present-day value of the winner's check of about a quarter of a million. But that was just the tip of the money iceberg, at least in theory. A thousand times it had been written that a win in the Masters or the U.S. Open was worth $200,000, $500,000, perhaps as much as a million dollars, in endorsement and exhibition fees. Almost everyone believed it.

Vinny Giles did not concern himself with the cash he'd make if a miracle occurred. As an amateur, he couldn't accept prize money or payment for endorsing golf clubs or car batteries. But for a few thrilling moments on Thursday, he was forced to contemplate the possibility that he might win. "Leading the Masters at this time," called out Leo Beckman, the green-coated announcer by the ninth green, "at three under par, a young amateur from Virginia, Vinny Giles!" Applause from the gallery, a nervous smile from the young amateur from Virginia. "I was makin' putts you can't make," recalls Giles. "From thirty feet on one, from *forty* feet on five. I only had twelve putts."

Vinny had a decent crowd because he'd gone to the University of Georgia and the campus at Athens was not too far away, but his wife and parents got only a little extra company on the back nine (he shot 38, two over). Everyone noticed it: Despite the beautiful weather, the crowds were not only smaller than in previous years, they were very, very quiet. Martin Luther King had been buried in nearby Atlanta just two days before. Chastened and inward looking, on Thursday, April 11, 1968, people did not seem ready to get all giddy about a golf tournament.

Who watched? The same cast appeared year after year. Most were golf fans from across the country who came to see and adore Arnie. They wore green, rectangular badges marked SERIES on top in black and $20 in the lower left. Corporate big shots and golf insiders displayed thirty-five-dollar clubhouse badges on shirts or lapels, red metal rectangles with a window in the middle showing the wearer's name, typed in all caps. Robert Trent Jones, the biggest name in golf course architecture, scored red badges for his wife, sons Robert, Jr., and Rees, and their wives. Robert Junior had been elected as a delegate to the upcoming Democratic Presidential Nominating Convention, which would be held at summer's end in Chicago. A significant number of beer-fueled U. of Georgia students came to party by the sixteenth green (they shouted "Go Dogs!" when Giles played the hole). Dotted throughout the grounds were people from TV, radio, the newspapers. In and out of the Quonset hut were scores of scribblers from lowly dailies, a dozen or so big-name columnists like Furman Bisher of the *Atlanta Constitution,* and three writers from Mount Olympus—Wright, Jenkins, and Herbert Warren Wind of *The New Yorker.* An agent from Akron named Bucky Woy trolled for clients and shook hands on behalf of this interesting guy he'd just signed, Lee Trevino. The tournament director, an owlish former MP, Colonel Homer Shields, monitored the committee chairmen and searched for inefficiencies. Everywhere were green-jacketed members of Augusta National; gung-ho representatives of the USGA and the R and A; proud and willing volunteers from Augusta Country Club, the National's neighbor on the other side of Rae's Creek; no-charge helpers from around the country who just wanted to do anything they could for this glorious event; and one-week employees of the club. No-nonsense security men from the Pinkerton's Detective Agency looked at the paying customers with thinly disguised suspicion.

Macky Mulherin, one of the cadre of recruits from Augusta Country Club, wore a bright red coat so people would attend when he walked onto the sixteenth green and called out the names of the approaching golfers. White high-school kids such as Sam Nicholson, the quarterback on the Richmond Academy football team, and Doug Engler, the halfback he handed the ball to, worked on scoreboards or in gallery control for ten dollars a day and a concession stand lunch of sandwich, chips, candy bar, and a soft drink. They wore golf clothes. Meanwhile, a quiet black army in white jump suits speared trash and cigarette butts almost before they hit the ground, keeping this the most immaculately clean golf tournament in the world.

Lots of locals remember being there: Jimmy McLeod, a member of the Augusta State golf team, took time out from school and his job at the Seven Lakes par three course in North Augusta to observe his heroes. Don Grantham loved Arnie like everyone else, but Yancey was a cousin of a friend so he watched Bert, too. An eleven-year-old named Jim Murrah lucked into a green badge for Sunday. Someone gave it to his father, the lost luggage man at the airport, and he gave it to little Jimmy, who wanted to see Gary Player.

Early in the afternoon, a member named Hiram C. Allen, Jr., took his position at a patio table near the eighteenth green. A likable and efficient man, his function was an unnoticed detail to fans but what he did was crucial to the players because Hiram C. Allen represented the finish line. After four hours and five miles of tribulation, each player sat at the little table by the eighteenth green, signed his scorecard, and handed it to Mr. Allen. None entered Masters heaven—or hell—except by him.

Cliff Roberts oversaw everything. Bobby Jones remained in his white house near the tenth tee.

In the Quonset hut, Al Ludwick peered through his glasses at the leader board as if he might be tested on all the names and numbers. In a way, he would; Robert Eubanks, his editor at the *Augusta Chronicle,* had a rule that a story had to be written about anyone who turned in a first-round score of 69 or less. Leaders with something interesting to say made his job much easier and reduced the anxiety of creativity on deadline. Over the years Ludwick had heard too many sunburned golfers observe that they felt great and the course was in great condition. It was hard to weave prose that snapped from such skimpy thread.

Casper finished early, with a 68. OK, Ludwick thought. Not the best, not the worst. He knew Billy was no quote machine but the hooks were obvious: his religion, his putting, and his diet. He entered the press building and took a seat at a table in front. "I feel great," the Mormon elder said in his uninflected baritone. "I'm perfectly at peace with myself." He putted well, even for him—only two or three others were in his league with the short stick—and he talked about how he walked alongside his putt as it rolled toward the hole on seventeen, and when he'd gone about twenty feet the fifty-five-footer fell in. Regarding food: nothing unusual today, Billy said. For breakfast he'd had a steak and a papaya.

Ludwick caught a break when Nicklaus rolled it in from eleven feet on eighteen with his unique-looking putter, "White Fang," a Bulls Eye with its brass head painted white. The birdie gave him a 69 and an invitation to the press center. At age twenty-eight, Jack already had years of practice with the media and a good idea of what writers find interesting. He reflected on his embarrassment of a year before, when as defending champion he shot 72-79 and missed the cut. "Maybe I'm getting older," he said. "But I was more nervous than I normally am . . . I didn't calm down until the fourth hole." This tidbit gave the *Los Angeles Times* a catchy subheadline—MASTERS JITTERS.

Tommy Aaron shot 69. Ludwick scratched his head. Tommy was from upstate, Gainesville. Wore glasses. Age thirty-one. Quiet. Went to the University of Florida. He had a swing as fluid and consistent as a waterfall but his swing did most of his talking; if you could chat with him for twenty minutes you'd discover an interesting, intelligent man, but who had twenty minutes? NO SNOOZE FOR AARON AFTER 69 the *Chronicle* headlined excitingly, but the story that followed delivered only a couple of hundred words of bland: "Georgian Tommy Aaron, who has been concerned over the way he's been playing, wasn't lulled to sleep by a fine, three-under-par 69 in the Masters Golf Tournament on Thursday . . ."

Three other men broke 70, all foreigners, all with 69s: De Vicenzo, from Argentina; Devlin, from Australia; and Tony Jacklin, who Al Wright described as "the peppery young Englishman who had just become the first of his countrymen to win an American tournament since 1920." Tony's win at Jacksonville two weeks before the Masters was front-page news in *The Times* of London, and caused a significant migration of English sports-writers to Augusta. As Jacklin talked about how he made his birdies, you could see an ugly gash in his cheek, a wound suffered on Tuesday afternoon at Clark Hill Lake. For a bit of stress reduction, he'd taken his wife fishing. But when he tangled his line in a limb of an overhanging tree, and jerked it out, he hooked himself.

Jacklin and Devlin handled their debriefing with aplomb but they were as votive candles compared to Roberto, whose wit and accent lit up the room like a car's headlights on bright.

"You are surprise to see me, no?" he said with a grin when he took his place at a table in the cramped, windowless press room. Many writers—Ludwick not among them—quoted De Vicenzo's amusingly accented English phonetically: "peetching wedge," and "cheep and putt." Roberto described his round while the writers typed or took notes and tried to keep from cracking up. "I hole a twelve-foot birdie, wow. I hit a wedge four feet from hole on fifteen, make putt for birdie, wow.

"I be forty-five next Sunday. I buy everyone big Coke if I win."

Everyone misspelled his name: it's De Vicenzo, not Devicenzo, de Vicenzo, de Vincenzo, Di Vicenzo, or, as the British press often had it in the Open in '67, Vicenzo. Nearly everyone also mispronounced his surname: it's day-vee-senzo, not day-vin-senzo, not dee-vin-senzio, nor the Italianate dee-vin-chenzo. What no one missed, however, was what a good guy he was. A big man who didn't act big, his relaxed body language put people at ease. *The New York Times* pronounced him "colorful and popular." Ludwick wrote "likeable veteran." The most popular descriptive was "gay caballero."

UPI had sent out on its wire an unusually heartwarming story about Roberto and a lot of papers ran it on their sports pages this very day. In time, this anecdote—often embellished—became a staple of after-dinner speakers and Sunday morning sermons, including one by televangelist Robert Schuler. Undoubtedly, some of the men in the Masters press center had heard it. It happened in Dallas: With a long face and a heavy heart, De Vicenzo's caddie in the Dallas Open told his boss about his son. The poor kid had leukemia, he said, hospital bills were mounting, and all the money was gone. Roberto, a former caddie, had sons himself; he pulled out his wallet and dug deep, handing over almost all he had, which was several hundred dollars. Later, when someone told him he'd been conned—the caddie didn't have a son, much less one with leukemia—Roberto expressed relief, not anger. "That is the best news I have heard all day," he said.

On the day the '68 Masters began, the *Los Angeles Times* headlined BIG-HEARTED DI VICENZO FALLS FOR SOB STORY, BUT HE'S NO PIGEON.

While Roberto charmed the writers, Goalby pounded out more practice balls and Marble Eye picked them up. He'd played well, and would have had to entertain the press with the details of his 69, but he bogied eighteen and had to settle for 70. It all happened so fast: When old farts McLeod and Hutchison dropped out after a few holes, the second group off the tee zoomed around the National in three hours. Goalby and Trevino might have threatened the all-time record of one hour and fifty-seven minutes (Gene Sarazen and George Fazio, 1947) if not for that north wind. Bob puzzled for long moments with his hand on an iron, muttering numbers, scanning the treetops for clues about wind direction and strength. "One sixty-two to the front, pin's back, wind against. Or a little bit from the left. One sixty-two, is that what you've got, Frank? Huh?" Marble Eye stayed ready with his yardage estimates but Goalby didn't call on him very often. And except for cleaning his golf ball and tending the flagstick, he had no duties on the green at all. Goalby didn't ask him to read a single putt.

"Here they come." One ball rolled into view, then another. Doug Engler climbed the ladder leaning on the small scoreboard to the left of the tenth green. He'd already placed the plastic GOALBY and TREVINO placards in their places and how he put a green O next to the Goalby, indicating he was even par. The golfers appeared, walking fast down the steep green fairway. The short, dark-skinned guy took big steps and swung his arms emphatically from the elbows. Lee's breezy, rolling gait looked a lot different from Goalby's stride; Bob moved like a quarterback evaluating the defense as he walked to the line of scrimmage. A quarterback facing third and long.

From his perch on the scoreboard, Engler watched the golfers exit the green and hurry to the eleventh tee. What happened next is one of his two or three most vivid memories of the '68 Masters. Goalby stopped and motioned emphatically to Marble Eye not to follow him to the tee but to walk ahead, up *there*, hurry *up*, to the top of the hill, to watch the tee shots land. "He was so rude to that caddie," Engler recalls. "My impression to this day is 'what an asshole.' "

But he wasn't. "He was just hard on himself, kind of tense," says Marble Eye. "A hell of a nice guy, once you got to know him." He points out that his boss saved him a lot of steps by taking his driver after holing out at eight and ten and a couple of other greens, and having him walk ahead—not every player did that. Notwithstanding that bit of courtesy, golf was a battle for Goalby, not a figurative fight, but an actual conflict that caused him to exhort or berate himself constantly. He was also "a bit of a loner"— his words—who practiced as much as anyone since Hogan. And his willingness to offer an opinion on almost anything related to professional golf earned him a behind-his-back nickname, "the Bulldog."

"Bob was a go-to kind of guy, as honest as the day is long," says Ford. Goalby had the respect of his peers, and a no-bullshit charm. Members flocked to him for lessons or a beer during his days as an assistant pro, and pro-am partners appreciated his sincerity and his effort. But the best proof of the pleasing side of his personality was how he smiled and talked his way into the arms of a babealicious TWA flight attendant named Sarah Dillaha. He was thirty-four, she was ten years younger. They met on October 22, 1962, an easy date for her to remember, because precisely two months later, they were married.

"It was an early Los Angeles-to-St.-Louis flight, and he was the last one on board," Sarah recalls. "The agent slammed the door on his back and he flashed his smile at me. 'Where can I sit?' he asks. We're on a 707 with a total of thirteen passengers. I say, 'Anywhere you want.' He says, 'I'd like to sit with you.'"

Because of his age, she thought he was married. But by the end of the flight, Bob had her number—she wrote it in his checkbook—and he called her until she agreed to see him. Things went well for a month and a half but Bob wanted to escalate. "I was staying at a Holiday Inn in St. Louis and he called me from Florida," says Sarah, "and he says, 'I've got two questions: Do you mind if I don't get that Cadillac we talked about? Lincoln's giving me a new car. And what about getting married before Christmas?' Well, we threw a wedding together in two weeks.

"Why did it happen so fast? I've thought a lot about that. I think it was an indication of the success he was feeling at the time. He'd had two wins on the tour that year and was feeling good and confident and complete in his adult life."

He'd come a long way. When Goalby finally quit college and football and committed to golf, he hung a tarp on a clothesline in his parents' backyard and hit balls into it hour after hour. *Whack-thump. Whack-thump* . . . He sold Fairlanes, Falcons, and T-Birds for Auffenberg Ford in the morning and again at night. Between shifts with tire kickers who said, "I remember that pass you threw to beat East St. Louis," he kept a golf club in his hand. St. Clair Country Club charged just twelve dollars a month for a junior membership. He joined.

Golf, a job, no significant financial or personal obligations, and a goal in sight—another young man might have enjoyed this year-and-a-half-long interval. Goalby did not. Walking in the front door at the club seemed so odd, like he was a caddie posing as a member. "I felt like a bum," he recalls. "What was I doing with my life? Golf? I'd have to be crazy to think I was going to beat Hogan and Palmer and Snead."

In the money games on tough, tight St. Clair, he'd discovered his emotional liability. "I had a temper," he recalls. "Guys would say I couldn't make it [as a golfer] and that just pissed me off more."

The *whack-thump* in the backyard continued, and it paid off. A great athlete with, at last, focus on one game, he won the Kansas Open and the Tri-State Open and the St. Louis District Amateur and the Irvin S. Cobb Invitational in Paducah, Kentucky—"and a bunch of other little shit. Everything I played in, damn near." His identity became more secure. He turned pro and snagged an assistant's job at Wee Burn Country Club in snooty Darien, Connecticut, for thirty-nine hundred dollars and a room above the pro shop. When snow fell and the club closed, he stuffed everything he owned into his '54 Plymouth Savoy, a blue two-door with a heater but no radio, and drove to Florida. In the final event on the tour of 1957, the Mayfair Inn Open, he shot 64 in the last round to tie George Bayer, Art Wall, Walter Burkemo, and Leo Biagetti for last money. "We split one hundred dollars five ways," Goalby recalls. "Leo Biagetti. That was a crazy son of a bitch.

"So now I'm qualified for the next tournament, see? But the L.A. Open (the first event of 1958) is on the opposite coast. I'll never forget that drive—they charged forty-five cents a gallon for gas in the desert. It was twenty-something in Florida."

At least until it warmed up back in Connecticut, Goalby exchanged the safe poverty of the assistant pro for the glamorous poverty of the touring pro. "I could get by on $150 a week," he says. "The Holiday Inn was $12.95, divided by two because I'd have a roommate. Forty or fifty bucks for a caddie for the week. Meals at Morrison's Cafeterias."

After Goalby shot 71-69-69-66 and won the 1958 Greater Greensboro Open—and two thousand dollars—he decided not to go back to Wee Burn and the little room above the pro shop.

The first big-time player to befriend him was Doug Ford, a scrappy little guy with a dime-store swing and a short game from Neiman-Marcus. Like Goalby, he knew cars, and occasionally reconditioned luxury vehicles to sell at a nice profit. Ford's moment in the sun had come at the '57 Masters, when he holed a bunker shot on the final hole for a 66 and a three-shot win over Snead. "On a drive from Oklahoma City to Hot Springs in '59," Goalby recalls, "that was when Doug told me how to play every hole at Augusta National."

When financial success visited him for the first time in his life—he won about $25,000 in '59, the same in '60 and $31,300 in '61, good money in those days but hardly a fortune—Goalby did two revealing things: He bought his mother a new car, and he built his parents a house. The car was a Volkswagen, which cost $1,312 and which his mother loved. The house was a nice-looking two-story over on the good side of St. Clair Country Club, far from the racket from the railroad track. His generosity didn't leave much in his own bank account, so after the wedding, Bob and his new bride lived with George and Helen—Bob's folks—when they weren't on the road. "He remained *terribly* tight with his parents," says Sarah.

The nomad's life seemed like a lark at first but the fun faded quickly. Sarah wanted to talk with someone, anyone, outside of golf—or to at least have dinner with another couple, like Don and Pat January. But it seldom happened. "Bob had his group of older buddies. Art Wall—oh, he was fun. He did not like me. It'd be mid-July and he'd be in a wool sweater and want the AC off. Doug Ford was brusque but underneath a sweet guy. And Gardner Dickinson, always doing a caricature of Ben Hogan."

"We'd been married four or five months when I became pregnant. I was dying to nest, carrying these ornaments around to make hotel rooms feel like home, and I made loud noises about getting a house." Bob found a little lot he liked in a shady neighborhood in Belleville, a block from his sister Shirley's place. "She was *extremely* tight with Bob," Sarah says. The house they built for themselves was smaller than the one Bob had built for his parents.

She didn't like Belleville; he wouldn't live anywhere else. She wanted to see the world; he hated to leave the U.S.A. and never played in the British Open. She sensed that her in-laws wished he'd married a local girl. He dedicated his life to his craft but she wasn't really into golf; her lack of interest in the game disappointed him deeply. "Now *there* was a conflict," Sarah says. "Duh."

The duality of her husband's personality presented another problem. Sometimes Bob got so mad on the golf course that he was harder to watch than a Steven Seagal movie. Sarah remembers walking up the eighth fairway of Augusta National in '67 with *St. Louis Post-Dispatch* golf writer Bill Beck, who she calls "a wonderful, understanding person who never held a grudge." But Beck had written something Bob didn't like, and when Bob went dead left off the tee and then saw the offending writer, he snapped. "Now, you son of a bitch, you can write about how I hooked it into the woods," he said. Mortified, Sarah walked back to the clubhouse with Beck.

On the other hand: At Doral one year, Goalby was in contention with an itinerant caddie named Walter Montgomery on his bag, a caddie who lost track of his position relative to his boss's ball and accidentally kicked it. Montgomery started to apologize for causing the momentum-killing penalty stroke but Goalby wouldn't hear it. "You didn't mean to do it," he said, and put an arm around the caddie's shoulders. "Let's go, we'll get it back." Montgomery always told that story to trump anyone's Angry Goalby tale.

After a couple of children were born—Kye in '64 and Kel in '67—following Bob on one of his marathon business trips became less attractive than ever. In that pre-daycare era, the families of touring pros were more refugees than the honored guests they are today. Entire weeks were spent by motel swimming pools. At the course, one young mother would play with several sets of kids in the parking lot while the other mothers watched their husbands in the tournament. Then they'd switch.

So Bob usually left home alone, in his four-door Mercury stuffed with clubs and clothes or from the St. Louis airport on airlines that no longer exist: TWA, Eastern, National. His earnings slumped in the first few years of the marriage but in '66 he won fifty-five thousand dollars and in '67 he won seventy-nine thousand dollars, tenth most on the tour. Bob the Ironman played in as many as twenty-nine seventy-two-hole events a year. Back in Belleville, Sarah the Golf Widow took care of the kids and the house and waited for his nightly phone call. He'd tell her what he'd shot, where he was staying, describe what he was working on, and ask her if she'd fed the dog. On days when he just wanted to give her his score—for free—he'd call collect and speak in code:

Operator: I have a collect call from Tommy Shaw. Will you accept?

Sarah: Tommy Shaw? Oh, dear. No.

"Doug Ford" and "Tommy Bolt" were good scores—69 or 70, they forget which—but for some reason, "Tommy Shaw" indicated a terrible number, like 78.

Bob's calls to his wife during the '68 Masters were to Arkansas, where Sarah and the kids were visiting her parents. She felt glad to be there, dyeing Easter eggs and letting her mother help with diaper changes. Besides, to her Little Rock "was a metropolis compared to Belleville." Looking back on all of it—her isolation in her adopted home town, the bad vibes from her new family, her husband's immersion in a game she didn't care for—Sarah Goalby says yes, their marriage was in trouble in 1968.

Good Friday, April 12

Casper 68

Aaron, De Vicenzo, Devlin, Jacklin, Nicklaus 69

Goalby, Pittman, Zarley 70

Yancey, Floyd, January, Giles, Sugimoto, Keiser 71

The death chart on the front page of the *Augusta Chronicle* reminded readers that 279 Americans had died in Vietnam the previous week, and 5,507 had been killed thus far in '68, bringing the total to 21,054. These sad stats appeared beneath the main story, the announcement by Secretary of Defense Clark Clifford that 24,500 more Reservists were ordered to join the battle in Southeast Asia. The local angle: The 174 men of the 319th Transportation Company of Augusta were included in the call-up.

It was a gorgeous day, with a high of seventy-six recorded at the airport, and the wind a mere whisper. The course sped up and the fairways remained perfect. In the unusually benign conditions, first-round Masters leader Billy Casper shot 75 and blamed it on "something I consumed"—a peach, possibly a sausage. Bruce Devlin, the tournament leader at six under after nine holes, went bogey–quadruple bogey on ten and eleven. On eleven, he hooked his three-iron second shot into the hazard in front of the green. From the drop area, he tried to shave it too close and left his lob in the high grass on the bank. He slipped when he swung at that one, missing the Dot completely or driving it closer to the center of the earth; it was hard to say. For a moment after his swing he teetered above the still water like a drunk on a curb, but he twisted athletically and dove back to shore.

Four-time Masters champion Arnold Palmer played with a distracted air, as if he was straining to make out the words of a song only he could hear. With his horrendous 72-79, scores identical to Jack's in '67, Arnie missed the cut (by two) for the first time since he made his Masters debut in 1955. He offered no explanation or excuse. "I'll be back next year to try to . . . make the cut," he said with a wan smile, irony from Arnie, the four-time champion. He still signed the autographs and still met the press, so different from the post-traumatic-round conduct of the best player of the early twenty-first century. For the silent thousands in Arnie's gallery, this Masters was over. Nineteen sixty-eight was a bummer, all right.

The second round wasn't all pratfalls and tummyaches, however. Frank Beard, then in his third or fourth year of alcoholism, according to his later calculations, shot 65. Player shot 67 for a

139 total and tied for the lead with January. "I'm the fittest man here," Gary said to a writer who had admired his physique. Goalby, Nicklaus, and Beard ended Friday one shot back. Aaron was two back at three under. Three back at two under were De Vicenzo, Yancey, Devlin, Floyd, and Jacklin.

Goalby felt like he was dreaming: 70-70; he'd never done this well at Augusta before. His "little mental gimmick" as he called it, the mantra that kept him from snap-hooking his driver, continued to work—but not perfectly and not every time. "We had a little incident in the second round on number eight," recalls Marble Eye. "He quick-hooked it and he said somethin'." Someone in the gallery who thought he was the target of the remark looked up with a "what the hell?" look but Marble Eye said, "He wasn't talkin' to you, sir," and that was it. The evil hook appeared again two holes later, a few yards from Bobby Jones's window. You've got to curve it right to left off the tenth tee to have a second shot of reasonable length, and Goalby did—but too much. Gallery guard Sam Nicholson, the high-school quarterback, arranged the ropes and the spectators so they wouldn't interfere with Goalby's second shot from the orange pine straw beneath the towering pines. "He comes down the hill and he's just airin' it out," recalls Nicholson. "One expletive after another. But then he hit just a miraculous shot." Goalby threaded a low hard hook through the trees, past the fairway bunker and onto the green. He made the thirty-foot putt for an unlikely birdie. This was an excellent sign: Making chicken salad from chicken shit is what winners do.

Bob signed his card, spoke briefly to the press ("I'm very pleased with my game as a whole but there is still room for improvement"), then marched to the practice tee. Marble Eye retrieved balls in the fading light, alone in the practice fairway except for Willie Peterson, doing the same duty for Jack. It was almost dark when Goalby waved his man in.

"He may have said, 'I'm gonna win this,' that night or the next, I don't really remember," says Sarah. "I was excited for him just because it looked like he'd finish high enough to qualify for the Masters the next year. That was always a struggle. I'm a natural pessimist—qualifying for the '69 tournament was as much as I could hope for."

As usual, Roberto didn't phone home. Calls to Argentina could take hours to complete and were very expensive. Besides, he had no particular news for Delia. He started late on Friday afternoon and shot 73 in the company of the dyspeptic Casper. "On number three, I played like a monkey," Roberto told the press. "I was in the trees to the left and the trees to the right. On fifteen, I hit my second shot into the water. I played that hole like a duck." The deadline writers loved this, of course, quotes that didn't need a lot of written upholstery to seem interesting. "He's fast becoming one of the most popular players in the tournament," they wrote in the *Chronicle*.

Yancey had had an interesting pairing: Arnold Palmer. Playing well with Arnie required an extraordinary amount of concentration because his fans rushed to the next hole like Tokyo commuters as soon as he putted out. Golfers used to still backgrounds had to adjust or suffer. The King's gallery also made a lot more noise than was considered quite proper but his double bogey on twelve and his triple on fifteen quieted the usual war whoops and rebel yells. Yancey didn't seem to be bothered by any of it. He shot 71.

"Bert was always stoic, a little humorless," says Bill Yancey of his twin. "I remember after his first Masters (in '67) when he finished third, I went up to him all excited but he never responded one way or another. He said, 'OK, we'll be back next year,' or something like that. I would have been devastated."

At the Los Angeles Open in January, Bert had noticed that a good-looking blonde had been following him for a couple of days. He asked his sister-in-law if she knew who she was. "Faye Dunaway," she said. "Don't you remember? You went to high school together." Bert, clueless, said hello and asked the actress what she was doing in L.A. "I live here now," said the costar of the hottest movie in the world, *Bonnie and Clyde*.

Immersed in a competitive cocoon, especially the one he cultivated at the Masters, Yancey could say hi like "hi" meant go to hell. Or he could look right through you. He and the straight-ahead Goalby didn't like each other. "I thought he was an ass-hole," Bob says. De Vicenzo remembers the time he spent with Yancey in Africa for a "Shell's Wonderful World of Golf" match. "Very good player," Roberto says, "but . . ." He wrinkles his nose and holds up his right hand and moves it from side to side, like the Queen Mother greeting a crowd. "But kind of in a fog."

Yet no one could be harder to describe through anecdote than Bert Yancey and no one deserves gentler treatment. For who could pretend to know which behavior was him and which was his disease, and which was a blend of the real Bert, manic-depressive disorder, and lithium? As a sufferer of an incurable sickness of mood, and a self-medicator, he played a game much tougher than golf and for higher stakes than the biggest tournament. "Back then, they didn't know as much as they do now [about drug therapy]," says Scott Yancey, Bert's third child, a golf pro in suburban Philadelphia. "My father believed he was smarter than everybody, including the doctors. He wanted to see how little he could take."

Legend has it that the therapeutic effects of lithium carbonate were discovered by a Christian missionary to Latin America who noticed the very even-keel nature of the people he was trying to convert. He analyzed the water and found the unusual presence of Li_2Co_2, the white, powdery salt of the lightest known metal. They've noticed this in El Paso, too: There's a relatively high concentration of lithium salt in the water and a low local incidence of mental illness. But a sufferer of mania with depression can't just swallow a pill of the stuff and expect to stop blowing through the ceiling and disappearing through the floor. It takes weeks to work, which was what made Bert's experimentation so dangerous, and put him in danger of another "nervous breakdown." But he hated the drug. It dulled him, gave him a slight hand tremor, and as he told his twin, "made life really boring." Without lithium carbonate, he could live where life really felt like something, in a world called hypomania, a creative, exciting state of mind just this side of madness. That was where the models of the greens at Augusta National resided, and the best books, and the most intuitive thinking, and the least sleep, and the best golf.

But if he went too long without his medication or if the doses were too small or too infrequent—disaster. In the grip of mania, he once attempted to climb into the control tower at LaGuardia Airport in New York, a point from which he believed he could contact billionaire recluse Howard Hughes, with whom he was sure he could find a cure for cancer. He told someone who came for him in an ambulance that he had found the center of the earth. It was under a penny at Niagara Falls.

But those breaks with the real world were still a few years away. Now, he was this ethereal golf pro with a smooth walk and a smoother swing and a putting stroke from God. When he won the Portland (Oregon) Open in '66, he used his black-shafted Cash-in putter only 102 times, a tour record. That he'd almost won the first Masters he played in amazed his peers, and now, in his second, he was contending again. He was two under after two rounds, with two birdie twos on the sixteenth. "You couldn't win or even do that well in your first five years," says January. "You had to know where to drive on what day and what pins you could shoot at. There were no pin [hole location] sheets, remember. And the greens were so demanding."

Yet here was Yancey, defying the odds with his putter, with chessboard strategizing, and with ardent desire. He told Gary Player before the tournament that he wanted this as badly as he'd ever wanted anything. "I think I would almost be willing to retire if I won the Masters," he said. He was twenty-nine.

Yancey's second ex-wife, Linda, doesn't remember exactly what they did that Friday night. You wonder if he got the Play-Doh models out from under the bed and mulled the ramifications of a back right hole location on the eleventh green. Maybe he stood in the front yard of the Masterses' house, so close to the course of his dreams he could smell it, and watched the total eclipse of the moon.

Saturday, April 13

The first time De Vicenzo and Goalby breathed the same air and played the same course was at the Houston Open in February 1958. Roberto shot 70-70-71-71 and finished tied for second, one shot behind Porky Oliver. "That was the first time I ever thought I might win a tournament," Goalby says. "I was in the second-to-last group on Sunday. But Porky shot 67 and I shot 80." In their second event together, two months later, at Greensboro, Bob shot 71-69-69-66 and won for the first time on tour. Bob and Roberto think they may have been paired a couple of times in early sixties, they're not sure. But there was enough contact for each to have formed an opinion of the other.

"I liked Roberto," Goalby says. "A good guy. Crazy like a fox. Snead says he spoke better English when he first met him in '45 than he did ten years later."

"Very clever fellow. I like Goalby," says Roberto. "He intelligent. Went to university. Make good presentation. Well dress. Look good."

At 1:12 Saturday, with the temperature rising toward its daytime high of seventy-nine on another gorgeous spring day, Goalby and De Vicenzo played the third round of the '68 Masters together. Bob wore rust-colored Sansabelt slacks hiked to bellybutton level, and a white shirt. Roberto had an off-day sartorially, in brown trousers, a red shirt, and old-man's black-and-white brogan golf shoes.

"Now drivin'. Roberto. Devinsenzio!" Like the title character in the movie *Gladiator*, Roberto liked to feel the ground on which the battle was about to take place, so he almost never used a tee for his first shot of the day. No one hit the driver (or a brassie) off the deck as well or as frequently, a shot that required a looseness and confidence that few other players possessed. He learned the shot as a kid because, he says, "We were too poor to afford a tee."

Roberto's strength and length impressed Marble Eye. "He hit it really big, as big as Larry Ziegler or Nicklaus," the caddie recalls. "He hit it past Goalby all day." Except once: On the thirteenth tee, the boomerang-shaped par five, Goalby hit his nightmare shot, a pull hook. He watched in horror as the ball curved toward the woods and the thin, dark stream beneath the pines . . . but he'd whacked it so hard that the ball got around the corner, took a big bounce and a long roll, and he had only a seven iron left to the green. By forty yards, it was the longest drive he ever hit on thirteen. The resultant two-putt birdie got him back to even par for the day, four under for the tournament, and tied for third.

On fifteen, Goalby showed how well he was strategizing. He had a long way to reach the green of the par five in two; should he lay up or go for it, and risk not clearing the pond in front of the green? He settled on a third course, and hit more or less on purpose into the gallery to the right of the green. Human backstops were better than trees or earth, because they had to move out of the way if your ball stayed among them. And those who parked to the right of fifteen at Augusta National were known as a friendly bunch. Balls often trickled out of the tangle of feet and handbags toward the greens. Once cameras caught a man slapping Arnie's ball toward the green like a handball player. No shenanigans were evident, but Goalby's ball rolled from the people to a couple of yards from the green. He chipped up to about five feet and made the putt and was tied, briefly, for the lead.

Throughout the round Marble Eye observed his opposite number with professional detachment. The word was that Roberto's caddie could read a green like it was the top row in an eye chart. Although it was plain that Crosshanded Henry Brown was not the brightest bulb on the Christmas tree, he seemed to see slopes others missed and he had the emotional intelligence to prod or cajole golfers into hitting good shots. Marble Eye knew this physically graceful man from previous Masters mostly because it was hard not to know Crosshanded Henry Brown. "He was talkative, very talkative, but he didn't always know what he was talkin' about," Goalby's caddie says. "He'd say, 'Hey man, I'm *right*. This is how it is, this is how it's gonna be.' And the *way* he talked, he was hard to understand. No, I never had a drink with him. He was not a regular kind of guy you want to spend time with. He took things too hard. Not like me, I'm kind of easy-goin'."

But De Vicenzo and his caddie clicked. Fractured syntax didn't bother Roberto, who improvised English himself, and

Crosshanded Henry Brown's firm opinions on the club needed for the next shot usually gave Roberto a little shot of confidence. Marble Eye noticed that the other golfer and caddie literally put their heads together before every putt, while Goalby hadn't asked for his opinion all week.

After the round, Bob and Roberto shook hands and walked to the back right side of the green to sit under an umbrella with Hiram C. Allen and sign and return their score cards. Only a green-and-white gallery rope separated the round metal table from the spectators, an informal setting for a solemn occasion. Goalby had scarcely begun his hole-by-hole review when De Vicenzo signed on the line marked PLAYER, rose, and said, "Good luck, Bob, I'll see you later." To Goalby's surprise, Roberto didn't seem to examine his card at all before he signed it.

Third rounds have acquired the nickname "moving day," implying that this is time to get out of town if you've missed the cut, or, if your prospects are rosier, to put yourself into position for the Sunday finale. Moving day it was, for Arnie. That morning, he rode in Bobby Jones's old seat in Cliff Roberts's cart. It may have looked like penance for missing the cut, but it wasn't; Cliff and Arnie really liked each other, and Arnie enjoyed seeing his public in almost any circumstance. After an hour or two of this, Palmer went out to Daniel Field and revved up his jet. He dipped a wing when he flew over Augusta National, then headed north, to Latrobe, Pennsylvania. He'd be home in time to watch the Masters on TV.

As for the contenders, this was a moving day with no progress. No one asserted himself convincingly, or played so poorly as to have no hope on Sunday. Had Player not made an S-shaped downhill thirty-footer on eighteen, a putt he was merely trying to get close, the final day would have started with a six-way tie for first. Nine players were within two shots of the lead, and sixteen of the best were within four, including Trevino and Nicklaus. "Four shots is nothing on this golf course," Jack said. By far, this was the closest Masters in history.

When it was over a day later, one of the leading men would cry, one would smile, and one simply got in his car and drove home. A fourth one got so angry he looked around for someone to punch.

CHAPTER FIVE

BOBBY LOCKE, INTERNATIONAL MAN OF MYSTERY

Drive for show, putt for dough.

—ARTHUR D'ARCY "BOBBY" LOCKE

He killed a man who demanded his wallet and was convicted of manslaughter, sentence suspended. He won four British Opens, the last in circumstances that remind you of the '68 Masters. He piloted scores of World War II combat missions in a four-engine B-24 bomber, and survived. He got hit by a train and only barely survived. He came to the United States from his home in South Africa in '47 to play the tour and positively highjacked first place, which didn't please Hogan, Demaret, and Snead. In '48, he won the Chicago Victory Open by sixteen shots, still the largest-ever winning margin on the U.S. tour. In '49, on a flimsy pretext, the PGA banned him. He hooked every shot, including putts. He was the greatest putter ever. After he was gone, his wife and daughter committed suicide together and died holding hands. He coined one of golf's most famous phrases. His nicknames—Old Muffin

Face and The Archbishop—spoke to his doughy countenance and to his slow procession down the world's fairways, a pace that put you in mind of parade floats or ocean liners. In an increasingly casual fashion era, he always wore a long-sleeved white shirt, a sleeveless sweater and a dark tie above enomous plusfours, which flapped around his birdy legs. No one who saw Bobby Locke ever forgot him.

"He didn't look like an athlete at all," comments Ben Wright, once the golf writer for the London *Financial Times* and later an announcer for CBS Television. "Bloodhound's jowls and a purple face. His swing was a very strange rolling motion around his belly. But no one ever putted as well. We played a round at Moor Allerton [in Northern England] and he hit the hole all eighteen times. Nine of them stayed in for birdies. 'Oh, that happens quite a lot,' he said."

He had a wicked sense of humor, always delivered deadpan. When Wright left an important putt short, Locke sighed and said in his clipped South African accent, "What a tragedy we asked you to bother."

In the time of Hogan, Nelson, and Snead in the United States, the three best in the rest of the world were De Vicenzo, Peter Thomson—an Australian—and Locke. The latter two owned the Open Championship in the first decade after the war, each having won three. Form held in '57 at the Old Course at St. Andrews, as Peter and Bobby fought to the finish. What happened at the end of that emotional day by the North Sea—or after the end—recurred eleven years later in Augusta. A golfer did one thing and recorded another, television produced an irrefutable record of what actually took place, and wise men debated what must be done. Presented with similar facts, the tribunal in Scotland and the one in Georgia returned opposite decisions. Both cited the same rule book.

Rules ruled in 1957. In April, the PGA made a splash by suspending Don January, Ernie Vossler, George Bayer, and Doug Higgins for deliberately shooting high scores. When they were not allowed to withdraw from the third round of the Kentucky Derby Open, the four professionals played but gave something less than their full effort. The PGA gave them thirty days off.

In June, the USGA debarred Harvie Ward, one of the best amateurs since Bobby Jones. Ward played (a lot) and worked (a little) for golf gadfly and USGA Executive Committee member Eddie Lowery, a Lincoln-Mercury dealer in San Francisco. Ward won the British Amateur and two U.S. Amateurs and he might have sold a car or two. But Harvie, no rich kid, admitted that he had twice accepted reimbursement for tournament expenses from his wealthy patron. Mustn't do that, the USGA said, and disinvited him from its competitions for a year.

The biggest brouhaha came at the end of the month. On June 30, Mrs. Jacqueline Pung of Hawaii stepped off the final green of the U.S. Women's Open, hugged her daughter, Barnett, and smiled her beautiful smile. In an event filled with the best-known pros, like Mickey Wright and Betsy Rawls, Jackie had won—or had she? The scorecard she'd signed had the correct total—she shot 72 that day at Winged Foot—but one of the individual holes was wrong. On the fourth hole, where she'd made a six, a five had been marked. The rules were clear on this: The player is responsible only for her score on each hole. If your scorecard shows a number on a hole lower than that actually taken, and you sign that card, the penalty is disqualification. And that's what happened to Jackie Pung, who burst into tears when they gave her the bad news. Lincoln Werden, the golf writer for *The New York Times*, passed the hat for the sad young lady from the fiftieth state and his hat came back with $2,500—some reports say as much as $3,000—by either account a good deal more than the first place money of $1,700, which went to Miss Rawls.

Locke came to the eighteenth tee at the Old Course with a two-shot lead over Thomson, who had already finished. Harsh sun and wind had reddened faces all day, but now the breeze had died and mellow sunshine shone on the unusually large crowd surrounding the home hole. It had already been an unforgettable day for Locke's playing partner, a wunderkind named Bruce Crampton. In his second Open, Crampton, twenty-one, had played superbly to get in the final group for Friday's double round (this was the first Open in which the leaders went off last). But something went haywire in the young Australian's rhythmic swing so that he had to endure a golfer's worst nightmare, the equivalent of the wearing-only-underwear-at-the-formal-ball dream—the shanks. He hit six laterals in the final round, and shot 78–79 for the day.

Meanwhile, Locke was at the height of his powers. "On number seven, a dogleg right par four, the wind was blowing very hard from right to left," Crampton recalls. "With his big hook, I thought there was no way he could get the ball near the hole with his second shot." The flagstick waved in the wind in the front right of the green, the most difficult possible spot for a hooker like Locke. Bobby had a go with a nine iron, aiming east to go north. His shot curved through the air so much it appeared to be coming backward at the end, like a boomerang returning to its thrower. The ball's semicircular journey ended eight feet behind the cup. Locke took his hook stance and his hook stroke and the ball rolled obediently in.

"That one tried to get out, Cap," he remarked drily to Crampton. He called everyone Cap.

Two strokes ahead, one hole to play: Bobby drove far left on the final hole, a short par four bordered by history and ten thousand highly involved Scottish golf fans. The crowd was allowed to stream in behind the final group after the tee shots were away.

Crampton looked over at his companion and was startled to see tears streaming down his face.

The young Australian hit his second shot, not a particularly good one, well above the hole. Locke composed himself, then pitched his ball as if he was pitching horseshoes. He almost got a ringer; his practically perfect running seven iron finished two feet below the hole. Another deep-throated roar from the crowd, another tip of the hat from the about-to-be new Champion Golfer.

Crampton went for his putt, missed, and had a four-footer coming back. Still away. "Would you move your mark please, Bobby?" he murmured. Locke obliged, putting the club head of his hickory-shafted magic wand next to his silver coin. He picked up the coin and placed it carefully opposite the toe of the club, out of young Bruce's line.

After holing his putt, Crampton walked toward the wooden scorer's table at the back of the green. He heard, rather than saw, the inevitable: Locke made his putt and the crowd erupted. Bobby had won by three over Thomson. Minutes later, The Archbishop stood in the sunshine on the stone steps of the Royal and Ancient's clubhouse, his hair plastered to his scalp, a light-colored jacket complementing his usual white shirt and dark tie. Mr. H. Gardiner-Hill, captain of the R and A, wore tweed, as you must when your name is H. Gardiner-Hill. He handed Locke the Claret Jug. In front of the two smiling men stood a black microphone the size and shape of a baseball. Locke cleared his throat. . . .

Crampton and a number of the other golfers took a train to London that night, then flew to Paris the next day for the next event on the tour in Europe, the French Open. There in a hotel lobby they watched a television replay of the last few holes of the Open. Something they saw startled them: After Locke moved his coin on the eighteenth green, and Crampton holed out, Bobby *forgot to move his coin back.* The implications were enormous: He'd breached Rule 22–3. For placing his ball in an incorrect spot and playing it from there, he should have been penalized two strokes. Which meant that the new champion shouldn't be the new champion. He deserved a five on the last hole, not the three he signed for. Thus, he'd signed an incorrect card, with a score on a hole lower than what he had actually made. Remember Jackie Pung? Disqualification was automatic. Wasn't it?

No. After it learned what had occurred, the R and A invoked the rarely used Rule of Equity, Rule 1–4, the rule you use when you can't figure out what rule to use. It was written to address "any point in dispute that is not covered by the rules." The gist of it was, when in doubt, you do what's fair.

The sense of the championship committee was expressed by its chairman in a letter to Locke:

My dear Locke,

You will already have heard from the Secretary of the Royal and Ancient Golf Club that the championship committee intend to take no action with regard to the incident on the last green which appears in the television film of the Open. Your winning score remains at 279.

A penalty may, in exceptional cases, be waived if the committee considers such action warranted.

This committee considers that when a competitor has three for the Open championship from two feet, and then commits a technical error which brings him no possible advantage, exceptional circumstances then exist and the decision should be given accordingly in equity and the spirit of the game. Please feel free to show this letter to anyone.

With all best wishes,
Yours sincerely,
N. C. Selway

Locke had naturally been shocked when he learned what he'd done. Now relief filled his heart over the charitable handling of his case. "He felt that his private gratitude should find expression in some overt gesture," wrote Peter Dobreiner in *The Book of Golf Disasters*, "some mark of humility which would daily remind him of his debt to the committee's compassion." So to show the world how much he appreciated the R and A's decision, Bobby took off his pants. All his life he'd worn plus-fours on the golf course, a quaint fashion statement that had become his trademark. But from the day he received Mr. Selway's letter, he never wore plus-fours again.

Somehow, the affair of the '57 Open remained buried in golf's back pages. The newspapers never picked up on it, and the sensational British press would have loved to turn the incident into a scandal. Thomson, the runner-up, didn't mention it in his Open recap in the Melbourne and Sydney newspapers. Pub debaters argued about other things. "I was not aware that any discussion took place that day," says Crampton. "No one contacted me to discuss it, then or ever.

"And in the case of the '68 Masters, I doubt that what happened [with Locke at the British Open] set a precedent. The USGA and the R and A were not joined then, as they are now."

But they were joined. A unification conference had taken place in 1951, in London, at the House of Lords. Leading the American side was the vice president of the USGA and its Rules Committee chairman, Isaac B. "Ike" Grainger. Ike was a member of Augusta National. He never missed the Masters. He was there in '68.

CHAPTER SIX

SPLIT SCREEN

In my view, where the Rules of Golf are concerned,
fairness is everything.

—ISAAC "IKE" GRAINGER, CHAIRMAN,
USGA RULES COMMITTEE

Saturday night: Alfred Wright wrote. He could work ahead a little bit in the hours before the final round, and maybe not have to
parse and peck all night to hit his pre-dawn Monday deadline
with the *Sports Illustrated* copy desk in New York. He cranked
a sheet of paper into the Olympia, set his fingertips at a-s-d-f-
j-k-l-; and the metallic clacks from his machine joined the others
in the Quonset hut. "There is probably no way to re-create what
happened on Saturday for those who were not there and even for
those who were," he wrote, referring to the unprecedented
closeness of this Masters. "Inasmuch as the leader boards
around the course hold only 10 names, the gallery sometimes
had no notion who was ahead."

Over and over the daily deadline guys seated in the room trot-
ted out shorthand that referred to "skinny Bruce Devlin, the one-
time plumber" and "Bob Goalby, the handsome tour regular who

looks like a football halfback," and "Roberto De Vicenzo, the balding Argentine," but *SI* demanded deeper stuff. "To Player, [this Masters] seemed almost a crusade," wrote Wright of the third-round leader. "Above all, he wanted to vindicate his contention that he is one of the all-time greats of golf, as indeed he almost is."

Bert Yancey listened. At the cramped dinner table in the Masterses' kitchen someone observed that Bert had played the sixteenth hole in six shots—three consecutive birdies. Amazing! "You know, Bert, if you shoot 65 tomorrow, you could win," another diner said. Linda doesn't remember who made that prediction—his brother Jim, her parents, his father Malcolm—but she does recall that everyone agreed. Sixty-five, that was the number her husband needed.

Wilda Gwin planned a party. It wasn't as if the executive secretary to the tournament director didn't already have a lot to do, but Wilda had become very fond of her house guest, and Roberto would be celebrating his forty-fifth birthday on Sunday. A number of other people from the club were in on the surprise party, including Cliff's tournament secretary, Kathryn Murphy. Roberto had charmed them all. Someone baked a cake.

Lee Trevino simmered. A blue-collar pro in a white-glove atmosphere, Trevino shot 71-72-69 and trailed the leader by just two, an extraordinary performance for a Masters rookie. Lee was the next big thing: The world didn't know it yet, but he was a genius with a golf stick and an off-brand ball. In two months he would win the U.S. Open. Nor did the galleries appreciate that this public jokester was a private brooder, the classic clown who liked to be left alone after his performance.

Despite his score, something about the place bothered him. "I remember when we were driving up Magnolia Lane every day, he was just uncomfortable," recalls Bucky Woy, then

Trevino's agent. "No matter who you are, you're in awe your first time at the Masters. For someone with Lee's background, even more so."

After his round on Saturday he asked tournament officials for extra tickets for the casual friends he was always making, and he was told no so sternly and perhaps so condescendingly that his discomfort with the place became sharper and deeper. On Sunday, when virtually every contender sprinted to the finish, only Trevino retreated. The entire field would average 71.29, a fraction under par. Lee shot 80, the worst score of the fourth round. He doesn't want to talk about it even to this day.

Marble Eye stayed out late. He and his cousin James fell in with a group of caddies who fell into a vat of beer; the next thing they remembered, it was three in the morning. Late nights and liquor were not part of Frank Stoke's usual behavior. Back home in Atlanta, he was a family man who lugged suitcases as a bellhop when he wasn't shouldering golf bags at the country club. He didn't have time to party, didn't even like alcohol that much. Had a week of retrieving balls for the endlessly practicing, self-flagellating Bob Goalby make him want to cut loose? Did observing cocky Crosshanded Henry Brown's close working relationship with De Vicenzo fire up a case of envy that might be extinguished with Schlitz?

The man once known as Marble Eye balks at this line of questioning. He can't remember or won't say where he and the other caddies went on Saturday night. "I had maybe one beer," he says. "And no, I wasn't down. Him not asking me for advice didn't bother me. I never did make myself bigger than the golfer."

But Frank Stokes was a big man, bigger than most anyone in the Masters. There was something important about him, something he didn't mention to Goalby or to anyone he didn't know well: His wife, the former Doris Chapman, was the oldest of eleven children. When her mother died in 1965, her eight youngest siblings needed a roof, a meal, a family.

"Can we take them in, Frank?" Doris asked.

"Yes, that sounds like something we could do," Frank replied.

The math went like this: three plus eight minus two. They already had three kids of their own; add eight orphaned brothers and sisters, and then deduct two of the newcomers who eventually decided to try life in a less crowded house. Nine was too many kids to allow Doris to work outside the home, but it was plenty to keep Frank holding down two jobs. Caddying in the Masters was both a career accomplishment ("Being inside those ropes was more than an honor," he says) and a lottery play. If he didn't get a bag or if his man didn't make the cut, or was a cheapskate, he'd make less money than in a regular week at home. But if he won, no caddie could use it more. Winners in professional golf traditionally gave their caddies 10 percent of first-place money. First place paid twenty thousand dollars in the '68 Masters.

Win or lose, the cousins were heading straight back to Atlanta when the tournament was over. As they packed their clothes on Sunday morning in Fireball's rooming house, Marble Eye said something strange: "I don't feel like goin' out today."

"Man, you got to go," James Blandenburg said, incredulous. "You could win."

He went. The Riviera rolled into the caddies' parking lot at about 11:30. Goalby arrived around noon for his 1:16 starting time. Marble Eye looked at him like a trainer looks at a horse before the big race. He liked what he saw. "Goalby wasn't tight at all. He was loose," Marble Eye says. "He says, 'We got one more day. We're gonna make it.' "

Late on Saturday, Goalby had hit balls after his round and putted; the putter felt especially good in his hands. When the light began to fade, he got in the Buick, turned right at the end of

Magnolia Lane, and returned to the not-luxurious Towers Motel near the Savannah River in downtown Augusta. He called Sarah. Had a quick dinner—probably at the Townhouse, probably with Wall and Ford. Back to his room for some TV before bed. He liked variety shows, and ABC aired *The Jackie Gleason Show* on Saturday nights. Maybe he watched that, he doesn't really remember.

He remembers this, though: On Sunday, before he had a chance to hit the most important club in his warmup before the most important round of his life, someone shooed him away. They wanted to park cars on the range, starting right now. So Goalby and Marble Eye walked across Magnolia Lane to the auxiliary practice area. In the bright sunshine of the third consecutive perfect day at the Masters, Bob fished two Dots from the shag bag, teed one up, and aimed for the woods. The squarely hit balls sizzled through the air and tore into branches and leaves like bullets.

A short iron shot away, Bobby Jones lay in his bed in his cabin. Was this the day he'd kiss his baby, his tournament, goodbye forever?

Easter Sunday, April 14

Player . . . .-6 (210)

January, Devlin, Beard, Goalby, Floyd . . . .-5 (211)

De Vicenzo, Trevino, Barber . . . .-4 (212)

Aaron, Pittman . . . .-3 (213)

Nicklaus, Yancey, Henning, Boros, Weiskopf,

    L. Hebert . . . .-2 (214)

Starting times:

        Henning, Yancey—12:36

        Nicklaus, Pittman—12:52

        Aaron, De Vicenzo—1:00

Barber, Trevino—1:08
Floyd, Goalby—1:16
Player, Beard—1:24
January, Devlin—1:32

Roberto sweated through his tan-colored shirt in his warmup and went into the cool locker room to change into an incongruous gray one. He read the only telegram in his locker. It was from Delia, in Spanish. *Feliz cumpleaños,* it read—"Happy Birthday. Good luck to you and we all love you."

He stayed inside for a while, putting on the clubhouse carpet while talking to friends. A Pinkerton guard interrupted. "Excuse me, sir," he said. "But your caddie says there isn't much time left."

"What time is it?"

"A quarter to one."

"Then is time for me to go."

He walked to the practice green, hit exactly six putts, then strolled down the hill to the first tee. When the man called his name at one o'clock, De Vicenzo rolled his Maxfli onto the ground, no tee. He swung aggresively and caught it perfectly. The ball stopped in the center of the fairway about 280 out, 120 yards from the hole. He took a nine iron and didn't swing very hard. The ball landed dead on line, took three bounces, trickled about a foot, and went in. The crowd erupted. Roberto took off his hat for the walk to the green, preceded by his playing partner, Tommy Aaron, a body-double for Davis Love III. As Roberto gently removed the flagstick, Crosshanded Henry Brown took the ball from the cup, kissed it, cleaned it in a white towel, and handed it to his boss. The gallery started to sing:

Happy Birthday to you
Happy Birthday to you
Happy Birthday Ro-bert-o . . .

The fun was back. War and riots and assassination were forgotten for a few hours.

On the second tee, the sheltering trees resounded with the crack of persimmon on a hard rubber ball. De Vicenzo smoked his four-wood second shot just over the green, then chipped very close. Then he tapped in from a foot with his no-follow-through stroke for a birdie. On three, a short but dangerous par four, the big man danced his second shot around the cup and had his second birdie—almost a second eagle.

Happy Birthday to you

No fist pumps or grins resulted from the birdies or the serenades. Instead, De Vicenzo looked pleasant, though preoccupied, as he took the lead in his umpteenth championship. But a bit funny, too. Those yellowish socks inside his geriatric black-and-white brogans must have been the last clean pair in his suitcase. And his hat: Purposely or not, his white ball cap often rested on his mostly bald head at an angle, like a beret, or with the brim a little bit sideways. An outsized embroidered crocodile sunned itself on the front of his lid. The croc was the corporate symbol of Lacoste, the French clothing company. Logos were starting to catch on in '68—Goalby wore Munsingwear's stylized penguin on his shirt—but they were usually small and chaste. Roberto's giant reptile looked like a joke.

But four under for three holes was no joke. Player had lost his lead before he'd stuck a tee in the ground; he, January, and Trevino soon fell by the wayside, while a handful of others charged to the finish line like milers on the gun lap. The most unexpected charger had to be Vinny Giles, the freckle-faced amateur from Virginia. "I started the fourth round birdie-birdie and three pars so I think, 'Man, I've got nothin' to lose,' " he recalls. "Then I look at the leader board at De Vicenzo and Devlin and I said, 'Man, I'm goin' backwards.' "

Vinny's 3-4-4 start put him three under for the tournament. Roberto's 2-4-3 and Devlin's 3-4-3 tied the two foreign golfers for the lead at eight under.

Giles faltered after his glance at the scoreboard. On seven he hooked his tee ball into the trees, and, as he prepared to chip out sideways, his fellow competitor approached. "What are you doing?" Dave Marr asked in stage whisper. "Take a three iron and hit it at the green. There are so many people up there they can't all move."

Marr had a heart of gold, but his intervention constitutes what the Rules of Golf call Advice. You can't give it—except to your partner in a team competition—or ask for it, except from your caddie. Marr's breach of Rule 9 should have resulted in a two-stroke penalty, which would have given him a 73 instead of a 71. Since he signed his scorecard showing a bogey five on the seventh, instead of the seven he really had, he should have been disqualified and the $2,050 he won should have been redistributed to the rest of the boys, as everyone would have moved up one place. The fact that players as accomplished and intelligent as Marr and Giles didn't know Rule 9 was both incredible and not the least unusual. No one memorized every corner of golf's complicated and legalistic rulebook. But everyone would learn a little more about the rules by the time this day was over.

Goalby and Marble Eye marched down the hill to the first tee. Goalby entered the arena hatless, collarless, and beltless—he wore a white Munsingwear shirt, blue DiFini slacks, black shoes. The caddie wore white tennis shoes, a white jump suit with the numeral 21 on the front, and a green hat, all of it provided by the club. Bob shook hands with his fellow competitor for the day, Raymond Floyd, and rehearsed his simple plan for the one-thousandth time. It was the same plan that had kept him within three shots of the lead every moment since the tournament began, an incredible feat given his history in the Masters. With the driver, he'd try to sense a downswing path that prevented his bugaboo, a wild hook. Putting was a roll of the dice, but he could count on his irons, the strength of his game. If he needed to take a chance, it was more likely to be with a three iron than with a twenty-foot putt. The overall strategy would be not to think about winning, but just to play.

Twice before Goalby had contended in a Major, and both times he'd finished second. At the PGA Championship at Aronimink in 1962, he shot 67 in the final round but fell one shot short of Gary Player, an experience that taught him only that Player was tough to beat. But at the U.S. Open the year before, he'd learned another type of lesson: "In the third round on the fifth hole [at Oakland Hills], I hit a full five iron to eight inches. I took the pin out myself. I said 'I'll putt it, Kel'—I was paired with Kel Nagle—and I putted it, and I missed. Should have marked it, because there was mud on the ball I didn't see. Dumbest move I ever made."

Gene Littler won by one, and from then on, Goalby tried not to let emotion make him rush. Tried: Every year he became more a golfer and less a football player playing golf. But when he did something stupid or something stupid happened to him, his rage mocked his self-control.

He parred the first and hit three perfect shots on two to set up a two-foot birdie putt, but he hit it too hard and the ball lipped out. He looked unhappy but he didn't erupt. After two more pars, Bob had lost four shots to Roberto and had fallen into a tie for third, three shots behind De Vicenzo and Devlin. Then his simple plan began to work. A six-iron second shot on five stopped in exactly the right spot, seven feet below the hole. He made it. On six, a downhill par three, he again hit six iron, and, again, hit it flush. The ball flew over the hole cut in the front left and stopped on the fringe, about six steps above the cup. This would be an impossibly fast putt today. But while the greens were significantly slower then than now, they were still fast and didn't hold at all. When Goalby rolled this one in, he raised both hands over his head, as if signaling that the field goal was good. Now the handsome tour regular who looked like a football half-back was just one behind the skinny onetime plumber and the balding Argentine.

Despite the pressure of the moment and the bizarre detail of people singing to him, Roberto continued to walk slowly, his ex-pression that of someone about to be introduced to someone at a cocktail party. "After eagle one, birdie two, birdie three, I get a good feeling," he recalls. "You walk different, look different. Maybe the 'Happy Birthday' is why I start feeling good. Who can tell how you get inspiration? But I know when you lose it, it can be disaster."

While Goalby was hitting his third consecutive iron close to the hole—he missed from ten feet on seven—De Vicenzo pre-pared to chip his third shot from the front of the eighth green to the hole in the back right. He believed in self-fulfilling prophe-cies on the golf course so, as a matter of policy, he talked to his ball. "The birdie come because you tell the ball the place you want to putt," Roberto says. "You control the ball with the swing and the mentality."

His mentality requested an uphill birdie putt of a foot or so, and he got it. He stabbed it in and for the first time he had the lead to himself at nine under. For the day he was five under after eight holes with three tap-in birdies and a hole-out. The least re-liable club in his bag, the putter, had not been tested.

Goalby talked during battle even more than De Vicenzo. What did he say after his third shot on eight, a mediocre pitch from forty yards? He doesn't recall. What did he say after he made the putt from eighteen feet, his third birdie in four holes? He said, "Now, godammit, you make a couple more and you've got a chance."

With nine holes to go and Roberto (-9) and Bob (-8, tied with Devlin) straining for the wire, two new horses entered the picture. First was television. "Live from the Augusta National Golf Club in Augusta, Georgia," said a familiar voice, "the Masters." The speaker was Pat Summerall, whom millions of CBS viewers knew from his pro football announcing. This was just his second day on the job; he hadn't done much golf before, had never worked at the Masters, but now he was making his debut in the most visible and audible way possible, as the lead announcer. Summerall had a deserved reputation for economy in speech and for being a cool hand in a crisis. Back in his days with the University of Arkansas and the New York Giants, he'd kicked many critical field goals and extra points, and he described football games clearly and calmly no matter what the circumstances. Today his grace under pressure would get another test.

Producer Frank Chirkinian felt the heat, too. A perfectionist with another perfectionist looking over his shoulder—Cliff Roberts—Chirkinian had to break in the new anchor man, a new hole (they hadn't televised the thirteenth before), and a new man to describe the action on the new hole. "Thirteen was an immediate hit," says Chirkinian, "the most critical hole on the back side. But that analyst turned out to be a one-time deal, a newspaper writer from Scotland. He had a brogue so thick no one could tell what he said. Can't remember his name."

His name was Bob Ferrier, his newspaper was the *London Daily Mirror*, and Cliff Roberts fired him quickly. "I couldn't. Understand a *fucking*. Word he said," commented the excruciatingly deliberate chairman a few years later, when interviewing another new announcer, Ben Wright.

Sarah Goalby switched on the TV in her parents' den in Little Rock and tended little Kel and Kye for the next two hours without losing eye contact with the screen. She watched the announcers introduce themselves and the holes that lay beneath their green-painted towers. There was slow-talkin', will-he-ever-get-to-the-point Cary Middlecoff sitting with Summerall on eighteen, dramatic John Derr on fifteen, the pure Texas twang of Byron Nelson next to Derr, enthusiastic Frank Gleiber on seventeen, and droll Henry Longhurst manning the mike on sixteen, drinking from the flower vase that was always at his right hand. The flowers were plastic and the liquid in the container was gin, no ice. His colleagues called him Longthirst.

Delia De Vicenzo didn't watch—couldn't watch—Argentina had no live coverage of the event, just irregular reports on the radio. Doris Stokes, Marble Eye's wife, didn't turn on the TV until the very end. It was Easter Sunday, and Doris and all the kids spent the day at Atlanta Bible Baptist Church. Linda Yancey watched in person as her husband tried to shoot that 65. Remarkably, he looked as if he might.

Yancey became the other eleventh-hour subplot, the only other name to take note of at the end besides Goalby and De Vicenzo. Although he'd started the day from farther off the pace than Rob and Bob, Bert had one small advantage: He'd finish before them. One of golf's best dramas occurred when a dark horse shot a hot final round and gained the psychological advantage of being the leader in the clubhouse. Sometimes the other guys made bogeys when they knew the precise number they had to beat.

Yancey was paired with his bridge partner Harold Henning. Two groups ahead of Roberto and four ahead of Goalby, he wore yellow, a color that would look good with a green jacket, his customary white visor, and kept his customary cool.

Bert birdied the second and eighth holes, which got his name on the leader board. He was four under, four shots behind the leader, De Vicenzo. Then he birdied nine, followed by birdies on thirteen and fifteen. But all these birdies amounted to a net gain of only one shot on the lead. He stood on the sixteenth tee, a pale and visibly calm man in golf's most picturesque and emotional caldron. Thousands of overheated fans breathed and whispered, their silhouettes reflected in the pond. They'd cut the pin in its most inaccessible spot, more or less on line with Longhurst's green tower, in the right center rear.

None of the pressure or excitement of the moment seemed to register with Yancey, in part because he'd made a time-motion study of his golf. For hours at a time on the practice tee, he'd have his caddie click a stopwatch as he took a club from the bag and walked to the ball with a specific shot in his mind; the practice swing came next, then the set-up, the address, the hit. By routinizing and timing the entire procedure, Yancey fought the random thoughts that pressure brings.

Yancey got his yardage, tested the wind, pulled a club: tick . . . tick . . . tick. Could he birdie the sixteenth for the fourth consecutive day? With a solid iron shot and a perfect putt—Linda Yancey doesn't recall the distance, only that it went in—he'd made four twos on the sixteenth. No one had ever done that before, or has ever since. Now Cool Bert was eight under, two shots behind with two holes to play. The crowds on the back nine were swooning.

"This is more golf tournament than I can stand," Cary Middlecoff said on TV.

As Yancey moved with that gliding walk to the seventeenth tee, his wife and fans and family and friends scurried along with him. They were so excited by the moment, they could hardly contain themselves, but Bert looked inscrutable, as self-absorbed as a jazz musician, making his music for himself, not for you. He knew the notes to hit on these last two holes. With a birdie and a par, he'd have that 65 and the lead in the clubhouse—nine under and nine under wins the Masters.

In the basement floor of the Thomas Butler Cabin, Vinny Giles, trying not to grin too much, held a Co' Cola in a cup and watched Yancey and the others on TV. Vinny had slumped a bit after his fast start and shot 73, but he'd won the tournament within the tournament he'd been thinking about since he made the thirty-six-hole cut. His 288, even par, beat the second-lowest amateur by seven shots. This meant he'd be presented with a cup and a medal and a silver cigarette box, and that he'd be interviewed on TV in front of a cold fireplace in the makeshift CBS studio. Mr. Roberts always did the introductions of the winner and the runner-up and the low amateur but he was so stiff in front of the camera he looked like he needed oil, and Mr. Jones did the best he could given his condition. It was always an awkward ceremony, but everyone who played in the tournament wanted to be a part of it. Vinny watched the last forty-five minutes of the race on a monitor in the cool of the basement, living a dream in the only place on earth he wanted to be, the Butler Cabin at the end of the Masters.

Vinny and every other TV viewer got to see more of the course than they'd ever seen. Although covering the twelfth hole had not been part of CBS's mandate, Chirkinian ordered one of the new cameras on thirteen simply to swivel a bit and show balls landing on the green of the best par three in the world.

The tournament leader walked slowly up the hill from the eleventh green to the twelfth tee, concentrating so hard that he scarcely acknowledged the gallery that, in Arnie's absence, had chosen to love him. Roberto had one stroke on Goalby and Devlin and a shot to play that would reveal everything about how he felt about his game, this tournament, and himself. The twelfth, a rooftop-to-rooftop par three played through mysteriously swirling air, induced dry mouth and nervous swings in almost everyone who played it. Its green resembled a reclining supermodel, narrow, with subtle curves, and not an ounce of fat. Hit it short, long, or right and you're dead because of Rae's Creek, bunkers, and azaleas. The left side was relatively safe but the pin was cut in the right corner. Roberto went straight at the flag. As his mile-high six iron hung in the air, it occurred to everyone that the line he'd chosen risked the tournament if his judgment and luck were even slightly off. They weren't. His ball just cleared the bunker and stopped about ten feet from the jar, leaving him a straightforward putt on the least contoured green on the course. De Vicenzo betrayed no nerves as he lined it up, and his stroke looked smooth and assured. A second after the ball fell in, he held up his right hand in the briefest of waves to acknowledge the cheers. Ten under now, in the lead by two.

Goalby, two groups behind Roberto, proceeded cautiously for a few holes. He missed the greens on ten, eleven, and twelve, but he missed in the right places so that he could nudge the ball up close for pars. On thirteen, he laid up short of the continuation of Rae's Creek that snakes in front of the green, then hit a superb pitch from a hanging lie to about eight feet, and then he drained the putt.

Up ahead, Yancey made three on seventeen, his third bird in a row. He was nine under.

Roberto birdied fifteen. Eleven under.

Goalby birdied fourteen. Ten under.

Color deepened in the late-afternoon sky, sharpening the edges of high, thin clouds that looked like the iris of a gigantic eye. The day seemed to get hotter while the politely contained excitement in the fans, the TV announcers, and the leading men increased. Roberto hadn't danced or otherwise celebrated all day, but when he made his ten-footer for birdie on fifteen, he slapped the air with his right hand, sidearm. After Goalby holed from about fifteen feet from the fringe on fourteen, he dropped his putter, repeated his field-goal's-good! gesture from earlier in the round, and walked around in a tight circle, like a pony in a paddock. Floyd, in tight royal blue trousers, looked displeased to see someone else making all the putts.

Yancey's second shot to eighteen fell off the left edge of the green and rolled down into the trampled brown grass beneath the gallery's feet. With his shirttail out, he putted up the hill and left it twelve feet short. But Yancey was an artist with his old Cash-in putter, a painter with a brush. He stroked, the ball rolled . . . when it went in, Bert raised his right fist but did not raise his head, a gesture that reinforced the idea that this had been a private battle. He'd won, in a way, since he'd shot the 65 he thought he needed. But who could have predicted that two of the guys in front of him would also play out of their heads? Yancey's charge had fallen short. He would finish third for the second year in a row. It was a two-horse race now.

Goalby, pumped, hit his longest drive ever on fifteen, and had only a three iron left to the green, the least he'd ever hit. De Vicenzo played seventeen almost simultaneously. He, too, crushed it from the tee, and needed only a wedge for his second shot. But which wedge? The rivals stood in sunshine on adjacent hills, feeling the pressure and the thrill of a once-complicated battle now simplified to me-versus-you.

Bob took the three from Marble Eye, took two practice swings, and then a cleansing breath.

Crosshanded Henry Brown said something to Roberto, who looked at the hole and touched first his pitching wedge and then his old reliable, a scarred 1942 Wilson Leo Diegel Contestants

Model sand wedge. It had little holes punched in its face instead of grooves.

The chromed steel shaft of Goalby's three iron flashed in the sun. His ball hung in the air, one second, two seconds, three, a high, slightly hooking shot. It cleared the pond, thumped audibly onto the front of the hard green, pitched forward to within eight feet of the hole, and the crowd around the green whooped. Maybe this was the best shot Goalby ever hit. Jones thought it was the best second shot ever hit on the fifteenth, and he was there on the day in 1935 when Gene Sarazen holed out from the fairway.

Roberto heard the yell and paused in his deliberations. Goalby, he thought, that has to be Goalby. I cannot get rid of this man.

Bob walked quickly to the green while Roberto, perhaps remembering the first hole, pulled the nine iron from the bag. He hit a little punch shot, and his head bobbed up and down, watching the ball, referencing the ground, then back to the ball, his crocodile hat turned sideways a little, his eyes squinting in the bright sun. One second, two seconds, three . . . the Maxfli landed gently near the hole, skidded, and stopped three feet from the flagstick, a magnificent response to the bulldog, Goalby.

In the CBS production truck hidden in the woods adjacent to the tenth hole, Chirkinian looked at the monitors showing the last two men standing. "Show me fifteen. Get tight on Goalby . . . John, throw it to seventeen . . . Frank, how long's Roberto's putt? Cary, which way does it break?" Chirkinian barked orders and questions into scores of headsets, his eyes wandering a bank of monitors, his mind racing. These putts would probably decide who would win and who would not, and both had to be shown live. If both made, there'd be a tie for the lead at twelve under. If Goalby made but De Vicenzo missed, Bob would have the lead. If

Roberto made but Bob missed, the man from Argentina would be one ahead with one to play.

Chirkinian had developed an acute sense of how long an individual golfer took to hit a shot. Cary Middlecoff, for example, the analyst in the tower on eighteen, had been the slowest of the slow. He'd stand over the ball as if ready to hit, and then begin an almost endless cycle of look at the target, scrunch down, look, scrunch, look, scrunch. Twenty-eight reps once, Chirkinian says. Doug Ford, possibly the fastest player, simply took a club, picked a target, then hit the ball. Bob and Roberto played fairly quickly, but the numbing pressure on this Sunday afternoon slowed both of them down a bit.

As Goalby lined up his eight-foot putt for eagle and De Vicenzo conferred with Crosshanded Henry Brown about his short try for a birdie, Chirkinian realized that they would finally hit their putts at almost the same instant. "Split screen," he said. "John, we're gonna come to you for both holes."

Perfect: No one conveyed snippets of golf drama better than John Derr, the announcer in the tower above the fifteenth green. Derr had been following Goalby's ascent with particular interest because of his lucky five-dollar bet in the *Sports Illustrated* calcutta. "I couldn't *not* think about it," Derr says. "But I didn't let it interfere. I remembered doing a horse race once with a newspaper columnist who'd made a little wager, and in the home stretch he says, 'Here comes my horse!' "

The split screen was novel for golf but was itself not brand-new technology; CBS had used it on Dodgers baseball games Derr had worked in the fifties, with one-half the screen showing the opposing pitcher and the other half a shot of base-stealing star Jackie Robinson dancing off first base.

As Bob and Roberto addressed their putts almost in unison, Derr looked only at his monitor and not down below at Goalby.

Click . . . click. The Dot and the Maxfli rolled simultaneously. The birdie putt fell in first then the eagle. Two roars filled the air as if from adjoining football games. The allegedly emotional Latin hardly reacted while the supposedly stoic son of Illinois dropped his putter, raised his arms, and ran a few steps.

Sarah Goalby screamed at the TV and tried to explain to little Kel what an eagle was.

They were tied for the lead now, with one hole left for Roberto, three for Bob.

Goalby stayed aggressive with his shot on sixteen but the ball spun way back. He two-putted for par. But boldness got lost on his walk through the pines and the people to the seventeenth tee. Nerves and worry and shortness of breath suddenly found the quarterback. "I was actually nervous," he recalls, "not the nervous you get when you're not playing well, because you don't choke as much when you're winning. Anyway, it was the first time I backed off all week." He took a three wood instead of a driver, and, too fearful of a ruinous hook, he blocked the shot to the right. The Dot clipped the top of a loblolly pine and fell into the fairway about seventy yards behind where Roberto had driven a few minutes earlier.

Derr watched his horse play sixteen, then he and Byron Nelson climbed down from their tower and walked up the tenth fairway toward the clubhouse. Derr told Nelson about his potential winning ticket, and how he'd acquired it so cheaply.

"Do you think I should find who backed De Vicenzo and offer to split the money?"

"No," Byron said. "You've come this far. Why not go all the way?"

Roberto drove straight but short off the eighteenth tee. When he got to his ball, paralysis struck. An avalanche of variables seemed to fall down the hill from the green and, for a long moment, he couldn't move. The flagstick was stuck on the left in the lowest of the three tiers in the stair-step green. He couldn't see the bottom of the stick because the shot was uphill and because of the dazzlingly white sand in a huge intervening bunker. A shot too short would be disastrous but long might be worse; the pages of Masters history were crammed with sad stories of three-putts from above the hole on eighteen. Adrenaline might make him hit the ball too hard or uncertainty could cause a weak shot. He knew he wanted a three, a birdie, not a mere par, because this Goalby back there just wouldn't let up.

As usual, Crosshanded Henry Brown knew exactly what to do: Hit the five, he said. Aim right, away from the bunker. But after a day of firing at pins, caution just didn't feel right to Roberto. For the only time all week, he overruled his caddie. He took a four iron and aimed it over the bunker and straight at the hole. As on twelve and seventeen, and especially on one, he'd shown he could be deadly accurate with a three-quarter swing.

But he hooked it.

"He wanted to hit one less, I wanted to hit one more," De Vicenzo says. "I hit it too strong and I go over the green. I wanna make three and I make five. If I listen to [Crosshanded Henry Brown], maybe . . ."

The ball landed hole high in the left fringe, bounded forward, and then kicked sharply left. A Pinkerton guard plunged into the twelve-deep gallery in a comical attempt to locate and protect the fugitive Maxfli, but the ball eluded him like a mouse scurrying around and between dozens of ankles. Finally it rolled free on the brown trampled hardpan, hole-high, about thirty feet from the flagstick. The guard broke out of the scrum and stood over the ball like a mother hen, while the marshals quickly carved a corridor into the crowd from the ball to the green.

Ralph Hutchison walked onto the green as Aaron and De

Vicenzo approached. Hutchison turned to address the throng: "At twelve under par, from Argentina, and celebrating his forty-fifth birthday, Roberto De Vicenzo!" Roberto acknowledged the standing ovation by taking off his hat and nodding. But when he looked at the shot he had left, he looked more discouraged than resolute.

The two leading men continued to act in tandem: Back on seventeen, Goalby was cracking. "I was really shook about the tee ball," he recalls. "Then I didn't hit a good second shot." His six iron crawled onto the front left of the green, at least forty feet from the hole. He looked at the scoreboard by the green and saw that he and Roberto were still tied. He putted way short, as nervous golfers almost always do, then missed to the right from seven feet. His first bogey of the day (and his first three-putt) dropped him out of the lead. But only for an instant, because just as Bob 'n' Rob had made crucial putts in lockstep a few minutes before, now, they missed them.

De Vicenzo played the smart shot for his very difficult third on eighteen, with a putter. It was the same choice Yancey had made half an hour earlier. A tough shot, though, with all that was riding on it: The ball needed to go up a hill and then down the other side while traversing two colors and three thicknesses of grass. With his big Ray Cook mallet, Roberto whacked it up the brown hill and through the green fringe to about six feet, a good shot under the circumstances.

Pressure filled the air like humidity. As they stood behind the putt, Crosshanded Henry Brown inclined his head conspiratorially close to Roberto's and held his right thumb and index finger about an inch apart. Just play that much up to the left, he said, and don't forget to hit it.

In churchlike silence, Roberto stood over his putt. The anxiety in his body language couldn't be missed. He aimed left but not far enough, and hit the ball firmly but not firmly enough. The ball hit the right edge and lipped out.

Roberto tapped in, took off his hat, and tried, but failed, to smile. He knew he'd just lost the Masters. Goalby would never make a bogey . . . but a few moments later, Goalby made a bogey. They were still tied. Roberto and Tommy Aaron shook hands, then walked to the side of the green to sit with Hiram C. Allen, Jr., at his little scoring table.

Mistakes were made.

Scorecards are required to have two signatures at the end of the day, from the competitor and his marker. Aaron took De Vicenzo's card from his pocket and filled in his last two scores, a four and a five, signed on a line on the bottom left, then pushed the scorecard across the table. But for some period of time—how long is in dispute—Roberto didn't even look at the folded rectangle of paper. He sat staring at nothing, exhausted by the physical and mental stress of the day, contemplating the gravity of his mistakes on eighteen. If only he had listened to Henry Brown. Or if he'd waited for a minute or two before his par putt, he might have known from the gallery's groans that the unshakable Goalby had finally wobbled with a bogey on seventeen. That might have helped. . . .

Roberto filled in Aaron's scores on the final five holes, signed the card, handed it to Tommy, and slumped back. While Aaron went over his scores again and again, like a good and industrious student, his playing partner just sat there, like the kid who doesn't care whether he flunks.

"I was angry," Roberto says. "I start feeling that I open door for Goalby."

Aaron looked across the table at De Vicenzo not looking at his scorecard. "I wanted to say, 'Look, Roberto, I'm checking each of my holes and I think you should, too,' " Tommy says.

A green jacket walked up behind De Vicenzo and interrupted his fugue. The member told Roberto that he'd like to take him to the Butler Cabin for an interview with CBS as soon as he was finished. Roberto snapped back to the present. He scanned his card but the only number he really saw was that devastating five on eighteen. Then he scratched his name on the line above PLAYER and below the words I HAVE CHECKED MY SCORE HOLE BY HOLE. He stood and walked to a waiting golf cart. They whisked him away to the Thomas Butler Cabin.

Roberto says he actually spent little time lost in thought. "I sit down only one second and a guy in a green coat is behind me," he says. "The guy says 'Come on, Roberto, we gotta go to press room.' I think I go too quick."

Through his black-framed glasses Aaron continued to examine the twenty-one numerical entries on his own scorecard. Counting the eighteen penciled-in scores, the eighteen yardages, the numbers of the holes, and the totals of yardages and strokes taken on the front, back, and eighteen, a scorecard could have sixty numbers in a fairly small area. But the card Roberto signed did not have The Number—what he'd shot. Since the rule was that players are responsible only for the scores on individual holes, and not for adding them up, some competitors simply left the square marked TOTAL blank. Neither Aaron nor De Vicenzo added the 2 plus 4 plus 3 plus 3 and so on to arrive at his correct aggregate, 65. More than anything, that caused the disaster that followed.

After seven or eight reviews, Aaron signed his own card, and handed it to Hiram C. Allen, Jr.

As Aaron remembered it in 2002, Roberto's scorecard sat in the center of the table. He idly picked it up and noticed a very big mistake. Someone—probably Allen—had added it up. The box for the eighteen-hole score was marked 66, and Tommy knew De

Vicenzo had shot 65. He remembered it slightly differently for Sam Blair of the *Dallas Morning News* two weeks after the incident. Aaron said then that he heard someone comment that the number on the leader board didn't match the number on Roberto's just-turned-in scorecard. But in both versions, Aaron grabbed the card and asked, "Where's Roberto?"

"The press room," someone answered (actually he was in the Butler Cabin, getting ready for the TV ceremony). Aaron handed the card to Hiram C. Allen, Jr., and alerted him to the problem.

According to Alfred Wright, "That green-coated gentleman [Allen] snatched up the card and rushed off with it to a nearby cottage where the ailing Bobby Jones, president of the Augusta National Golf Club and cohost of the Masters, was watching the tournament on television." Probably he didn't; no other account mentions Allen's taking the initiative to involve Jones. But this passage in *Sports Illustrated* was the smoking gun for Roberto's fans, since it depicted an officious little functionary grabbing some perverse glory for himself when he "snatched" the scorecard and "rushed" away with it.

"It was almost like a 'gotcha,' " says one ardent De Vicenzo supporter. "I've seen them go into the parking lot to get a player who'd forgotten to sign his card. You don't suppose this would have happened with Jack or Arnie, do you? This guy could have said: 'I'm not accepting this card until Roberto reviews it.' "

But there's no dispute that walkie-talkies suddenly crackled with urgent, startling messages. The press room was told not to post De Vicenzo's score, which made the deadline writers ask what the hell was going on. Just minutes after the green jackets escorted Roberto into the Butler Cabin, they escorted him back out. "For the thirty minutes after De Vicenzo finished, an atmosphere of cloak-and-dagger suspense prevailed," wrote Ron Coffman in *Golf World*.

Back at the scorer's table next to the eighteenth green, Roberto, Aaron, and Chief Rules Official Ike Grainger examined the scorecard. It had three errors: the totals for the second nine (35 instead of 34) and the eighteen (66 instead of 65), and, most important, the score on seventeen. Although Roberto had made a birdie three on the next-to-last hole in front of millions on TV and thousands in person, Aaron had entered a four. Such mistakes are so common in tournament golf as to be almost routine; Julius Boros, for example, had a reputation for making at least one mistake on every card he kept. But when De Vicenzo signed on the attest line, he declared that the four was correct.

"I'm sorry, Roberto," Grainger said, his finger on the infamous four. "You made a three on seventeen."

"It is my fault," Roberto said then.

"Tommy Aaron tried to correct," De Vicenzo recalls. "But guy [Hiram C. Allen, Jr.] says no. This is official. Everything happened too quick. With another rules official? You never know."

"People all around were wondering what the hell was happening," recalled Grainger in 1993, still cogent at age ninety-eight. "I remember Aaron expressing great regret and Roberto holding his head in his hands. I knew what the ruling had to be. Every competitor is responsible for the correctness of the score recorded for each hole. If he returns a score for any hole higher than actually taken, the score as returned shall stand." Grainger would take the card to Jones because, he said, "I wanted Roberto and everyone else to know we were giving him every benefit of the doubt."

But what doubt? The law in this case was as plain as the nose on Cliff Roberts's face—if you sign a card with a higher score than the one you actually shot, that higher score stands. It's not a rule that needs interpretation. But they went to talk to Jones for a very good, always unstated reason: They'd found some give in the rules in the Masters before, and maybe they would again.

For example, Finsterwald: In 1960, Dow shot 69 in the first round. Only he didn't: During the second round he discovered that he'd breached a local rule the day before when he hit a practice putt after holing out on the fifth green. When he realized his mistake, he turned himself in immediately. But as he had signed for a 69 when he had actually shot 71 (the penalty for the extra putt was two shots), disqualification was automatic. Wasn't it? No. The committee decided, without precedent, to change Finsterwald's first-day score to 71 and allow him to continue.

Another, more famous example involved Arnold Palmer and his final-round duel with Ken Venturi for the 1958 Masters. When Arnie's ball buried in the soft ground behind the twelfth green, he applied for a free drop from the rules official on duty and was turned down. Furious, he played from the crater and chunked it into some casual water. A drop, another chip, two putts, and Arnie had a double bogey five. He'd lost his lead to Venturi, with whom he was paired. But then Palmer informed the official that he was going to play a second ball, and chip from a spot near where the first ball had embedded. With that ball, he made a three. Which would count? The three, the committee ruled; Arnie had his lead back, and he won his first Masters. But if they'd strictly followed Rule 11-5, he should have had a five on the twelfth. Arnie didn't do that second-ball thing right.

"The rules say you're supposed to play a second ball *before* finishing the hole with the original ball," Venturi said, and has said a thousand times. "You can't play out and then say, 'I didn't like that score; I'm gonna play another ball.' What if your ball buries on the tee shot on a par five? Do you play the hole, then walk back three hundred yards to play your second ball?"

Why, in these two cases, did the Masters waive the rules? Two reasons: Both Dow and Arnold were great guys and great players, and respectful of the institution. Second, the tournament administration had some culpability in the mistakes, and they knew it. In Arnie's case, the official on duty on the twelfth green had been dead wrong about at least one thing, the golfer's right to put another ball in play when there is "Doubt as to Procedure" (Rule 11-5). When Arnie announced his intention to play a second ball, the official said, "No sir, you cannot do that." He could and he did.

Finsterwald, a rules expert, had asked on the first tee before the first round if any special rules were in effect, and he was referred to a mimeographed sheet that mentioned nothing about practice putting, which was not against USGA rules. They'd put the local rule prohibiting practice putts on the back of the scorecard, not the usual place for such information.

The classic case of an inventive ruling at Augusta occurred in 1972 in a bunker on the second hole and, again, it involved Palmer. When Arnie failed to get his ball out of the pit with his first swing, he angrily swatted the sand again, a plain violation of Rule 33: "The player shall not touch the ground in the hazard . . . with a club, or otherwise." But officials came up with some folderol about why no penalty was assessed, which outraged players like Gardner Dickinson.

Would lawyer Jones find that the club was partly responsible for Roberto's error because it had not provided a private place for competitors to mark their cards? Or an authoritative third party to review the scores? Or an area without someone standing behind any golfer, telling him that the press was waiting? Would he decide that justice demanded that Roberto get what he actually shot and not what Aaron wrote and De Vicenzo mistakenly approved? Did he recall Bobby Locke at the '57 British Open, or Finsterwald and Palmer at the Masters? Or was this a day for the letter of the law? Would he—*could he*—cite precedents that backed up either position?

While the delegation hurried to the Jones cabin, all eyes focused on Goalby.

On the eighteenth tee, Goalby felt the hummingbird heart and the spaghetti spine of panic. He didn't know Roberto had bogeyed, didn't know that they were still tied. He assumed he needed a birdie to get into a playoff. But eighteen at Augusta National, a narrow, uphill dogleg right, was a hole that fit him about as well as his wife's shoes.

He teed his ball low and took a three wood from the big red bag. As he drew the club back, fear of hooking rose like fear of drowning, and his right hand just wouldn't release. His soft blocked shot flew sickeningly to the right, straight at the magnolias and pines. "Same damn thing [as on seventeen]," he said to himself through clenched teeth. Again, his ball nicked the top of a tall tree on the right, and again it came to ground in the fairway—good luck but not great luck. His ball sat on an upslope with a hook lie, and he'd obviously have to cut it. The ball would have to traverse about two hundred yards and begin its journey very low to keep from hitting an overhanging limb.

In his moment of crisis, Goalby badly needed a sounding board, a confidant, someone to encourage him. He had such a person and had had him all along: Marble Eye. It was, says Frank Stokes, the only disagreement they had all week—and their longest discussion:

"I think it's a four wood," Goalby said when they reached the ball.

"That's too much. Hit a three iron. You can make a four from short."

"I'm gonna hit a two iron," Goalby said.

"No, you got my money on this now. A two iron might end up in the clubhouse."

"If you're wrong, you know where this club is going," Goalby said.

Goalby doesn't remember the back-and-forth specifically, only that his caddie had become "as nervous as a whore in church." At any rate, Marble Eye's counsel helped. Bob hit the two, but not as hard as he might have if he hadn't asked for a second opinion. And perhaps just talking flipped his competitive switch back on. Because the shot he hit—a low faded bunker-dodging two iron, with a major championship on the line—was every bit as good as the most famous long iron to a final green. That being Ben Hogan's one iron to the eighteenth at Merion in the 1950 U.S. Open.

The ball stayed under the tree limb, curved gently right—that alone made it a helluva shot for a hooker from a hook lie—landed on the right fringe between the bunkers, and skidded to the back of the green. From the seat at the table he had so recently vacated, and to which he had returned, Roberto watched morosely as the ball rolled toward him, and stopped on the green fifteen yards from the hole. He pulled on his lower lip. He tapped a scorecard against the arm of his chair.

In the tower above De Vicenzo's uncovered bald head, Summerall heard the weirdest words through his headset. "Don't announce a winner or talk about a playoff," Chirkinian said. "There's a problem with Roberto's card." Here was tough duty for a rookie lead announcer in the last few minutes of an exciting Masters: Talk about anything but the outcome.

Grainger, the smooth and smooth-haired president of Chemical Bank in New York City, had walked to the Butler Cabin to confer with Cliff Roberts, who was preparing for the green-jacket ceremony. Giles noticed Cliff but didn't see him slip out with Grainger for the visit to the Jones cabin.

Roberto continued to sit at the little round patio table by the eighteenth green. "I think of nothing," he said. "I cannot think. I cannot even move or maybe I would have gone to the club-house."

The old quarterback marched up the hill to the green. He paid little attention to the applause and a lot of attention to the scoreboard. The game was tied, apparently. Fourth down. No time-outs.

Meanwhile, Goalby's golf ball was a lonely white Easter egg on an acre of green. "I'm forty-five feet, the pin's left front and I'm right rear," Goalby recalls. "And there's so much break, I've got to play it at almost a right angle." In the hush, Bob carefully lined up the putt. Summerall and Middlecoff murmured into microphones. Marble Eye walked to the back of the green and sat down on the base of the golf bag.

Like Bobby Jones, Goalby did not believe in keeping his body perfectly rigid during his putting stroke. Bob's head and upper body moved fractionally forward when he hit the second-biggest putt of his life. It rolled, turned right, and died four feet below the cup. Four feet—vomit distance.

Floyd played his final shots but no one really cared. All eyes were on Goalby. Were his lips moving? Before the biggest putt of his life, Bob had two conversations: one with himself, and another with Marble Eye.

"You're kidding me," the caddie said to himself when Goalby motioned for him to get off the bag and read his first putt of the week. A caddie couldn't have a longer or more dramatic walk than the one Marble Eye now took. He squatted behind the ball.

"What do you see?"

"I don't see nothin' but the bottom of the hole." Exit Marble Eye.

Now Goalby gave himself one of his gruff pep talks. "You chokin' son of a bitch," Bob said to Bob after one practice swing. "Now get up and hit this like a man." He did. It went in, with perfect speed, dead center, the putt of a lifetime.

A tie! A playoff tomorrow! In a living room in Arkansas, Sarah Goalby clapped her hands together and wept tears of joy. In Augusta, hundreds or thousands made plans to extend their stay an extra day. Gallery guards went to the tournament office to volunteer to miss another day of high school. Two more groups had to finish—Player-Beard and January-Devlin—but they were out of it unless they started holing out from the fairway. Marble Eye took the putter from Goalby and put it in the bag. "Nice putt," the caddie said, and trudged off through the slowly departing crowd to the caddie shack to call Doris.

Bob walked to the scorer's table and saw that with Aaron and De Vicenzo and a gaggle of green jackets, every seat was taken. But he didn't wonder why; he couldn't get out of competition mode quickly enough to be curious, especially after shooting 66 in the last round of the Masters. He shook hands with the closest guy, De Vicenzo, who didn't get up but managed a genuine smile. Goalby hunched down into a catcher's crouch to start checking the card he kept for Floyd, at which point one of the members came to and gave up his seat. What a scene: Floyd, Goalby, Aaron, Roberto, the green-jacketed hosts of this unfolding nightmare, each alone with his thoughts, each feeling emotion so pure it could be a color, and no one saying a word.

Bob ground away on the math and discovered an error he'd made on Raymond's card. He emphatically crossed out the 3 he'd given him on sixteen and replaced it with a 4, initialing the change.

Above their heads in the green tower, Summerall read the eighteen-hole scores and final totals of everyone on the leader board, and then he did it again. He spoke somewhat vaguely about a problem with De Vicenzo's scorecard. He seemed to say not much at all for a long time, but Chirkinian insists it was only three or four minutes.

Gay Brewer remembers looking at Roberto, still at the

scorer's table well after his round, his head down. What the hell's he doing? he wondered. He shouldn't still be there and there shouldn't be all this confusion. This is the *Masters!*

After Goalby signed his card and left the table, Snead approached his good friend. "You're gonna win that playoff tomorrow," Sam said. "Roberto's a fuckin' choker." He wasn't, of course, but it was a beautiful thought.

De Vicenzo continued to sit silently by the umbrella table, looking up in the air or down at his feet, looking utterly alone. And thinking to himself *que bolludo yo soy.*

Marble Eye shook some hands and chatted with other caddies for a couple of minutes, then he called Doris. "I gotta stay an extra day," he said. "I'm tied."

"No, I don't think so," Doris replied. "I just saw on the TV they might have a winner. Someone messed up his scorecard." Fearful that that someone was Goalby, Marble Eye hung up and hustled over to the pro shop—still with the bag on his shoulder—to find out what in the world had happened.

Jones sat in his wheelchair in his bedroom, watching the tournament on TV, still too ill to go out. With him were his wife, Mary, his son Robert T. Jones III, and granddaughter Mimi, then age twelve. "All of a sudden I just remember the cabin door opened and this parade of green-jacketed men coming in to seek his counsel on how to handle this," Mimi Jones Hedwig told ESPN in 2000. "And my grandfather said Goalby has to be the winner. Even at his most infirm, people still looked to him for this kind of wisdom."

The parade little Mimi saw consisted of Hord Hardin, John M. Winters, Jr., and Grainger, all former USGA presidents and all members of Augusta National, as well as Cliff Roberts.

Grainger re-created the conversation thus:

Jones: What's the Rule, Ike? Did he violate it?

Grainger read Rule 38-3. "No Alteration of Scores: No alteration may be made on a card after the competitor has returned it to the Committee. If the competitor returns a score for any hole lower than he actually played, he shall be disqualified. A score higher than actually played must stand as returned."

Jones: There's nothing that can be done about it?

Grainger: No.

Jones: Ike, I agree with you.

Mimi's and Ike's versions contradict. Was it Bob's call or Ike's? Jones never spoke for the record about his role, but Grainger grew fond of calling it "the easiest and the hardest decision I ever had to make"—easy because the rule was so clear, hard because Roberto was such a good guy. Sometimes Ike portrayed it as his decision, sometimes as Jones's.

But the meeting couldn't have been as succinct as Mimi and Ike imply. What did they talk about for a quarter of an hour? Concession stand revenue? Football? Here were four accomplished men of the world, including a lawyer, an investment banker, and a former bank president, all of them members of the club, deciding something crucial with a very loud clock ticking and a TV audience of about 20 million waiting to hear. They'd like us to believe that they didn't discuss liability, image, or their entire range of options. If they talked of precedents—Locke and Finsterwald, for example—none of them ever admitted it.

A third account of the extraordinary meeting seems most credible. As Jones confidant Herbert Warren Wind wrote in *The New Yorker* (May 18, 1968), Bob "made it very clear that his primary concern was to find some way, if there was a way, of waiving the rule that would cost de Vicenzo [sic] a tie and the chance to win in a playoff." They talked about it; Grainger concluded there was no precedent. "The only way that Jones could have done what he wanted to do was to place himself above the rules of golf, and he would never do that," Grainger told Wind. "I should think this must have been the unhappiest hour of his sixty years in golf."

Another grandchild, Robert Tyre Jones IV, was eleven, one year too young to be in the cabin, according to the club's policy then. But he was a sharp kid, and a golfer, so he found out all he could from his sister, father, and grandfather about what was said in the cabin that day. And what wasn't said: "I've always been surprised that given the number of R and A people around there, that no one brought up the Bobby Locke case from the British Open in 1957," says Bob IV. "That's the kind of thing my grandfather loved, a conceptual discussion. It's still an intriguing question. But no, I don't know what side he would have taken if someone had brought it up."

Whoever and however they did it, they made their decision and then decided how to spin it.

Grainger walked back to the eighteenth green and told Roberto the news: The higher score would stand, the score he didn't actually shoot. He had not tied for first in the Masters, there would be no playoff tomorrow, there would be no million dollars, and the possibility of glory for winning this great event was gone. De Vicenzo's eyes welled up, but he accepted the bad news with grace. Not grace alone but also despair, because, as he says, "My English wasn't good enough to argue the situation."

TV got the word and Summerall struggled to explain what had happened. Pat knew golf but was aware that the majority of viewers didn't. Most were very casual fans who'd been attracted to the game by golf's first action hero, Arnie, and to this broadcast because everybody had heard of the Masters and didn't that golf course look amazing in color? Most of them wouldn't know Rule 38-3 in the Rules of Golf from Rule 3-38 in the IRS code. And they listened to Summerall's words with growing incredulity and for many, growing outrage. We saw him make a 3 but he's got to count a 4? Because of an accounting error? Talk about a technicality! What kind of game is this?

And the viewers noted who benefited—the homegrown fellow who scowled when he played, not the pleasant-seeming foreigner. When they saw Goalby sitting at the scorer's table with poor Roberto, they recalled that this same handsome but fierce man had been paired with poor Roberto. Or was that yesterday? Whatever, the avuncular Argentine was getting the shaft—and on his birthday, no less. Did Goalby cheat him somehow? The explanations for why Goalby had won sounded like the secretary of defense insisting why more of our boys had to go to Vietnam. What viewers saw, they did not like.

And when they saw the nice man cry and the grim man smile, they liked it even less.

CHAPTER SEVEN

THE MILLION-DOLLAR BONER

The reputation of a thousand years may be determined by the conduct of one hour.

—JAPANESE PROVERB

Time dripped. Clocks melted. Salvador Dali played through. In the surreal aftermath of the '68 Masters, no one knew where to look, what to say, or what to do. The end of the tournament had always been the beginning of a celebration, but as the sun reached the top of the pines on this Sunday, no one wanted to party. And what should you say if Bob or Roberto walked past? Congratulations? Condolences? No words seemed adequate. Nothing felt right.

The institution shuddered like a big ship hitting an iceberg. The men in charge of the best-run tournament in the world had been exposed as a bunch of green-coated dilettantes, at least in the one really important thing they were supposed to do: determine a winner. Both Jones and Roberts despaired. They liked Roberto and they loved the Masters, but through bad luck and inefficiency, they'd perpetrated a crime against both.

Damage Control sprang into action, as crisply as the Pinkertons or Parking or any of the other committees. Fifty members did not talk to fifty reporters about what happened or what should have happened because, as usual, the club spoke with one voice. This one voice made it easy to stick to the message: The club was not to blame. The club's hands were tied. Not abiding by a strict interpretation of Rule 38 paragraph 3 would be an even worse mistake than the one conjured by Roberto and the United States Golf Association.

Volunteers, uncertain about whether they'd be needed to guard galleries or monitor restrooms for the Monday playoff, gathered at the bottom of the stairs leading to the tournament office at one end of the clubhouse. Presently the tournament director, a mournful-looking man with big round glasses, came out of his office and stood on the steps. Many Masters customers on their way to the parking lot paused to hear his announcement.

"After Roberto De Vicenzo had signed and returned his card to the scoring committee," said Homer E. Shields, the former MP, "it was discovered that there was an apparent error in his card. Under the Rules of Golf, a scorecard signed and returned to the scoring committee is official if the player has left the final green. This, in fact, was the case. Therefore, the committee has no alternative but to accept the scorecard as signed."

Roberts positioned the truth in almost the same words for the cameras making the official Masters film: "This tournament is always played in accordance with USGA Rules. Although Roberto De Vicenzo made a birdie three today on the seventeenth hole, he signed and returned his card, which showed a four on that hole. Under the Rules, this score as returned must stand. . . . I make this announcement on behalf of the Masters Tournament Rules Committee."

Cliff repeated the message several more times that day.

It's not our fault; their rules, not ours; we're powerless to do anything about it. This, of course, was mere spin. *Should they* and *could they* are two different issues, but there's no question they'd have found a way for Roberto to correct his card if they'd wanted to.

USGA president Hord Hardin read an announcement to the press in the Quonset hut that sounded just like the other two. None of them—Jones, Roberts, Grainger, or Hardin—chose to recall Finsterwald in '60. His score was corrected a *day* later but Roberto's error, they decided, could not be fixed *five minutes* after it was discovered.

Goalby was among the people milling around during the limbo period before the verdict from Grainger and Jones. For twenty minutes he shook hands, signed autographs, accepted congratulations, and talked with Snead. The mass confusion was "the goddamnedest thing you've ever seen," he recalls. "The Masters usually had everything under control and written down. But they weren't ready for this."

Gay Brewer still insists that he was the first to tell Bob he won, because, as defending champion, he was in the heart of it all. Goalby says Gay's full of it; Middlecoff gave him the shocking news. Cary came down from his TV tower and tapped Bob on the shoulder.

"You won this tournament, Bob," he said.

"What the hell are you talkin' about?"

"Roberto screwed up his card."

Goalby's first reaction? "Between you and me," he says now, "I didn't care if he screwed it up."

Freddie Bennett, the caddiemaster, delivered the bombshell to Marble Eye. "Congratulations, man, y'all won," Freddie said. The man with koala bear eyes stood there by the pro shop, incredulous for a moment, then started to believe as more and more of his friends came by with handclasps and backslaps. But there was a dark side to this scene: The caddies were sure a conspiracy had just taken place. "That was a setup!" says Mark Eubanks, Gary Cowan's caddie in '68. "They didn't want no foreigner to win."

Carl Jackson doesn't remember whose bag he had that year, but he'll never forget being outside the pro shop with Marble Eye when the news spread like smoke through the air. "Man, it was a shock," Jackson says. "My first thought was, 'They done tricked that man out of the Masters.' Being a minority in those days made you think they weren't too ready for a foreign winner."

Such sentiments seem preposterous unless you remember the context that informed them. Dr. King had been murdered a week before in Memphis. The Kennedy brothers were perceived as friends to the black man, and President John Kennedy had been assassinated four and a half years before, and Robert F. Kennedy, the presumed next president of the United States, would be taken down by a man with a handgun in less than two months. Probably the war in Vietnam added to the paranoia. . . . Everyone knew but no one could prove it was all a conspiracy. If "they" could kill the Kennedys and King, stealing a golf tournament was nothing.

But Marble Eye didn't listen to any of it. He leaned on the big red bag with the white lettering and the white bird-on-a-ball logo as though he owned it, and in a way he did. He'd carried this sack for eight days, half that time under the considerable pressure of serving a temperamental athlete having the best tournament of his life. Sure, Frank Stokes hadn't exactly been a copilot, not like Crosshanded Henry Brown; but on the seventy-second hole, when Goalby finally needed him, he'd said precisely the right things. With satisfaction, Marble Eye did what caddies always do, he waited for his man.

When they got the word in the tournament office, Kathryn Murphy threw out the birthday cake for Roberto's surprise party.

One of the few people on the grounds who celebrated with unalloyed joy was John Derr. He kept his eye open for Bill McPhail and later found him in the clubhouse. The president of CBS Sports and the treasurer for the *Sports Illustrated* calcutta counted out $2,515 and put it in Derr's hand. Longhurst wrote a column about it in the *Sunday Times,* lamenting that Derr hit the lottery on a day when the pubs were closed.

History does not record who informed Crosshanded Henry Brown of the decision of the Rules Committee. But a number of witnesses attest that he shrieked and flailed for a minute, in the let-me-at-'em, somebody-stop-me way that people do when they're filled with impotent rage. Henry Brown swore he'd kill that goddamn Tommy Aaron.

Aaron endured a peculiar agony from the moment he discovered the scorecard error. According to the Rules of Golf, scorekeepers are accountants with no accountability, since no penalty attaches to their mistakes. Only the competitor is responsible for the numbers on the card. Still, your marker has an implied duty to supply accurate backup, so Tommy couldn't help but feel terrible about what happened. In a vain effort to rectify this car wreck of a finish, he'd stayed at the scorer's table during the endless interval before the result became final. But when it was over, he didn't stick around. Ron Coffman of *Golf World* found him in the locker room, packing up his stuff.

"In all the confusion, I marked down 4-5 instead of 3-5 for the last two holes," said Tommy, who'd had a good, almost great tournament, shooting 69-72-72-69 for a tie for seventh. "Roberto just glanced at it and signed it. As soon as I got another look at the card I knew I was wrong, and I told the committee to get Roberto back. I thought the fact that I was still there might make a difference, but . . ." And then he was out the door.

More reporters intercepted Aaron on his way to his car and they were not kind to him for his seeming haste to leave. In the stories they were about to write, they used verb phrases like "tried to flee," "scurried for his green Cadillac," "zipped up the windows" of his car, and when he'd had enough, he "roared up the driveway." Sandy Grady of *The Evening Bulletin* in Philadelphia mistook Tommy's low-keyed personality for a lack of concern. "He was without remorse," Grady wrote. "You would have figured he made a little mistake in a gin rummy score instead of costing a 45-year-old fighter the most prestigious title of his life."

A red-faced man walking past Aaron and the writers shouted "are you the————who marked De Vicenzo's card wrong? You ought to be shot"—an incident Grady reported.

Vinny Giles watched events unfold from the basement of the Butler Cabin, watching the air go out of the TV presentation he'd been so excited about a few minutes earlier. "There started to be these rumblings that something wasn't right," he recalls. "Then someone said the problem was with Roberto's scorecard. There was an indication that he was rushed—that the member whose job it was to take him to meet the press had said, 'Mr. De Vicenzo, we've got to go as soon as possible.'

"Then Roberto walks in. He looks—no, not angry—distraught. In shock. And he's muttering that exact comment he became famous for—'What a stupid I am.' He also said, 'But in my country, what you shoot is what you get.' "

With CBS about to switch to its 6:00 P.M. Eastern programming, Roberts looked at the camera and started to talk when its little red light went on. With his thick glasses, halting speech pattern, and lack of natural warmth, Cliff did poorly on television on his best day. And in trying to explain what had just happened in this tournament, he was clearly overmatched. Jones watched this sad performance from his cabin, the first time he did not participate in the TV ceremony.

"Roberts was a little confused," Goalby recalls. "Well, not confused as much as, 'How do I say this?' " Cliff had brief comments for Bob, Roberto, and Vinny, who had very brief comments of their own, not much more than "thank you." Goalby thought the chairman made more out of the achievement of the runner-up than he did of the new champion. Then 1967 winner Gay Brewer entered from stage left armed with a green jacket, a full head of dark hair, and in light of events, an incongruously broad smile. Bob stood, Gay held the jacket, and Bob slipped it on. When the red light went off, so did the coat. Goalby would put it on again during the real presentation on the practice putting green, which followed immediately.

Like altar boys preparing for a high mass, the clubhouse staff had assembled the setting for the final ritual. A long, narrow table was placed in the same flat part of the practice green, year after year, and it always faced down the first fairway, with the clubhouse to the right of the participants. On the table they placed a green velvet cloth with yellow string ties at the four corners and, on top of that, the brown lectern set precisely in the middle. They lined up three armless wooden chairs with cushioned seats at one end, for the winner, runner-up, and defending champ, and a single chair at the opposite end for the low amateur. Behind the table were placed neat rows of folding chairs for the derrieres of honored guests, mostly insiders from the USGA, the R and A, and the PGA. They strung a long extension cord and plugged a hand-held microphone into it. While Cliff made his introductory remarks, a solemn black man of mature years walked slowly onto the scene, carrying something. The man was Bowman Milligan, the club steward since its opening in 1932, and the something was the new champion's green jacket. Bowman's march always struck a perfect note, a half-chord between dignity and joy. But nothing could save this party.

"It was like a funeral," says Jimmy McLeod, a local college kid.

"There was just this pall over everything," recalls Giles. "It had been a really exciting time for me; then, all of a sudden, it wasn't."

As Roberts said a few words to the small and unenthusiastic crowd, Goalby looked almost as glum as Roberto. His blood was in this win today: All the hours on the practice tee, all his discipline, sacrifice, and competitive fire had combined to create the best round of his life. No winner at Augusta had ever shot a lower final round, and his 277 total was the fourth best in the thirty-two-year history of the tournament. But as badly as he'd wanted to win, he realized now that he didn't want it this way. For a moment he put a consoling hand on the runner-up's knee, but Roberto could not meet his eyes. He didn't want to start crying again.

Goalby put on the coat and took the mike. It was unfortunate the way it ended today, he said. I'd have rather won in a playoff, he said. It was just one of those things, but a rule is a rule. De Vicenzo didn't speak.

After the ceremony, Roberts approached Roberto. Would he care to join us for dinner tonight here at the club?

"Yes, Mister Roberts, I'd be happy to."

Here was a significant break in tradition: unless Arnold Palmer was involved, the runner-up did not attend the dinner for the new champion.

Roberto remained stunned, adrift. He has general impressions of what he said and did for the next few hours but few specific memories. He must have gone back to the Gwins' house for a shower and a change of clothes, but he doesn't recall doing so. He must have talked to the press because the next day he read what he said.

Goalby went from the presentation to the locker room to change out of his golf shoes. He called the Towers Motel to see whether he could check back in—he could. He canceled his flight for Sunday night and got another one leaving at six in the morning, Augusta–Atlanta–St. Louis. He had a drink. He walked down to the Quonset hut to meet with the press. De Vicenzo arrived just before him, with, for the first time all week, an interpreter. As Roberto entered the barnlike building, Al Wright and the other writers gave him a standing ovation, a very rare honor in a press room.

"I feel very sorry for me," Roberto said. "I am so unhappy to make five on the last hole, and Bob, he gave me so much pressure on the last hole that I lose my brain. I play golf all over the world for thirty years, and now all I can think of is, what a stupid I am to be wrong in this wonderful tournament. Maybe I am too old to win."

Roberto, we heard that someone was pressuring you to finish your card so you could get to the Butler Cabin for a TV interview. What happened?

"When I finish, I am at the eighteenth green and someone says to me, 'When you finish here, you come with me.' I tell him OK. No, I do not know if he is from television or from where. But it was not his fault about the scorecard, it was mine."

Bob, how do you feel?

"I'm very, very happy to win the Masters," Goalby said. "I'd be a liar if I said anything else. But I deeply regret the way it had to be done."

Ever have a problem with your scorecard, Bob? a writer asked.

No, Bob said. "I play each hole over and then I back check each one. If you look on my card you find two checks by each hole."

But Bob, do you think this rule is fair?

"I leave the rulesmaking to the USGA. They do a pretty good job of it."

Augusta National spun. Augusta National member Charlie Coe stepped forward to declare on behalf of the club that before a card is accepted at the scorer's table, each player is asked, "Are you sure this is correct?"

Were you asked that question, Roberto?

No, Roberto said, he wasn't.

Coe quickly changed the subject.

Cameras, microphones, and autograph nerds surrounded Bob and Roberto as they emerged from the building. Roberto wandered off to find Crosshanded Henry Brown and his golf clubs. "I'm feeling like a chicken who jumped in the river and comes out on the other side," he recalls, in Spanish. *Qué? No comprendo.* "It means depressed, defeated. *Todo el mundo* is slapping me on the back. 'I'm sorry, I'm sorry.' But for me there are no words to say."

The light faded. Roberto walked slowly to the unpaved parking lot in front of the clubhouse, leading a cortege of reporters. One by one the silhouettes walked off until there was only the golfer and the caddie at the open trunk of the rental car. Crosshanded Henry Brown put the clubs in and slammed the lid. The collaboration was over.

Goalby found Marble Eye, still waiting by the pro shop with a few of the other caddies. He got out his checkbook and started to write.

"There's a little extra for that club on eighteen," he said. Frank Stokes looked at the number and grinned. How much, how much, the other caddies asked. "Twenty-five hundred," Frank Stokes said, as his friends whistled and asked for loans.

Marble Eye put the clubs in the locker room. He and Goalby shook hands and that was it. Neither man was a hugger. In a few minutes the caddie got in his cousin's Riviera for the two-hour drive back to Atlanta. They got something to eat on the way, so it was close to midnight when James dropped Marble Eye off at his house. Doris and the older kids had waited up for their hero, and they had a little party.

The next day Frank Stokes bought his wife a washer, a dryer, a ring, and a wristwatch. For himself, he went to Friedman's Shoes, which was next door to the downtown hotel where he worked. He selected a pair of alligator loafers, green ones, the same green as the color of Bob Goalby's new jacket. On Tuesday he returned to work, carrying the bags of high handicappers at East Lake in the morning and the luggage of new arrivals at the Garden Hotel at night.

"He was a good caddie," says Goalby. "Experienced. You didn't have to tell him where to stand. He could take a little shit, you know what I mean? You could say, 'Goddamn, you're no better than me,' and he'd know you didn't mean anything by it.

"The caddies weren't that good in those days. If you could find a guy who didn't make you mad, that really helped."

In Augusta National's lengthy apologia, entitled *The Making of the Masters* (Simon and Schuster, 1999), author David Owen maintains, no surprise, that the club acted flawlessly before, during, and after the mess of '68. Roberts "never doubted the correctness of the ruling, and he never regretted that it had been made," Owen writes. "But he quietly worked behind the scenes to make things right for both men."

It's a curious mishmash of thoughts. If the decision was correct and unregrettable, why did anything have to be made right?

Cliff apparently did three things to correct the injustice that wasn't an injustice. First was his invitation to the runner-up to attend the Champion's Dinner. A fiasco. "Very awkward," Goalby recalls. "No one knows what to say," agrees De Vicenzo, who made a conscious decision to drink very little to prevent saying something he would later regret. Roberts, Grainger, and the two golfers stared at the potatoes and steaks on their plates, making theirs the only really quiet table on a busy night in the dining room. Cliff told Roberto during dinner that he and Bob Jones "want you to know that we would love to declare two winners this year."

Cliff's second gesture was to ask lawyer J. Richard "Dick" Ryan to get in touch with Bob and Roberto to offer his services as an agent. Ryan negotiated with CBS Television and the producers of the Masters annual highlight film on behalf of the club. Roberto met Ryan. They eventually became good friends and had a business relationship, but he hired Fred Corcoran to represent him. "Yeah, I called Dick Ryan once, that was it," says Goalby. "I didn't want to go to New York to meet him." Bob hired Bucky Woy, Trevino's agent.

Cliff's third attempt to make things right was to give Roberto a duplicate of the silver cigarette case that Goalby and every other Masters champion receives. It's a lovely keepsake, as well as historic, since the signatures of each of the players in that year's event are etched into it. For Roberto, however, a man with no shortage of silver and gold *copas* and *trofees,* this shiny box held memories of pain, not triumph. He kept it for a while, then donated it to the Argentina Golf Association's museum, in part because it was too expensive to insure, and he feared someone might break into his house to steal it.

How did it make you feel when you found out Roberto also received the silver cigarette case? Goalby was asked in the summer of 2003. "He did?" Bob replied. "I didn't know that. I wonder what they engraved on it. Mine says 'Roberto De Vicenzo, runner-up.' I wonder if they always put the runner-up's name on there." A mild reply, but a younger Bob Goalby would surely have pointed out that the winner's trophy had been devalued.

Who were these gestures meant for? Was Roberts trying to assuage the club's guilt or his own? Probably he just wanted to comfort Roberto and thank him for the brave way he handled a cruel situation. But the cynic's explanation for Cliff's making nice was that he wanted to keep Roberto from suing his ass.

Sue Augusta National and the Masters? The thought didn't cross De Vicenzo's mind—until he heard from lawyers by the dozen from all over the world in the weeks following April 14. His instincts told him not to go down that path, however. "If I say, 'I was cheated,' I damage golf and the Masters," he says. "This is why the Masters was so good to me. I never say, 'Tommy Aaron fault.' I say, 'It's my fault.' My profession would have been finished if I say this is cheating."

Sue the Masters? The very idea offends the professionals, low-handicap amateurs, and USGA and R and A members who are the sport's truest defenders, the people who often refer to The Game of Golf the way Fourth of July orators refer to These United States. But golf's rules did not come down from a mountaintop carried by Charlton Heston, and, though USGA rule-writing has quite naturally appealed to lawyers, there hasn't been an Oliver Wendell Holmes among them. Golf law lacks the brilliance of clarity:

> When proceeding under 26-2b, the player is not required to drop a ball under Rule 27-1 or 28a. If he does drop a ball, he is not required to play it. He may alternatively proceed under Clause (ii) or (iii).

A change in the yield of a debt instrument is a significant modification if the yield of the modified instrument is by more than the greater of 25 basis points or 5 percent of the annual yield of the unmodified instrument.

The first set of gobbledygook describes several of the actions permitted while playing from a water hazard, and the second outlines some of the tax consequences of buying 11⅞ percent bonds from *Telefonica de Argentina*. Which is clearer?

Roberto De Vicenzo v. *Augusta National Inc. et al.* might have provided an interesting sideshow in a year filled with more serious and violent conflict. Perhaps the lawsuit would have been couched in terms of medical malpractice and the scoring committee portrayed as country doctors attempting a complicated operation far beyond either their facilities or their training. Or maybe the suit would claim a simple breach of contract, the club's failure to keep the implied promise that this tournament—worth a million to the winner—would be professionally run. The complainant might produce a copy of a snippet from *Golf Digest* (July 1968) entitled CLOSING THE BARN DOOR:

The Masters Tournament is one of the few Professional Golfers' Association tour events at which the PGA tour staff is replaced by local committee workers. Had the field staff been operative at Augusta, Roberto De Vicenzo probably would not have been deprived of a chance at the championship because of a scoring error. "(Our) system insures that no player turns in an incorrect card," says PGA press secretary Bob Gorham.

The club's answer to the never-filed complaint is written in *The Making of the Masters*: "The scorecard rule is no less important and no more arbitrary than, say, the rules governing the accidental moving of a ball, (or) the grounding of a club in a hazard." It's not us—it's the USGA! Precedents for flexibility in enforcement, such as Locke in '57, Palmer in '58, Finsterwald in '60, or Arnie, again, grounding his club in a hazard, are of course not mentioned. Nor does the book address the half-assed scoring facility by the eighteenth green, the absence of an authority at that table, the lack of assistance, or the presence of the member who stood behind Roberto and reminded him that TV awaited. The rightness or wrongness of the rule wasn't really the issue but framing the debate that way was a good strategy for the club.

Because the problem hadn't been the rule. The problem was in how these once-a-year guys in green coats administered it.

The lawyer for the plaintiff might wonder aloud whether Mr. Roberts, Mr. Jones, and Mr. Grainger considered their own role in this tragedy based on their lack of control of the scoring area. Did it occur to them that they might be sued? And did they take the measure of Mr. De Vicenzo and determine that with this amiable man, for whom English is a foreign language, they could get away with a strict judgment? Raise your hands, ladies and gentlemen, if you believe things would have happened this way had Arnie been involved.

And in their meeting in the Jones Cabin, did these deeply conservative men look outside the gates for a moment, and observe the decline in the rule of law in the land, the riots, demonstrations, assassinations, the licentiousness and growing influence of the hippies, the burning cities—and decide "it stops here"?

Should we perhaps consider the mental agility of the men involved? Mr. Grainger and Mr. Roberts, both veterans of World War I, were from another century. Mr. Grainger was born in 1895, Mr. Roberts in 1894. In addition to being mortally ill with a neurological disease, Mr. Jones was further depleted by digestive problems brought on by flu, and was bedridden. So we have two old men and one very sick one. As Mr. Grainger has recreated it, no discussion of the tournament administration's role in De Vicenzo's mistake ever occurred in the high court in the Jones Cabin. There was no realization that the competition was still continuing when the scorecard problem surfaced, and no invocation of the legal doctrine of harmless error. In Western law, harmless errors, missteps that do not seek an unfair advantage, should not be severely punished.

To be sure, the lawyer for the defense would ask, "How *dare* you?" How dare you impugn the reputation of Mr. Jones, a man who called penalties on himself that likely kept him from winning at least one major championship, a man for whom the USGA's sportsmanship award is named. How dare you question the acuity of Mr. Grainger, who has devoted his life to forming and enforcing the Rules of Golf. How dare you look askance at Mr. Roberts, who enjoys a *considerable* reputation in the worlds of golf and high finance, a man who operates the most perfectly run tournament in the world. . . .

Cliff signed the check, and the somber celebrants walked to the door. It was about midnight. Augusta had clouded up and cooled off; a light rain had begun to fall. The men stood on the veranda for a moment and took stock of the night, as those who have recently dined often do. Grainger approached De Vicenzo. He was about to reiterate how badly he felt for the way things turned out, but Roberto spoke first. "I'm sorry I caused you so much trouble," he said—heartbreaking words Grainger never forgot.

Another USGA man went up to Goalby as he waited with his clubs for a cab to take him to the Towers Motel (he'd had to give up his courtesy car). Executive Director Joe Dey had just come from the Quonset hut, where the lights still burned bright and the clicks from typewriters filled the air. "Bob, I've seen what they're writing down there," said Dey, who would later become commissioner of the PGA Tour. "You're not going to like it. The best thing you can do is keep your mouth shut."

Sometime in the middle of the night, Alfred Wright put the finishing touches on his account of what just happened. "After some of the best pressure golf ever played at Augusta," Wright wrote, "the charming De Vicenzo and the handsome Goalby settled matters between themselves in a most sadly technical way."

Goalby and De Vicenzo got on the same predawn flight, and both watched from the air as the sun illuminated Atlanta. Bob walked through the linoleum corridors of Hartsfield International to catch the flight to St. Louis without causing a stir, but not so Roberto. UPI reporter Milton Richman observed the "infectious, instantaneous glow from all those around him as he came through the marbled main terminal of the airport. People who wouldn't have known him twenty-four hours before he was a victim of poor penmanship at the Masters now nudged each other and whispered. . . . There is no doubt that De Vicenzo, a man who makes friends easily and a man who has won more tournaments the world over than any other golfer, won more people to his side by what happened Sunday than he would have by winning the Masters title outright." The *Desert Sun* in Palm Springs, California, headlined the story THAT'S HIM . . . THAT'S HIM! NEW NATIONAL HERO—ROBERTO DE VICENZO.

Goalby walked to his gate and was not mobbed. He always wore a sports coat for air travel or to have dinner; he never forgot his humiliation when he was in high school and went to a banquet to accept an award, only to discover that he was the only male there wearing just a shirt and a tie. As he boarded his flight to St. Louis he didn't notice the little bald man with a dark suit and thick glasses, probably because Georgia governor Lester Maddox rode in first class and Bob sat in coach.

Governor Maddox, one of the last of the segregationist-and-proud-of-it leaders in the Old South, was a high-school dropout from a working-class neighborhood in Atlanta who met fame the day after the 1964 Civil Rights Act was signed into law. When black protesters attempted to get served in his restaurant, he chased them away with a pistol and an upraised pick handle, or pick rick, as he called it. He closed and sold his restaurant rather than serve blacks. Pick handles became his calling card and political symbol when he ran for governor and won in 1967. Between the pick ricks, his refusal to close the Capitol on the day of Martin Luther King's funeral, and his skill in riding bicycles backward for photographers, Lester Maddox became a national figure, a cartoonish man who always seemed to be in on the joke. The joke was on the governor, however, when he deplaned in St. Louis.

About twenty-five people had gathered on the tarmac to meet the new Masters champion, including someone from the mayor's office with the key to the city. "We arrived [from Arkansas] just before he did," recalls Sarah Goalby. "I was dressed up, and the boys were in nice clothes, and I was carrying a bouquet of red roses. The front cabin door opens and this little bald man stands there, waving, smiling, posing for the cameras. When he figured out we weren't there for him—God, that was funny."

The good times rolled: the neighbors in Belleville strung a banner across the street—WELCOME HOME CHAMP—and everyone in town wanted to shake Bob's hand or slap him on the back; it was as if he'd won the Big Game again. Writers and well-wishers kept the phone ringing, as letters and telegrams poured in. A couple of them were oddly vile, almost violent: "You're the worst American sportsman I've ever seen," and, "I hope you never win another tournament as long as you live." Sarah would read these, saying, "What's with *this* wacko?" and then hand them to Bob. The notes from the lunatic fringe didn't really dim the excitement, however—partly because there wasn't time. On top of everything else, the Goalbys were going to Las Vegas. Bob's win in the Masters had qualified him for the Tournament of Champions.

Sarah's feelings about going to golf tournaments hadn't changed, but this trip seemed worth taking. So she and Bob did six things at once during their day and a half at home—unpacking, packing, talking to the media, greeting friends, getting the kids settled in at Grandma's house, and booking the flight and the hotel. They arrived in Vegas on Wednesday, the day before the competition started. "So there's this ladies party, for the wives of the contestants," Sarah recalls. "And everyone says, 'Congratulations, we're glad you're here.' But then Dave Stockton's wife says, 'You must be *so* embarrassed.' "

Maybe that was the moment that being the wife of the '68 Masters champion ceased to be fun. "Why on earth should I be embarrassed?" Sarah replied. That week she found out why Katherine Fay Stockton assumed the Goalbys felt sheepish about winning the Masters.

"I do have a smart mouth," Sarah says. "Up to that point, I'd been saying, 'De Vicenzo just saved himself from taking a long walk for nothing,' by not having a playoff. Then I started noticing all these columns saying, 'Goalby wins the Masters with a pencil.' It took some of the joy out of it. This was the major accomplishment of Bob's career, and I saw people putting an asterisk with it."

But Bob never did. Not for a second, from that day to this, did he feel his Masters wasn't fairly earned. His certainty insulated him from the critics but that conviction isolated him as well.

After the first round of the tournament at the charmless Stardust Golf Club—Jenkins wrote in *Sports Illustrated* that it had all the natural beauty of a trailer park—Jim Murray of the *Los Angeles Times* visited the Goalbys in their room at the Stardust Hotel. Murray was the big time. Newspapers all over the country carried his column. Several times a week he comforted the afflicted and afflicted the comfortable in about five hundred words, often brilliantly, with lead-heavy sarcasm and irony. Sarah Goalby read him and liked him, but now felt "scared to death" at having his gaze turned toward her husband.

"Tommy Aaron was the only guy in the United States of America who thought [De Vicenzo] made a four on the hole," Murray had written in his first column on the Scorecard Incident. "Oh, we can expect to hear a lot of breast-thumpings now about the sanctity of golf and related eye-wash. But it's just plain ludicrous. There's no other word for it."

Goalby brought two interesting things to the interview with Murray: a sense of humor and some of that hate mail. The post-Masters TV interview in the Butler Cabin had been so morose, Bob said, that "it looked more like an autopsy than an awards ceremony. I kept looking around for the body." He also produced some of the messages sent to him in the previous few days, such as, "Why don't you give the green coat back?" and, "How dare you put it on?" and, "Arnold Palmer wouldn't keep it," and, "Why didn't you let Aaron add YOUR score?" Other men might have used such communiques to wrap fish or clean up the dog's vomit, but Goalby kept them, curiosities he might take out and show people, like a two-headed chicken. But the ugly words kept coming. Soon his sense of humor took a walk.

The *Los Angeles Times* headlined Murray's Friday, April 19, column WINNING MASTERS MAY BE GOALBY'S BIGGEST MISTAKE:

> . . . Bob is teetering on the brink of a place in history along with the guy who shot Santa Claus, ate with his fingers at the

queen's banquet, or put poison ivy in a Mother's Day bouquet—the kind of guy who would throw a brick through a Rembrandt. . . .

He's the only guy in history who won a major tournament with a pencil on the 18th hole, and the public is insulted. . . .

Bob Goalby had the colossal indecency to shoot 70-70-71 and 66 at the Masters, a brilliant burst of golf which made him a world-wide villain of the magnitude of Mussolini or Al Capone.

If Murray's essay was intended to get golf fans to give Goalby his due, despite the already tedious inaccuracy of "he won with a pencil," it didn't work. Anyway, it was only one of thousands of ruminations on what happened in Augusta on Easter Sunday.

DE VICENZO MAKES MASTERS FLUB, GOALBY WINNER (*New York Daily News*).

MILLIONS WATCH A MASTERS TIE, THEN GOALBY WINS ON AN ERROR (*New York Times*).

DE VICENZO GOOFS, GOALBY WINS (*Los Angeles Times*).

"Everything else there was so perfect," said Tom Weiskopf.

A jury ignores evidence and acquits a former football star of murder. A baseball manager is banned from the Hall of Fame because he bet on his own games. A famous basketball player tests positive for the virus that causes AIDS. A golfer with a circulatory disease sues the PGA Tour to allow him to ride in a cart. A feminist tries to force Augusta National to accept a woman member. . . . Every few years sports and society collide to produce a story that's simply irresistible: with the common elements of a hero, a villain (sometimes in the same body), and outrage. The Scorecard Incident, as it came to be known, filled the bill perfectly.

Like O.J.'s, Roberto's Mistake made the front page, the sports page, and the editorial page. Civilians wrote letters by the thousands to editors and by the hundreds to De Vicenzo and Goalby.

Big principles were involved. As Jim Murray had written, people were insulted. Evildoers needed to be named, and there were plenty of candidates.

Two editorial pages that rarely took notice of doings in the world of the perspiring arts made an exception. *The Washington Post* called this a TAINTED TOURNAMENT: "To a country which has made rather a fetish of 'sportsmanship,' the outcome of last weekend's Masters golf tournament in Augusta, Ga., must bring a feeling of chagrin and shame. . . . Few sportsmen anywhere in the world will think that Roberto De Vicenzo was dealt with generously, or even fairly."

The Op-Ed page of *The New York Times* wondered "if the game is, as Stephen Leacock said of Sunday golf, 'a form of moral effort,' should a man who increases his score be punished for it? Where is the justice in golf? Are the gods of the green completely without mercy?"

Sarah and Bob read everything they could about the Scorecard Incident that week in Vegas. $1M BONER, BUT ROBERTO MISSES COAT MOST—JACK, headlined the *New York Daily News*. The story quoted Nicklaus saying De Vicenzo cared more about winning than he did the money and that no one should be blamed for what happened. "Roberto is my friend and I could cry for him," said Tony Jacklin in the same story. "But it is his fault."

The *St. Petersburg Times* headlined MASTERS FOLLOWS RULES ON DE VICENZO'S "BUM DEAL" above an AP story based on an odd Monday interview with Cliff Roberts. "We've gotten quite a stack of [telegrams]," Roberts said. "And not one of them said we did the proper thing. [They] all say 'you gave that fellow a bum deal.'

"[Critics] don't understand the difference between golf and spectator sports, such as football and baseball. You must remember that baseball and football players have no responsibility about keeping score. In golf, this responsibility is pinned on the player, who must turn in an accurate score." It was a weak defense, but it kept the focus on the rules, and away from the club.

Cliff also told the press that he had investigated the charge that someone from the club or CBS had spoken to Roberto before he'd finished his card. The chairman's conclusion—that it hadn't happened—contradicted the testimony of eyewitnesses and of De Vicenzo. Maybe he hoped someone would believe him.

Sandy Grady of Philadelphia's *The Bulletin* certainly didn't. "You wonder if all those green-coated officials enjoyed their bourbon last night, knowing De Vicenzo had been robbed in the nit-picking confusion. You also wonder if the same outrage would have been perpetrated upon those Augusta idols, Nicklaus or Palmer."

Sports Illustrated printed letters about the affair for three weeks after the fact. "Masters officials ought to put Bowman Milligan in charge of the tournament and Cliff Roberts in charge of the kitchen," wrote Sam Krugliak. "I nominate Roberto De Vicenzo for Sportsman of the Year," offered Frank Allan. Denton Gibbes of Laurel, Mississippi, was succinct and calm:

> Sirs:
>
> The Masters officials have applied a rule with an inexorable finality the would be unexpected even in a court of law. Probably 5,000 persons witnessed the fact that De Vicenzo made a birdie three on the 17th hole. Millions of others witnessed that fact on their television screens, and even the tournament officials acknowledged it publicly. But then those same officials closed their eyes to the fact and accepted the myth that, instead of a birdie three, De Vicenzo really made a par four because that figure appeared in the appropriate square on his scorecard. I am disappointed in them.

In week three, Bruce Budner disagreed:

> *Sirs:*
>
> *I was greatly disappointed in reading the reaction of your readers. The Masters officials could have allowed Roberto De Vicenzo to correct his scorecard without penalty and without informing anyone of the error. Such an action would have avoided much criticism and controversy. However, Cliff Roberts and the rest of the officials were honest and honorable. They applied the rules of golf, fully realizing the consequences. Their action should be applauded, not criticized.*

A lot of what was written about the '68 Masters was cruel, inaccurate, and polarizing—a perfect fit for the country's mood, which had been made rotten by Vietnam and race riots and assassination. The *Los Angeles Herald-Examiner* ran a photograph of De Vicenzo slumped in despair at the scorer's table. The caption read BOY IF I COULD ONLY ADD. Virtually every game story the day after the event used Roberto's "what a stupid I am" quote, which led to snide jokes that De Vicenzo was a dolt.

Goalby got his full measure, too. "Bob must be prepared," wrote one columnist, "for the jokesters who, when they fill in their All-Star golf team in the future, will put Nicklaus down for the driver, Palmer down for the four-iron, Casper for the putter—and Goalby for the pencil."

Aaron was scorned as a careless incompetent who'd been an accounting major, of all things, back at the University of Florida. Most of the outrage focused on the USGA—on Rule 38. "The system is absurd," wrote another columnist. "No other sport has it. What a man writes with a pencil does not affect his performance in basketball or baseball or any other game. Professional bowling has official scorers, for Pete's sake. Why can't professional golf?"

Speaking with writers on the Monday after the Masters, a highly unusual occurrence, Cliff Roberts emphasized the main damage control theme. "We are operating a golf tournament—we do not operate the U.S. Golf Association," he said. "We just operate the tournament in conformity with USGA Rules." It wasn't us! It was that damn USGA!

On the whole, Cliff's misdirection probably helped obscure the club's role in the fiasco. Not that many commentators differentiated between the rule and the method of its enforcement. But some did.

The Rules Committee made "a grotesque mockery of the great piece of Americana that the Masters [has] become," wrote Arthur Daley of *The New York Times*. "Archaic rules and archaic presenters swept it into sport's dark ages. Something should be done about both."

"Don't offer us the lame 'rules are rules' excuse," wrote Hal Lebovitz, the *Cleveland Plain Dealer* sports editor. "Rules involve justice and common sense and your committee was guilty of ignoring both."

"At the scoring table behind the 18th green . . . were several high-ranking officials eminently versed in Rule No. 38, section 3," wrote Gene Ward in the *New York Daily News*. "Not one of those officials around the scoring table of this great tournament bothered to check De Vicenzo's card. Not one offered to help him in any way."

Dick Hyland in the *Palm Desert Post* seemed especially outraged—on behalf of Goalby, who represented a local club, Tamarisk, on the tour:

> De Vicenzo finished his final round while Bob Goalby was yet on the 18th tee and the Masters officials, from Chip [sic] Roberts on down, KNEW Roberto had goofed, knew his round's legal

score was 66 and not 65, knew Goalby needed but a par on 18 to win, a bogey to tie. They withheld that information from the official scoreboard. They denied Bob Goalby that important, vital information. That, to me, is awful. There can be no excuse . . . Chip Roberts, master mind of the Augusta National Club, even had the gall to say in front of Goalby that he and Bob Jones would see if there was not some way of having TWO Masters champions for 1968. . . .

The reputations of Chip Roberts and all 1968 Masters officials [are blemished]. Their place in golf's records is assured. They committed the most unsportsmanlike act in the history of major golf. If Bob Jones was present when the dirty deed was done it is no wonder he went home sick before making a television appearance, characteristically disassociating himself from the mess at the Unsportsmanlike Masters.

Building sympathy for Roberto to a tidal wave, the *Plain Dealer* printed—in boldface—a highly upholstered version of that Good Samaritan story. In this telling, De Vicenzo had just won a tournament in Florida, when a young woman ran up to him in tears. Her baby would die unless she found enough money for an operation, she said, whereupon De Vicenzo gave her his first-place check for ten thousand dollars. When someone tells him later that he's been swindled, that there is no sick baby, Roberto says that this is "the best news I've heard all day."

Amidst the firestorm, Grainger and Jones exchanged letters. On May 7, Bob expressed gratitude that he and Cliff had the guidance of great Rules of Golf men like Ike and a few others. "It was a tragedy for De Vicenzo, of course," Jones wrote, "but I cannot help thinking that it will contribute to a more widespread respect for the game and the people who guide it." Mr. Jones must not have been reading the papers.

• • •

In insular, unreal Las Vegas, Goalby and the others in the Tournament of Champions wandered the casinos in gold-colored contestants' blazers. Many of them felt uneasy about seeing their names listed like race horses at various sports books; except for the somewhat playful calcuttas at the Masters, they weren't used to being bet on. In this distracting fantasyland, with his wife along, with letter writers and columnists trying to tear the green jacket off his back, Goalby shot 70-70-66 and had the lead going into the final round.

"I've got timing and rhythm going for me right now," he said. "And maybe something to prove." But his putter cooled in round four for the first time in two weeks, and a couple of unwelcome hooks showed up. He shot 75, good for a tie for fourth. The Goalbys flew back to St. Louis for a week off. There were offers to consider for the new Masters champion and lots more mail to read.

When Delia De Vicenzo heard on the radio on Sunday night what had happened in the Masters, she sent her husband an encouraging telegram: "This result is bad luck but don't worry." Then she saw the pictures of Roberto in the newspaper the next day. When she suddenly understood the depth of his misery, she cried. She hadn't talked to her husband the entire week of the Masters. That wasn't unusual; international calls were such a pain. You had to crank the handle and ask for the operator, who asked for the operator in Quilmes, who asked for an operator somewhere else. Delia and Roberto finally spoke two days after the Masters, when Roberto called. It took him three hours to get through from Wilmington, North Carolina, where he was playing in the Azalea Open. Which he pronounced, "Azza lee-uh."

After the second round, he checked his scorecard carefully, then turned it in and walked away. A PGA official named Bob Gorham noticed that he'd forgotten to sign it, so he called him back.

Still feeling like a chicken who has swum across a river, he accepted an unending stream of sympathetic greetings and messages. People tried to imagine facing such a disappointment and knew that it would fracture their civility, if not their spirit, but Roberto's humility and grace awed them. A telegram from Argentina's consul general read, in part, "You have lost a million dollars but you have won a million friends."

Amid the flurry of communiques sent to Room 227 in the Waterway Motor Lodge were invitations to play here and there for pay, to increase his visibility with DiFini slacks and Etonic golf shoes, to drink and endorse Coca-Cola, to do a before-and-after ad for a toupee company, and to participate, perhaps within two weeks, in an eighteen-hole "playoff" with Goalby.

One intriguing telegram read: MISSION PRODUCTIONS WOULD LIKE TO PRODUCE A SPECIAL HEAD TO HEAD MATCH BETWEEN YOU AND BOB GOALBY, CASH AND GORGEOUS PRIZES AVAILABLE IF WE CAN GET TOGETHER A DEAL. MAYBE WE CAN DISCUSS ON THE TELE-PHONE.

Other entrepreneurs had the same idea. John Ross of Golf Promotions proposed that he would organize the showdown between Roberto 'n' Bob, NBC would televise, and Firestone Country Club in Akron would host (Augusta National having declined the opportunity). The purse would be the same as at the Masters—twenty thousand dollars for first, fifteen thousand dollars for the runner-up.

Roberto said yes to the exhibitions he could fit in; yes, thank you, to his slacks and shoes sponsors for paying him a winner's bonus; yes to Coca-Cola ($12,500 a year "and continuing thereafter for additional one-year periods as long as you shall satisfactorily perform your obligations"); no to the wigmaker; and yes to the mock tiebreaker with Goalby. Despite his nonchalance about money, he was only human. The $1M Boner bothered him, as it would anyone, as he had a family to provide for and high travel costs. Who likes to leave cash on the table? "You see the money fly over your head," he said. "But you cannot catch it." A little payoff from a playoff seemed only fair.

Doug Ford was a good friend of both men in the drama. "Roberto says to me, 'Tell Bob he can win, I just want the second-place money,' " recalls Ford. "But Bob thought, what if he gets beaten? That would mean he hadn't really won the Masters.

"Did he believe that stuff about a major being worth a million dollars? I don't know—it may have been worth a million to Arnold or Jack but not to anyone else. I told him, 'Bob, you're not gonna make twenty cents off that title. I didn't.' "

Goalby declined the TV match, telling the Associated Press that he couldn't think of any good purpose it would serve. But interest in the concept remained high and other offers came for higher stakes, as much as ninety thousand dollars to the winner; still Goalby said no. He believed that a win in a faux-playoff wouldn't really validate what he had won fair and square and a loss would confuse things further, as well as jeopardize the financial bonanza he still expected.

"Here's the man who turned down five thousand dollars a hole," said Jerry Barber the next time he saw Bob.

Roberto shrugged and played on. After the Azza Lee-uh, he'd play in two events in Texas. He was not depressed; sad, yes, but he did not seem to have the wiring to allow a descent into a chronic funk. He soldiered on in Wilmington and in Dallas, finishing tied for nineteenth and tied for thirty-fifth, winning $550 both weeks. After the Houston Champions International, he'd fly back to Buenos Aires and spend a month with family and friends before returning for the U.S. Open.

In Texas, more than anywhere else in the country, they thought it was funny to quote Roberto phonetically. "Some-atang should be done," wrote Bob St. John in the *Dallas Morning News*. "All I know es what 'appen es bad por everybodee. Es bad por me; es bad por Goalby; es bad por Aaron, and por the gallery who feels dis tang es not finished yet. My sponsors give me de bonus money but still et es not settled." St. John, Mickey Herskowitz in the *Houston Post* ("I cannot keel myself because I do the wrong theeng") and Nick Seitz in *Golf Digest* infantilized De Vicenzo with this treatment, which eventually annoyed him deeply.

Goalby played at Houston, too, but not particularly well: his 72-69-71-75 got him only a tie for thirty-third, and no memories. But Champions, a very long course with very big greens, suited Roberto. There he shot 67-68-71 and wound up in a dogfight for first with his final-round playing partner Lee Trevino—the real Lee Trevino, the publicly happy one, not the scowling misfit seen in the fourth round at the Masters.

You could see how comfortable Lee was to be back in his native Texas by his roly-poly walk, his stride so big his nascent beer belly faced east then west as he walked north or south. He was Tex-Mexican and others with the same ethnicity filled his gallery. A couple of times someone yelled, "Tamale Power!" No one appreciated it as such then or since but, as Trevino tried to win for the first time on the tour and De Vicenzo for the last, the '68 Houston Champions International had the import of regime change.

Lee led by two with three to play. When De Vicenzo made a

birdie two on the sixteenth, he whispered to his marker, the third member of the threesome, Al Geiberger. "You see I made a two? Don't put down a three."

Lee bogeyed seventeen, Roberto parred it, and they were tied. A TV sound man bothered Trevino when he hit his second shot on eighteen, a long par four, and he blew it way right. Then he pitched on, four feet from the hole. De Vicenzo hit the green in two, about thirty feet from the flagstick. He rolled his first putt three feet past, and then he did a clever thing. Instead of marking and waiting for Trevino to putt, he kept going, as was his right under the rules. When Roberto made his three-footer, Lee, who admitted he'd been unable to spit for several holes, missed his putt badly to the right.

Roberto had shot 68 and won. But there was still the paperwork. After checking his card repeatedly, he handed it to PGA Tournament director Jack Tuthill for further review before he signed it. They asked him about it in the press conference afterward, naturally. "Before I sign, I call my lawyer," he told the writers with a grin, which got a good laugh. He'd gotten a haircut since the Masters and looked ten years younger than the pointy-haired man who'd gotten in so much trouble three weeks earlier. His smile at the trophy and check presentation lit up the day. And in Houston they're still talking about the victory party held in a member's backyard.

Sometimes it's difficult to summarize an event in a few words, but this one was easy. That night headline writers from *The New York Times* to the *Springfield Shopper* used a variation on: IT ADDS UP FOR ROBERTO.

But what about Bob? While De Vicenzo seemed to have already recovered from that mess in Augusta, nothing seemed to add up for Goalby. His fate and his journey would prove to be the oddest, saddest, most unexpected aspect of the Scorecard Masters.

CHAPTER EIGHT

THE BOOK OF BOB

*He teareth me in his wrath, who hateth me; he
gnasheth upon me with his teeth; mine enemy
sharpeneth his eyes upon me.*
    *They have gaped upon me with their mouth; they
have smitten me upon the cheek reproachfully; they
have gathered themselves together against me.*

                                      —JOB 16:9–10

They say Americans love a winner, but they didn't love this one.

"Roberto was popular, Goalby wasn't," says Frank Chirkinian, the CBS TV producer, and even his explanation for the bile directed Bob's way contains an explanation. People were immediately and automatically on a first-name basis with De Vicenzo, but that unsmiling grinder who used to play football was just Goalby. Bob had hidden strengths superior to mere charm, but 1968 was not a time for subtlety.

No one much cared for nuance. Americans in the late sixties labeled each other and themselves constantly, a bumper-sticker mentality that assumed an opinion on one topic indicated an entire worldview. We called each other hard hat or hippie, peacenik or redneck, freak or crew cut. The dinner-table defender of Goalby had to be pro–Vietnam War, antiprotest, My Country Right or Wrong. If you thought De Vicenzo had gotten a raw deal, you must also be a draft card-, flag-, or brassiere-burner. It was an angry atmosphere that allowed people to be incredibly or stupidly wrong about almost anything, in print or at the top of their lungs.

Oh, the things Goalby got to see and hear because he won a golf tournament. Imagine perfect strangers writing to tell you that "you're nothing better than a cur," that "you're the worst American sportsman I've ever seen," and that "I hope you never win another tournament as long as you live." Letters to the editor were slightly more civilized but just as painful to read. "De Vicenzo is the real Masters champion and Goalby cannot be publicly accepted as such," wrote a certain C. W. McAnally to *Golf Digest*. "Bob Goalby knows that he did not win the Masters," offered Frank Wilson to the readers of *Golf World*.

Something strange was happening. People wanted a face and a name to blame, and facts and fairness didn't seem to matter. Seldom-seen Cliff Roberts wouldn't do as a scapegoat and neither would Bobby Jones, whose positive public image and physical state made any criticism unlikely. The USGA and the Masters Rules Committee were ultimately too big and amorphous to be satisfying targets, and no one knew Ike Grainger. Tommy Aaron got some grief but not all that much, ditto TV for its agent at the scorer's table possibly rushing Roberto into his big mistake. So the attack dogs lined up against the one really blameless person in the drama—Goalby. In a perverse zero-sum game, each bit of compassion for Roberto was offset by an equal amount of resentment of Bob. People had a contradictory desire for more smiles from the new Masters champion and more contrition. He couldn't do both. He wouldn't do either.

When he missed a three-footer in the process of missing the cut at the Atlanta Classic in late May, someone in the gallery yelled out, "Here's a pencil, you can change your score." Any other year, they'd be cheering the new Masters champion in Georgia. "I'll keep the score for you," shouted another voice. "That's another way you can win."

Goalby's progress toward wealth was going about as smoothly as his public relations. After his unpleasant rounds of golf in Atlanta, he sat with the agent he'd hired a month earlier, a go-getter from Akron named William "Bucky" Woy, a charming, fast-talking former golf professional. "In those days, you win a Major, a million was what everyone talked about," Woy says. "I'm not saying Bob could have made a million off that Masters, but he was certainly marketable."

This, their first big meeting, did not go well. Woy was new to the still-new business of athlete agency and was as exuberant as Goalby was glum. He'd developed six or seven opportunities for Bob to look at and couldn't wait to tell him: "That was the mistake I made when I approached him with all these deals. I had to learn to wait until he had some time to get off his game suit and unwind." Bucky recalls that he pitched contracts worth forty thousand dollars with Amana, Munsingwear, *GOLF Magazine*, and Bellows Valvair, an outdoor sign company, as well as various exhibitions. Goalby said no to each one.

"You'd bring him a piece of business and he'd reject it," recalls Woy. "He was upset with the public, and he took it out on me. Maybe some psychologist could explain that." The explanation was simple: Bob had decided to follow the advice Joe Dey delivered on the veranda at midnight the day he won the Masters. No matter what the provocation, he'd keep his mouth shut in public. A couple of times he vented to writers, but otherwise galleries and sports-page readers didn't know how much he was hurting inside. Sometimes, as with Woy, the poison had to come out.

"Bucky wasn't really my kind of guy, know what I mean?" says Goalby. "And the deals he brought me weren't worth that much. It was a couple hundred here, five hundred there. I'd have to go here and go there and, meanwhile, I've still got a family and I still want to play golf."

One offer he accepted was a series of exhibition matches with 1964 U.S. Open winner Ken Venturi in upstate New York. But only twenty people showed up to watch the first match, and, at promoter Bob Murray's suggestion, everyone went home after nine holes. Goalby assumed the entire thing had fallen through and didn't appear at any of the subsequent scheduled matches. At the Western Open in August, Murray sued Bob and Bucky. He dropped the lawsuit a few weeks later, but the entire episode reminded Goalby how far wrong things had gone.

"Bob was a very straight and narrow guy," recalls Doug Ford. "We had dinner with a guy I knew from Sears, which owned [club manufacturer] Golfcraft. Those were perfect clubs! They had me, Phil Rogers, Dick Mayer. . . . Anyway, this guy from Sears took a liking to Bob and asked him if he'd be interested in a signature line of golf clubs. Bob says, 'No, I don't want my name on a department-store club.' I said, 'Jesus Christ! They've got thousands of stores—think of the royalties you'll make!' In that sense, he wasn't that commercial."

Goalby remembers the flirtation with Golfcraft. "They wanted me as front man," he says. "But I didn't know if they'd kick Doug out if they got me." He couldn't do that to a buddy. So he didn't take it, and he never told Ford why.

He fired Woy—"Not that I had anything against him"—and went on with life as before, without an agent. But who wanted to approach Robert George Goalby after a round in which he'd heard someone in his gallery offer to paint a yellow stripe down the back of his new green jacket? Except for a few more exhibitions on Mondays, nothing much happened for him financially. Augusta National, as well as Jones and Roberts, had strong ties to Atlanta-based Coca-Cola; Cliff had spoken somewhat vaguely about an endorsement deal, but nothing came of it. Spalding raised his salary from four thousand dollars to six thousand dollars a year and featured him for a couple of weeks in their Ask The Man Who Drives One print campaign for the Spalding Dot. Munsingwear found a four-thousand-dollar salary for him, and there was a little something from DiFini, maybe a couple of thousand dollars.

"That part of my life, I didn't handle well," Goalby says now. "But I was busy enough. I never had a problem—I played as much on Mondays as anybody. I liked to play golf, and I liked my own time."

In the deeply disappointing aftermath of the biggest win of his life, Goalby often thought of a letter he received about ten days after the Masters. After reading it, he asked Sarah to have it framed.

> *Dear Bob,*
>
> *The privilege of welcoming a new Masters champion into a new green coat is something I have always reserved for myself. I was especially disappointed this year that a virus attack caused it to be impossible for me to make the presentation to you. I am sending you my warm congratulations on my first day back in circulation.*
>
> *Your golf in Augusta was superb in every way; I saw a good bit of it on the television monitor in my bedroom. I was particularly thrilled by those three great putts you holed on 13, 14, and 15 of the last round, and by your exquisite second shot to the 15th, which was the finest shot I have ever seen played on that hole.*

The scorecard mix-up was a tragedy for Roberto, but it was also one of equal proportions for you. I thought you both handled the situation in a most sportsmanlike and exemplary manner. I know you would have much preferred to go to a play-off. But I ask you to always remember that you won the tournament under the Rules of Golf and by superlative play. Indeed, I think overall it was the most beautifully contested tournament I have ever seen.

We in Augusta will always be proud of you as a Masters champion. I hope this will prove to be only the beginning of a wonderful year for you. I shall look forward to seeing you next spring.

> *With warmest regards,*
> *Most sincerely,*
> *Robert T. Jones, Jr.*

Goalby believed then and believes now that the delegation that went to Jones's cabin during the scorecard crisis wanted to convince him to allow Roberto to correct the mistake on his card. And he believed Jones, mortally ill though he was, had stood fast for a strict reading of the rules. In the midst of all the unfair crap he was enduring, he felt grateful to Jones for his insight and sympathy and proud, *damn* proud, that he'd won the Masters. He'd have preferred a more clear-cut victory, but he didn't think his win was the least bit tainted, either. Meanwhile, a lot of nuts seemed to hate him. It was a conflict he'd have to live with.

But he didn't live with it happily.

On the other hand, there was Roberto arriving from Argentina with a tan and a smile at the next big gathering of the tribes, the U.S. Open at Oak Hill Country Club in Rochester, New York. He called what happened at the Masters "one of those stupid things we do once in a while.

"People still write to me about [it]. They are so nice. They want me to know they feel badly about what happened to me. But I wish they would stop blaming others. What happened in the Masters was no one's fault but mine."

He seemed extraordinarily well-adjusted, as if he'd gone through all five of the Kübler-Ross stages of dealing with loss— Denial, Anger, Bargaining, Depression, and Acceptance—in six weeks. His win in Houston helped the natural sunshine of his personality re-emerge, as did the positive messages in hundreds of cards and letters and hugs and handshakes. "After the Masters, I should be shot," Roberto told the AP. "But people, the fans, they love me. . . . Suddenly, everyone is my fan. Everywhere I go, they say, 'Come on, Roberto. We're with you, Roberto.' They slap me on the back."

Relative to modern celebrity endorsers—$40 million for Le-Bron James, $90 million for Tiger—De Vicenzo did not turn his instant fame into a pile of money, partly because worldwide marketers like Nike didn't yet exist. There's some doubt he would have traded his time and freedom for cash anyway, regardless of the amount. He'd always said as much, and after his British Open win in '67 he put it in writing:

> . . . At this stage in my life, Fred, I really don't want to have a manager. I've reached a point where I expect to stop playing tournament golf before too long, and will play in a few selected tournaments more as a diversion than as a serious business matter.
>
> Such being the case, it wouldn't be fair on my part to have you work so hard to make arrangements for me to appear somewhere, and then I might not want to fulfill the commitments.

The Fred in the letter was Fred Corcoran, to whom Roberto addressed a different sort of letter exactly one week after the '68 Masters, obligating him to seek out "product endorsements, advertising and merchandising rights, motion picture, television and personal appearances, books, articles, syndicated columns . . . and all other activities generally engaged in by professional athletes." Fred's cut would be 20 percent. The sheer volume of requests for his time had virtually forced De Vicenzo to get an agent.

But there was no similar business groundswell for Bob, and people didn't coo his name as he walked past. He continued to play almost every week, continued to furrow his brow and grind and compete like a quarterback down a touchdown with time running out. Neither riches nor popularity had come his way, and those stupid sons of bitches with poison pens or snide remarks just made the whole thing very frustrating. Before the Open, he told columnist Milton Gross what it was like to be Bob Goalby in the summer of '68.

He felt, in the modern slang, dissed. "People seem to forget that I'm twelfth on the all-time money list," he said. "They seem to forget that I made eight birdies in a row in St. Petersburg for a record. You're lucky to get three in a row. I'm damn proud of that. If they'd check the record, they'd see that my win in the Masters wasn't quite as much of a fluke as people think."

Goalby believed the asterisks being put between his name and Masters Champion were completely unfair. "I did something I never thought I'd do, I won the Masters," he said. "Yeah, I won it. I'd be stupid if I said I didn't want to win it that way. He'd have taken the title if he won it that way. I don't have to alibi."

He had an explanation for why galleries were not warming to him: "When Roberto said on TV, 'Goalby made me so nervous I don't think too good, I lose my brains, what a stupid I am,' people thought I put pressure on him by needling him. All he meant was the pressure of the game, but people felt I deliberately did something to him.

"Hell, people keep saying it was such a terrible thing for Roberto. But it was a terrible thing for me, too. It was a terrible thing for Tommy. It's a shame the way they crucified him."

Goalby vented about the playoff ("Would it have been good for golf, for me? Hell, no") and hecklers ("Maybe I've developed rabbit ears"). He didn't sound like a man who'd won something; he sounded like someone who had endured a great loss. Someone who was stuck on phase two in the recovery process, Anger.

Tommy Aaron hurt his wrist and didn't play in the '68 U.S. Open at Oak Hill, but cynics whispered that the real reason for his absence was that he didn't want to relive the scorecard deal with the unsympathetic press. De Vicenzo and Goalby played but didn't come close to recapturing the magic they'd had in Augusta. Roberto shot 290 and tied for twenty-fourth and Bob had 293 for a tie for thirty-ninth. But two other faces from the Masters showed up in the spotlight, the brown-as-a-berry countenance of Lee Trevino, and Bert Yancey, who looked, as one writer said, "pale as a prison guard."

As at Augusta (except for Trevino's final-round 80), there was radar in their striking and confidence close to arrogance in the way they handled the putter. After three rounds, they separated themselves from the peloton so thoroughly that no one else had a realistic chance to win. Bert's 67-68-70 led Lee's 69-68-69 by one, and the rest of the field by seven.

The early part of Open week had been dominated by discussion of Rule 38. Gardner Dickinson said that the man who makes the error on the card should be penalized. Penalize both scorer and scored-for, said Johnny Pott. Each player should keep his own score, said Bob Rosburg and Tom Weiskopf. Just correct innocent errors, even when they're discovered hours later, said Frank Beard: "We know what our score is and what the other fellow has. No one can cheat."

Goalby, Don January, and a few others saw the real problem: not the rule, but its application. They wished for the simplest thing: some sort of structure in which to go over the final numbers in privacy. They got their wish, in spades. When each of the 150 competitors in the U.S. Open came off the eighteenth green, they walked directly into a three-sided tent (forest green), surrounded by stern signage ("USGA Only"), armed guards (three), and a cushion of space from the gallery (about five steps from the ropes). Two chalked lines ran from the edge of the green up to the tent, indicating ground reserved for finishing competitors. The lines were almost completely unnecessary, but they made a point that the marquee reaffirmed, and in it sat three no-nonsense officials from the USGA and their top gun with a Rules book, P. J. Boatwright. Please check your cards, gentlemen, Boatwright said to each group. Any questions? May I help? Would you read those scores back to me?

On the first tee, another official suggested to each player that he write down both his own score and that of the player for whom he was scoring. All of it—the tent, its isolation, the presence of rules officials, and the changes in procedure—indicted the casual club championship air of the scorer's umbrella table at the Masters.

"The De Vicenzo incident," said handsome Hord Hardin, the president of the USGA and a member at Augusta National, "has made us aware of what can happen here."

As for what could happen in the Championship itself, sharp students of the game might have seen what was coming—or who was coming. In the history of the U.S. Open, no one had ever gone as low as 205, Yancey's total for three rounds. Lord, he was a beautiful golfer, his swing smooth and flowing, holding his follow-through on full shots as if posing, his face a blank canvas. Trevino was also strumming Oak Hill like a virtuoso. But with his figure-eight swing and high-water pants—accentuating bright red socks on day four—he looked as though he didn't belong on the same golf course with the elegant Yancey.

"I remember that everyone assumed that Bert would win, and the writers started to prepare their stories as if he would," recalls his wife, Linda. "But the night before the final round, he asked me, 'Who am I to win the U.S. Open?'"

Linda, who was pregnant with Scott at the time, thinks this self-defeating thought indicated the presence of clinical depression. Scott disagrees: "No, he told me specifically that he thought he was going to win. Remember, he called Uncle Jim and all the family up to New York to watch. He just had a bad Sunday. He was still learning to play in the Majors."

Whatever Yancey's shocking comment meant or didn't mean, on the back nine Trevino passed him like a street sign. "All the blue collars came out, rooting for Trevino and booing Bert," says Linda. "It was awful." Trevino got member's bounces all day and made every putt, while Yancey lost his edge, his concentration—something. On one green, when Bert moved his coin to get it out of Lee's line, Trevino had to remind him to move it back.

Lee won, signed with agent Bucky Woy, and within six months made the Major winner's million dollars. Yancey slumped all the way to third, behind Nicklaus. At the end of the day, he didn't want to come out of the locker room. Trevino gave his speech, met the press, and the gallery went home; Yancey just sat there. As Arnold Palmer prepared to leave, he saw the forlorn man sitting on the bench in front of his locker, looking at the floor between his feet. Arnie detoured over to him. You're gonna have your chances to win Majors, Bert, Arnie said comfortingly, but you're not gonna win 'em all. You'll get 'em next time.

The next time Trevino saw De Vicenzo, he thanked him profusely—for beating him in Houston. He'd have never won the Open, Lee said, if he'd won in Texas the month before.

Roberto flew to Scotland in July to defend his British Open title. Goalby didn't go. Most Masters winners address the dream of winning the Grand Slam, but Bob didn't think of himself as either a world golfer or a potentially great one. "It's not that I have anything against the British Open, it's a fine tournament, I'm sure," he told the press. "But I've always played here in the United States . . . I'm going to play in this country instead. If you must know, I'm not too crazy about flying. I wouldn't want to fly all the way to England."

Sarah sighed. "I was so disappointed," she says. "We were invited everywhere, and we didn't go anywhere. Bob said, 'I'm not going over that goddamn pond.' "

So while Goalby traveled from the tournament in Detroit to the next one in Milwaukee, De Vicenzo put on his blue suit and prepared to be the Guest of Honour at the 1968 Open Dinner at the Bruce Hotel in Carnoustie, Scotland. The organizers must have known that his sense of humor had survived the Masters because the program depicted a cartoon Roberto walking down a fairway with five scorers: a little girl with an abacus; an accountant carrying a briefcase and an umbrella; a pinch-faced university professor; a "stick and notch" scorer from the R and A; and a blonde bombshell with an adding machine and a cocktail dress. "Relax, Roberto!" the caption read. "We have arranged the above team to tot up your scorecard—accurately!"

De Vicenzo did not play in the PGA Championship in San Antonio later that summer, so he and Goalby did not compete in the same Major event again until April 1969, the first anniversary of the Scorecard Incident. Adjacent, schizophrenic headlines in the *Augusta Chronicle* that week: B-52s BLAST BUNKERS, BASE CAMPS HELD BY REDS, and PEACE TALKS RESUME IN PARIS.

Like a birth, a death, a wedding, or a birthday, the '68 Masters would occasion a recap at regular intervals, or whenever a writer was assigned to ponder famous rules brouhahas or all-time worst athletic mistakes—the guy who ran the wrong way with the football, the baseball player who forgot to touch first base, the basketball player who shot at the wrong hoop. Inheriting a lot of rumor and loosely written contemporary accounts, latter-day reporters often got the story amazingly wrong.

"De Vicenzo really did not review his card carefully," wrote David Mackintosh in *Senior Golfer* (April 1998). "In fact, he turned in his signed card before Bob Goalby, who'd played in the group behind De Vicenzo, had even totaled his front nine. With De Vicenzo disqualified, Goalby won the tournament."

Jeffrey Forbes produced another howler in 2002 on golfinsite.net, in a piece about Jaxon Brigman, who signed for a score one higher than he'd actually taken in the PGA Tour qualifying tournament. The extra shot kept Brigman from getting his tour card. "[De Vicenzo] won the tournament," wrote Forbes, "but in the excitement of having just left the final green, he signed for one more stroke than he had actually shot. His partner had erroneously entered the wrong score on one hole. The trophy was taken away from Roberto and given to the second place finisher even though every single stroke of his final round had been witnessed and chronicled by thousands."

You'd expect a less egregiously wrong account in the *Augusta Chronicle*'s special supplement on the Sunday before the 1969 tournament. But you wouldn't get it. Speak No Evil was the paper's policy—it was owned by Augusta National member Billy Morris and his family—so they pretended the fiasco in '68 never happened. The eight-page souvenir tabloid, entitled MEMORABLE MASTERS '58, turned back the clock to a happier time, the year Arnie won his first green jacket. There were nostalgic features about the tournaments Snead, Hogan, Middlecoff, Ford, and Palmer had won. Nothing on '68 except an analysis on page five of the eleventh, which had been the toughest hole that year. Bruce Devlin made an eight there, remember? Good times.

Official Augusta may have cringed at the first anniversary of the Incident but the Goalbys didn't. "We decided to go and to rent a house because we said, 'Yeah, this is what Masters champions do,' " Sarah Goalby recalls. "Anyway, it was practically the only thing to do in that town unless you were willing to stay in a dump of a hotel. Which Bob always did because he was so thrifty."

Bob remembers it a little differently. "The kids couldn't go and she didn't want to go," he says. "Nineteen sixty-nine was the first and only time we rented a house." That week, the geological fault in their marriage reappeared: He was into golf like a scuba diver is into water, and she didn't much care for the game.

But they grinned as they rolled up Magnolia Lane that first day, with parking pass #1 on the dash. On Tuesday night Bob presided over the Champions Dinner, in which the defending champion is welcomed into the fold and picks up the check. Goalby didn't specify anything special like ham hocks or haggis, although it was his privilege to do so; the diners simply ordered from the menu (maître d' Wesley Ellis recalls with satisfaction that Bob slipped him a hundred-dollar tip, one hundred dollars more than the gratuity from the champ of a year before). Sam Snead told a couple of dirty stories. Byron Nelson, who had taken over as master of ceremonies in Ben Hogan's absence, harrumphed. "That will be about enough of that," Byron said. Goalby didn't much care for Byron.

And he wanted to hear more from ol' Sam. After the year he'd just had and the year he was having, he needed a laugh. His best finish so far in 1969 had been a tie for thirtieth at Greensboro. He'd broken 70 only once all year, and had won only about three thousand dollars. He amused himself in Masters practice rounds by revisiting the only flaw in his jewel-like final round 66 in '68, his three-putt on the seventeenth green. If he'd two-putted it, that would have changed everything. With Roberto's scorecard error, he'd have won by two, and by one without it. But after a few unsuccessful tries at the uncharacteristically slow and mysteriously breaking putt, Goalby said, "No wonder I three-putted."

When the competition started, things soured like old milk for Sarah. Other houses came with servants; not hers. One of their house guests was a chiropractor from back home who seemed to be obsessed with the tendons in everyone's feet. "Not a man with great social skills," she says. "I enjoyed Tuesday and Wednesday a lot, but the tournament was too tense and too busy.

"And I didn't like the snooty people there. Even the waiters acted like they were doing you a favor by letting you in the club-house. So different from a place like Colonial in Fort Worth, where they were always so gracious. Augusta National made so much money from their tournament, but they thought golf professionals were beneath them, and treated them like prostitutes."

Mrs. Goalby's perception that the Gentlemen of the Club acted superior was probably accurate; these guys *were* superior. Few other clubs selected members from around the country, and no other club owned one-fourth of golf's major championships. Besides, to many clubmen around the world, including this CEO-filled membership, golf pros were grown-up caddies, mere servants. Furthermore, Augusta National is mostly a men's club, a point brought home by the single-stall, claustrophobia-inducing ladies' restroom.

Roberto doesn't remember much about his '69 Masters. His golf had been spotty. With 65s in the first and final rounds, he'd won the Los Lagartos International in Colombia in February but played indifferently at his next two events, the Maracaibo and Panama Opens. He didn't get much going at Augusta National, either; his 75-75 missed the cut. Like a lot of people who've been injured in an accident or diagnosed with a disease, he'd begun to find all the sympathy a little stifling.

He also felt patronized by the tournament patrons. "Only two more times did I play good at Masters," he recalls. "Each year, I hear, 'Come on Roberto, don't forget to sign.' I hear a man say to his children, 'Look, there's the man who couldn't read his score-card.' It was like, 'See what can happen to you if you don't learn to read and write?'"

Bob made the cut but didn't play particularly well. His 70-76-76-75 earned him last-place money, fourteen hundred dollars. And his place as the villain of '68 earned him a few boos. He tried not to hear them, but with his rabbit ears, he couldn't help it.

After each round, Roberto and Bob and every other competitor walked into an ugly olive green Army tent to check and sign their cards. Miscellaneous volunteers were not permitted inside. Hiram C. Allen, Jr., had been replaced by two men, a local CPA and Joe Black, a PGA Rules expert. They would not permit a mistake.

Roberto won three of golf's most prestigious honors in 1970. In January, he flew from midsummer Buenos Aires to midwinter New York to accept the Bob Jones Award, given by the USGA annually in recognition of distinguished sportsmanship in golf. Before he spoke to those attending the seventy-sixth annual USGA meeting, the honoree found Ike Grainger. He put his big right arm around his shoulders, and both men grinned for the photographers. They were real friends and spoke highly of each other all the rest of their days.

"I play golf," De Vicenzo said from the podium. "Make some money, make some friends. Today . . . I have this wonderful thing in my hands. It means more than you think—for my family, my friends, my people in South America.

"To win a tournament you need just a hot week. To win an award like this you need years."

A week later, in the packed ballroom of the Americana Hotel in New York City, the Golf Writers Association of America presented Roberto with the William D. Richardson Award, which linked him to worthies such as Arnold Palmer, Bob Hope, and Clifford Roberts for his "consistently outstanding contribution to golf."

They handed him the trophy and the crowd grew silent. After a pause Roberto spoke. What he said brought the house down: "Golf writers make three mistakes spelling my name on trophy . . . maybe I'm not the only stupid."

Later that year, in the World Cup in Buenos Aires—a competition of two-man teams from around the world—the tournament was played in Roberto's honor. The World Cup—née the Canada Cup—was a big deal. Roberto and Tony Cerda had won the first one in '53. Hogan and Snead won it in '56. Nicklaus and Palmer won four times in the sixties. Over forty countries sent teams in 1970. And De Vicenzo won the individual trophy. In many ways, he was getting his heart's desire.

And what did Goalby get in 1970?

He got audited. The first thing the IRS questioned was his

five-hundred-dollar tab for dinner on a certain Tuesday night in April 1969 at Augusta National. It's called the Champions Dinner, Bob explained. The previous year's winner has to buy. It's a tradition. The clueless auditor said, "Prove it." So Sarah dug through some old copies of *Sports Illustrated* and found some references to the custom. The IRS finally allowed the deduction, but they kept auditing Goalby, year after year, as if he were hiding something.

CHAPTER NINE

YOUR SHADOW
FOLLOWS YOU

When Roberto's kids got older, and then they had kids, all three generations lived together in three houses enclosed by the same fence. When Delia's mother grew ill, she and her two nurses moved into the compound. Then Roberto's widowed sister moved in, followed by another sister. Meanwhile, on the other side of the fence, the government went to hell, people disappeared, and economic divisions sharpened. Argentina's middle class practically vanished. *"Yo no soy communista, pero*—I'm not a communist," Roberto said, "but why is it so uneven?" In his fifth decade he found more reasons to stay at home or at least to stay in South America, and, like old denim, he faded from the world golf scene.

In 1974, he didn't play a single event on the PGA Tour, breaking an almost uninterrupted run that had started in 1947. But he needed money, and he needed to see his friends, so he played, just not as much as before. As always, he won. He took the *abiertos* of Argentina, Brazil, Colombia, Mexico, and Venezuela in the seventies, and in the first U.S. PGA Seniors for which he was eligible, he won by three shots over Julius Boros and Art Wall.

His business life had its ups and downs. De Vicenzo wasn't really an entrepreneur, and Argentina, a country with no tax deductions, was suspicious of capitalism. But he tried. He bought an indoor parking garage in Buenos Aires and had his sons run it. It didn't work out. He invested heavily in a glass bottle factory and lost, says his friend Raul Cavallini, hundreds of thousands of pesos. On the plus side, the deal with Coca-Cola provided a nice income for three years. "Make Coca-Cola and the other products of the Corporation a natural and normal part of your every day life," the contract said, and Roberto did. "When playing golf, you should purchase Coca-Cola both for yourself and playing companions wherever and whenever practical." *Sin problema!* Roberto liked to buy the drinks anyway.

Cavallini hired him to play in his bank's pro-am tournaments. Here was a role Roberto was born to play: the graceful champion handing out the prizes, posing for photographs with the winners, perhaps giving a little speech. The banker and the golfer became close friends. "We ate for twenty years several times a week in the same restaurant in Buenos Aires, called Pepito," Cavallini recalls. "Later they called it Chiquilin. It was near the garage. Anyway, a queue of people always formed by the table, people coming to ask for money. Someone says, 'No wonder you ate there. You never paid.' No—we paid, every time. But they should have paid Roberto for all the business he brought them."

Once the Peronistas, one of the major political parties, asked De Vicenzo to consider running for mayor of his town south of the city. They hinted that bigger things than a mere mayorship would come his way if he accepted their nomination. So the potential mayor asked the Peronista leaders to come to his club for lunch. After they dined at Ranelagh, Roberto suggested they walk around the lush golf course for a couple of holes, just to see what it looked like. Then they went to his house nearby; there

Delia served them coffee. I do this every day, Roberto said, except that I also play golf. Is what you're offering better than this? Everyone agreed that it wasn't.

He taught golf, he played golf, a few companies paid him for being Roberto De Vicenzo, and his birthdays became almost a national holiday. The years diluted the pain of April 1968 to almost nothing. He had a nice life, punctuated by odd trips abroad. On one of these, in 1979, something significant occurred, as important in its way as that infamous Masters (cue the freaky music): Roberto had a flashback. For a few hours he was twenty again, with a head full of hair, and was playing the front nine at the golf course in Córdoba in birdie-birdie-birdie-birdie-birdie-birdie-birdie-eagle-par. In reality he was fifty-six, bald as a golf ball, and not in northern Argentina at all but at Onion Creek Country Club in Austin, Texas. And the tournament wasn't the *Abierto del Norte;* it was the first Legends of Golf. With his seven consecutive birdies, Roberto and his partner Julius Boros beat Sam Snead and Art Wall in an incredible shoot-out. People loved it. The television ratings went through the roof.

A few months later, in January 1980, the PGA Tour formalized plans for a series of tournaments for professional golfers age fifty and older. Representing the players in the meeting, which laid the groundwork for the Senior PGA Tour, were six veteran pros whom the others trusted not to give the store away: Dickinson, Sikes, January, Boros, Snead, and Goalby.

Bob had stayed on the road like a traveling salesman with a big territory. In the decade after the '68 Masters, he entered as many as twenty-eight events in a year—about the most anyone could stand—and he won three times. In the fall of '69, he took the long-forgotten Robinson Classic in downstate Illinois, and in '70, again in the fall, he shot 66 in the final round to win the much more prestigious Heritage Golf Classic at Harbourtown Golf Links on Hilton Head Island. In '71, he enjoyed his eleventh and final victory on the tour, in the season-ending Bahamas National Open. He's still the defending champ because the tournament was never held again.

But money won, tournaments entered, and miles on his Mercury may not be the best way to measure Bob Goalby's life. How about the number of times the least Gandhi-like man you can imagine heard or read an insult and reacted like a pacifist? Perhaps we should count explanations instead of years to mark his progress through life. You know: No, I didn't keep his scorecard. I wasn't even paired with Roberto; you see, I was two groups behind him. No, he wasn't cheated. No, it wasn't my decision. They were going by the Rules of Golf, see, which state . . .

Perhaps dogs. For some people, dogs mark the progress of time. When Goalby wasn't playing golf, he was often up at 4:00 A.M. and loading food, twenty-gauge shotguns, shells, and a bird dog into a truck, and then driving with his father or a friend to some distant winter field. The dog would flush, the men would fire, and the tasty, elusive quail would fall from the sky. The dogs laying the lifeless birds at the master's feet over the years were N-dog, then Jack, Dots, Dee, Jim, June, Sam, Dolly, and finally the current four-legged friend, another Dolly. The first four were English pointers, the rest, English setters. From golf, baseball, DNA, whatever, Bob was a helluva shot. The family ate well when he hunted.

Kids, including his own—Kye, Kel, and Kevin—motivated Bob, and he inspired them. Years before he married, he took a great interest in his sister Shirley's children, Jerry and Jay Haas. He took them to watch a couple of pro tournaments and introduced them to the great Snead. He gave them and their teammates at Belleville West High School clubs, balls, and lessons.

"Bob was a great supporter of our teams," recalls Dave Shannahan, then Belleville West's golf and basketball coach. "He bought the whole team golf shoes in '71, one of the three years we won the state championship in golf.

"During the nineties, we played a lot of golf together. He was a little bitter about some things from the Masters. He received more letters than you could imagine, some of which he let me read. One I saw accused him of cheating; another said he should be ashamed to wear the green jacket. Bob couldn't understand that even some reporters didn't give him credit."

The nephews became very good players. Jerry wound up as the golf coach at Wake Forest, where Arnold Palmer went to college. Jay was even better. He's won eleven times on the PGA Tour, same as Uncle Bob. "Jay was like a son to me," says Bob. "I didn't get married until I was thirty-four, you know. I took him to Greensboro when he was a junior in high school, and I took him to have a look at Wake Forest." Now Jay Haas has two kids of his own, Bill and Jay Junior, making waves at the highest levels of competitive golf. As a healer of wounds, time might remember Bob Goalby as the founder of a golf dynasty; it already remembers him for winning the most confused Masters ever held.

"For about ten or fifteen years, [the negative reactions to] that Masters really bothered me," Goalby says. Forbearance did not come easily to the man who had been the boy who fouled out of fourteen straight basketball games. He had few intellectual pretensions and found grammar to be one of the most difficult subjects in school, but because he was always being asked to recreate and analyze the infamous ending in Augusta in '68, he acquired a patient restraint and an almost lawyerly ability to explain. He grew, he changed. The temper mellowed a little bit. He passed through Denial, Anger, Bargaining, and Depression on the road to recovery and reached, if not Acceptance, at least its suburbs.

In 1977, someone with NBC-TV heard an interview he gave in Greensboro, and liked it. Larry Cirillo, the producer of NBC's golf telecasts, offered him a job. Cirillo had an idea: To make his show stand out from those offered by ABC and CBS, he'd put his announcers on the ground, walking with the players, not just in towers next to the last four or five greens. How about it, Bob? the high-strung Cirillo asked.

The timing was right. Goalby's career as a player was in unmistakable decline. He'd won roughly $50,000 in '73, $18,000 in '74, then $9,000, then $2,600. He turned forty-eight in '77, and was making ends meet with corporate outings, a new income stream for the golf pro. NBC wasn't offering much money and the job meant more travel than he wanted, but Bob saw the potential, so he took the job.

They wired him for sound and sent him and John Brodie, Bruce Devlin, and Tom Seaver out onto the golf course. The foot soldier/broadcasters didn't just murmur, "He's got 159 yards, not much wind, looks like a six iron," they talked to the players on air. Bob mentioned brand names more than the other guys, typically in questions such as "Steve, you're sure hitting that new Spalding driver well, aren't you?" Goalby was no Edward R. Murrow, but he was cool under pressure and didn't mind Cirillo's tendency to shout in his earpiece. He spoke clearly, and with pleasing enthusiasm. And, of course, he knew golf.

About the only things that bothered him in his twelve years as an announcer were a frequent wish that he was playing instead of watching—and Lee Trevino. NBC gave the voluble Trevino sixty thousand dollars per tournament—Goalby made a fraction of that—and a seat in the booth by the eighteenth green.

While the money disparity didn't bother him, Trevino's absolute refusal to say, "How do you think he'll play this?" to one of the foot soldiers—to "bring them in," in TV language—really annoyed Bob.

But, overall, TV was a very good thing for Goalby. "If you're on TV, people think you know something," he says, with his usual self-effacement. "It gave me a stature I didn't have before. I got adulation all around the country. . . . I think that's why they made me ramrod of everything. They'd think, 'Goddamn, he must be pretty smart to have that job.' "

Goalby helped bring the Senior Tour into being and soon was playing on it. Did pretty well, too; in '84, his best year, he won $114,000. He also had his TV announcing, regular corporate entertainment gigs with Amana and Nabisco, and his duties on the Player Advisory Council as well as the Division Board. He spoke out on behalf of the voiceless old touring pros who were struggling financially. "I don't agree with the attitude that says, 'I've got mine and if you didn't get yours, too bad,' " Goalby told *Golf Magazine* in 2001. "The guys who played before were just as talented, just as good, but we didn't have television money and we didn't have really big purses. . . . Even the guy who sweeps the factory floor gets a pension that recognizes the contribution he's made."

In addition to fighting the PGA Tour for retirement funds, he helped create the Grand Champions tour, a series of exhibitions for some graying old gents who played against Hogan and Snead and Palmer. "But let's be realistic," Goalby said, with his typical candor. "A lot of us have names and titles, but we don't have the talent anymore. We can't even impress the amateurs we're paired with at tournaments. And if you can't play, the BS and stories only go so far."

Bob was hardly desperate for the pension or a tournament

paycheck, but some of the old campaigners really needed the money. And boy, are guys like Howie Johnson and Al Besselink grateful. "Bob's the greatest son of a bitch in the world," Bessie says.

Years after he won the Masters, the prime of Bob Goalby finally arrived. Looking back, he believes he did get his million dollars from winning the Masters. "But I was doin' too much," Goalby says. "I was gone too much."

No caddie ever enjoyed a greater celebrity than Crosshanded Henry Brown in April 1975. That was the year Lee Elder became the first black man to play in the Masters, and Mr. Brown was given the honor of carrying his bag and guiding him through the subtle mysteries of Augusta National. An unprecedented crush of media and spectators watched every move Elder made, and they couldn't help but notice the animated man at his side.

But the seat-of-the-pants style that had suited Roberto so well didn't work for this employer. Elder was much more a modern pro in that he wanted precise yardages to the hole from wherever his ball was on the fairway. But Crosshanded Henry Brown couldn't or wouldn't provide them.

"He would tell me which club to use for approaches instead of telling me the yardage and letting me make my own selections," Elder told a writer with *The Washington Post* a few months after the fact. "I'd [always] be fifteen or twenty feet beyond the pin. I could have eliminated the problem by firing him and getting someone else after the first round."

But he didn't. His friends convinced him that doing so just wouldn't look good this historic week. "I'm not trying to use him as an excuse," said Elder, who shot 74–78 and missed the cut, "but it happens to be the truth."

Roberto and Crosshanded Henry Brown teamed up a few more times in the Masters after the '68 tournament, with only one good result, a tie for ninth in '71. But the Bob Goalby/Frank "Marble Eye" Stokes collaboration was never repeated. In one sense, it's no surprise. The self-reliant Goalby didn't expect much from his caddies and wasn't sentimental about them, even when he won. But caddies usually are very protective of the winning bag, especially when they've been well paid.

Instead of carrying the defending champion's sticks in the '69 Masters, however, Marble Eye worked for big Bob Lunn, a policeman's son from Sacramento. "I just wanted to spread my talent," Marble Eye recalls mysteriously and leaves it at that. What he probably doesn't want to say is that he didn't think Goalby could repeat the magic of '68, and with all those kids Frank Stokes had to play the odds. Goalby had played poorly in the spring of '69, while Lunn, who led the tour in sideburns, looked like the next Nicklaus. He was just twenty-four, hit the ball like a kicking mule, and had already won twice, at Memphis and Atlanta. After his success in '68, caddiemaster Freddie Bennett allowed Marble Eye to pick another man if he wanted to.

Lunn was a smart play that didn't work out. He shot 74–75 and missed the cut.

Marble Eye had two more notable experiences at Augusta National. In '76, he looped for another long-hitter, Larry Ziegler, who tied Jack Nicklaus for third. And in 1978, he watched with those big concerned eyes as his man Tsuneyuki "Tommy" Nakajima chopped up the thirteenth with thirteen strokes, an octuple-bogey, the highest score ever taken on that hole in the Masters.

He quit caddying in '82, at age forty-four. Bored with it, really. He'd been helping unload trucks at the shoe store next door to the Garden Hotel, the same store that had sold him his flashy green victory shoes after he won the Masters. When the hotel closed down, the owners of Friedman's Shoes offered a full-time position. He still works there—in shipping and receiving, security, building boxes, whatever. All his kids graduated from high school. He's a round man with round eyes who likes to wear sweat suits and looks way younger than his years. "Man, I can't believe I'm sixty-five," he says.

"What people fail to realize," he says, using his stock phrase, "is that Augusta has ended some people's careers—the White Shark, Ed Sneed. But a scorecard don't have no pictures on it. Just numbers."

There's one last point Frank Stokes would like to make, about the intertwining of destiny and character. You've got to go through this life with dignity and self-respect because "wherever you go, your shadow follows you."

Dear Betty: I am sorry. I love you. Cliff.

Now the chairman of Augusta National was ready to kill himself.

The '77 Masters had been hell for Roberts; he'd had to stay in bed for the entire tournament, just like Bob Jones at his last Masters in '68. And like his hero and partner, he had to endure an illness on his illness. Bob dealt with the stomach flu on top of his more serious disease. Cliff's burdens were age (eighty-three), stroke, and that week in April '77, an unceasing case of the hiccups.

His mother had been a suicide, in 1913, with a shotgun. Eight years later, his father walked in front of a passenger train—purposely, it seemed—headed south from San Benito, Texas, to Brownsville. Both Rebecca Roberts and her husband Charles de Clifford Roberts, Sr., were sick and despairing when they took their lives, and now, in 1977, their oldest son, Cliff, was very ill, too. But his actions were not those of someone crippled by hopelessness; he approached his last days in an ordered and organized way that was nearly businesslike in its efficiency. He sent pictures of himself to close friends a couple of months before his death. The day before he died, he got a haircut and a pair of new light blue pajamas. He had a waiter help him walk to the first tee for one last look. That night he ate one of his favorite dinners, lamb chops.

They found the body on the bank of a pond on the par three course at dawn the next morning, September 30. There was mist rising above the water and a wound to his temple; the .38 pistol lay on the ground by his hand. Precise and thorough even in death, he had slipped a copy of his medical chart into an envelope and put it in a pocket in his new pajamas. On the outside of the envelope, he wrote his succinct suicide memo to his estranged wife, Betty.

In the aftermath, Lawyer J. Richard Ryan recalled something Cliff had said during the Masters of '68. Roberts had just returned from a visit with Jones, who lay ill in his cabin, his limbs withered, his eyes bloodshot. "I will never let that happen to me," he said.

Some find it extremely distasteful that, as his last act, Roberts turned Augusta National into a crime scene. But Jack Stephens, a long-time member who would eventually succeed Cliff as chairman, saw his site selection as "characteristically thoughtful." Not so close to the club buildings that he might bother anyone's sleep with a gunshot but, as David Owen writes in *The Making of the Masters,* "in a well-traveled area where his body would be easy to find."

Cliff had ruled Augusta National and the Masters as thoroughly and effectively as a Mafia don or a nineteenth-century political boss. He got used to the power. The manner of his death

---

and its prelude proved that control meant more to him than just about anything.

With efficiency and command so important to him, the one time he and his organization screwed up so royally and so publicly must have been a torment.

Cliff's good friend on the Masters Rules Committee lived to be 104. Ike Grainger accomplished many things in his life, including the presidency of Chemical Bank, the presidency of the USGA, and membership at Augusta National. He may have been golf's greatest gadabout. It all started when he befriended Bobby Jones when Jones was just sixteen. That was Ike in the big black convertible next to Ben Hogan during the ticker tape parade for the Hawk in New York City in 1953 (at one point in the parade route, Grainger waved up to his fellow employees at the bank). That was him on the cover of *USGA Journal*—twice in 1954. As the organization's ranking rules expert, he was involved in high-profile U.S. Open disputes involving Nelson (in 1946), Snead (in '47), and Hogan (in '50), and, of course, that thing with De Vicenzo at the Masters in '68. The first of these, at Canterbury in Cleveland, in the first U.S. Open after World War II, resembled the Scorecard Masters in several ways.

In those days before gallery ropes, people walked along in the fairway with the golfers. When the crowd was big, the tournament provided marshals who held a piece of rope to keep the crowd back enough for a player to swing. Byron, the third-round leader, hit his second shot on thirteen, a downhill par five, and hundreds of spectators ran ahead to his ball. The marshals wormed their way through this human wall and quickly extended a rope. But they were too close to the ball. Byron's caddie fought his way through, ducked under the rope, took a step—and his toe nudged the ball about a foot. The rule was clear (a one-stroke penalty); Ike Grainger was there, the decision took a long time, the stakes were very high, the tournament administration seemed obviously culpable, and, as with the Masters twenty-two years later, the tournament administration took no responsibility for the error.

They gave Nelson his penalty stroke after he finished his round. At the end, he tied for first with Vic Ghezzi and Lloyd Mangrum. After two eighteen-hole playoffs in the longest U.S. Open ever played, Mangrum won by one over Byron and Vic.

"A few years ago, I had an opportunity to clear my conscience about this in a conversation with Byron Nelson," Grainger told the USGA Oral History project in 1991. "I said to Byron, 'Byron, I'm just distressed that I have to admit to you that Dick Tufts and I made a very bad decision at Canterbury Club in 1946.' He said, 'Yes, I know it. If you had told me what my position was I may have played the remaining holes differently.' " But Nelson was as amiable and sweet as Roberto. He said that he understood that a rule was a rule, without even mentioning that maybe it wasn't all his fault.

"Sportsmanship is a very difficult thing," said Grainger in that same interview. "It's like right and wrong. There are no shadings of right and wrong. If you're wrong, you're wrong. If you're right, you're right."

After Ike's death, J. Stewart Lawson, a former captain of the R and A, recalled in a letter that Grainger had "styled himself a maverick, a definition with which his contemporaries on the USGA would have agreed." But his independence manifested in a puny way, such as his belief that a ball entering a water hazard, which then goes out of bounds, should be treated as a ball in a water hazard and not as a ball out of bounds. Outspokenness on this and similar issues was enough to make Ike seem a regular riverboat gambler to his peers in the golf-administration business.

But had he been a real maverick, he would have done some-thing about golf's ridiculously arcane rules. A genuine maverick might have pushed the idea that the burdens of sportsmanship should fall on rules officials and tournament administrators, not just the players.

The Senior Tour practice tee is as sad and sweet as an old photo album. There's Gary Player taking mighty swings with every club in the bag, even the sand wedge, and bearing down as if each shot has some frantic importance. Here's Doug Sanders using the same abbreviated swing he employed thirty-odd years ago and wearing the same clothes. Literally the same clothes. Billy Maxwell's swing is still a wristy invention, Tommy Bolt's stroke is still pure though now he creaks, and Bob Goalby has that fa-miliar, impatient backswing except that it's shorter than ever. Probably the least-changed and best-looking stroke belongs to Tommy Aaron.

Standing by and in the practice bunker at the 2002 Legends of Golf in Savannah, the seventh-place finisher in the '68 Masters recalls the inspiration for his enviable swing. "When I was thir-teen, [in 1950] I went to a pre-Masters exhibition match in At-lanta," Tommy recalls. He's from Gainesville, Georgia, about fifty miles north of the big city. "It was Jack Burke, Harvie Ward, Frank Stranahan, and Sam Snead. I watched Snead and thought, 'That looks like how it should be done.' That exhibition was re-ally important for me to see."

He's not exactly gabby, but Aaron speaks easily about his old, old days. His father, he says, "did everything imaginable. He played in a dance band, worked in a hosiery mill and on a GM as-sembly line, and sold insurance. The last part of his life, he leased a golf course in Atlanta."

Tommy's life traced a much straighter line. It was strange and a bit difficult being the only kid in a little southern city who was hooked on golf, but that town to the southeast—Augusta—provided a goal. "The Masters was the only tournament I ever knew anything about," Aaron recalls. "There'd be something in the paper about the U.S. Open or the PGA but mostly, it was the Masters.

"Bobby Jones always followed my career. I met him in 1955 when I qualified for the USGA Junior at his club, East Lake. He invited me to come to his office."

Tommy lived his dream in 1959, while still a student at the University of Florida, when he played in his first Masters. He turned pro the next year and, in the ensuing decades, made a good living playing his game. He won two official events on the PGA Tour, but writers don't come out of the woodwork to ask him about his victory in the 1970 Atlanta Classic or how he shot a final-round 68 to beat Nicklaus by two in the Masters in '73. Writers, pro-am partners, and fans always want to ask about Roberto's scorecard. It annoys him.

"Naturally, I felt terrible about it," Aaron says, "but a rule is a rule. And it's a very good rule. When I won in '73, in the third round, Johnny Miller wrote down a five for me on thirteen when I'd actually made a four. *It's no big deal.* You catch mistakes all the time."

As his questioner continues to ask for more and more detail—what did you do after the mistake was discovered? what exactly did you say?—Aaron's speech becomes increasingly italicized: *"I'll say it again.* Roberto was *so* pissed off at making a bogey on eighteen he just signed his card and left.

"When is a card official? It's official when you sign it and leave the scoring area. *I thought you knew that."*

With a frozen smile and a polite goodbye, Aaron turns back to his work in the bunker.

The man to whom Aaron and the others handed their Masters score cards died in 1982, after hitting his tee shot on the par-three fourth at Augusta National. "It was the darnedest thing," says his son, Hiram C. Allen III. "Just ten days before, one of his friends had gone into one of the cabins at the National to take a nap, and he died in front of the fireplace with the TV on. Daddy said, 'That's the way to go and this is the place to do it.' "

Hiram III—"please call me Hikie"—inherited his father's name, his nickname, his alma maters (Georgia Tech and Phi Delta Theta), and his considerable charm. He also followed his father into the textile business; both had long careers with Graniteville, an Augusta-based manufacturer of heavy woven fabric for work clothing, and canvas for such things as tarps and sails.

Golf Digest reported in its 1993 retrospective of the Scorecard Masters that the senior Mr. Allen was devastated by the tragedy and volunteered to resign from the club. "I don't think that's true," says Hikie. "Some people blamed Daddy for that mess but he did what he was supposed to do. He checked the thing and then he made the point that Roberto had turned in an incorrect card. The criticism was that he should have been a USGA man. But you don't have to be in the USGA to take score cards."

In a letter to the *Golf Digest* editor regarding that story in '93, Hikie's son Hikie IV wrote:

> *Mr. Allen did not simply fade out from the Masters scene. He continued to remain active with the scoring committee which began work to improve its procedures. . . . The green tent erected in 1969 provided both privacy and an increased sense of formality for the card signing process. Contrary to your article, the players entering this tent continued to see Mr. Allen's familiar face as he served in the same capacity until shortly before his death in 1982. Hiram C. Allen was my granddaddy, and that green tent was his domain throughout my*

childhood and adolescence. His warm greeting marked the end of each
player's round. . . . It was perhaps a most fitting and divine reward
that death came to him suddenly and quickly during a round of golf on
a bright spring day on this grand old course that he and so many loved
for its many triumphs as well as controversies.

Marvin M. "Vinny" Giles III, the low amateur in the '68 Masters, played in his favorite tournament eight more times. Because he tended to arrive on the scene as early as possible to stretch out his time in golf heaven, he got to know Chairman Roberts reasonably well. "I remember asking him once, 'I'm qualified under four categories for the Masters next year. Can I save three of them?' He says, '*No.*' No, he didn't laugh. There wasn't a lot of levity in Mr. Roberts."

Giles finished law school, won the U.S. Amateur, and—this was unusual—did not turn pro. He was too smart for that. From his regular proximity to touring professionals, he saw just how difficult the constant travel was and how it corroded the home life for not that much money. He started an agency, Pros Inc., to negotiate endorsement deals for golfers including Tom Kite, Davis Love III, and Lanny Wadkins. The very successful company was subsequently acquired by a huge international marketer of professional athletes, Octagon.

The world didn't understand that other really smart man in the '68 Masters, and he didn't understand the world. Bert Yancey, golf's Vincent Van Gogh, didn't want to cut off his ear figuratively, or alienate friends, fans, and family. But he couldn't help it. His disease sometimes made any interaction with another human being feel like torture. Sometimes his faulty brain chemistry exhilarated him, giving him godlike insight and energy. On a few occasions, he suffered complete and completely devastating breaks with reality.

The worst of his disease, the mania, lay dormant for a long time. For years after almost winning the Masters and the U.S. Open in '68, Yancey continued to perform at a high level. He won over $80,000 for three consecutive years beginning in 1969. That was good money back then; his $84,205 in '71 put him twentieth on the money list. For a third and final time, he came close to winning the Masters. In 1970, he finished fourth, two shots behind Billy Casper. But he never won the tournament that obsessed him. The painted Play-Doh greens with plastic straw flagsticks were not enough.

A search for witnesses to Yancey's peaks and valleys during those years yields his regular tour caddie, J. D. Gardner. "Goddamn, he could putt," Gardner recalls. "All I ever told him on the green was 'buckle your knees and stroke it.' When he won in Atlanta in '69 he had 104 putts *for the whole week*. Which was a record." Actually, he set the record in Portland in '66 with 102 putts, but still . . .

They were quite a pair, the pale cerebral golfer and the cheerful black caddie. Sometimes that was an illegal grin on Gardner's face: After Yancey holed the winning putt in the Dallas Open in '67, J.D. ran out onto the green and tore his hat off in celebration. His under hat came off too, a tight, stockinglike do-rag that kept the hair-straightening chemicals on his scalp. Other stuff fell to the earth in the process: several unlabeled cigarettes and a double handful of pills in rainbow colors.

Today Gardner is almost seventy, and beat up. He's had a stroke—"You know, I wasn't always like this," he says, as he struggles with a knife and fork at a barbecue joint in Dallas. J.D. doesn't have enough money or health or teeth, but he's still cogent. "Yancey could laugh, but he was always serious," he says.

"He acted pretty level. But in the big tournaments, at the end, he'd start hittin' it funny.

"When he started acting crazy, it wasn't him."

As his ex-wife recalls, Yancey suffered his first manic attack since West Point in Honolulu, in, she thinks, December 1974. "He was up all night, his mind racing," Linda Makiver says. "From there he went on to Japan. Tracy [their daughter] and I stayed in Hawaii. When he got to Tokyo, he just lost it. He hadn't slept in so long . . . he tried to jump out his window at the Hilton. They took him to the hospital on the U.S. Air Force base in Tokyo and kept him for two or three weeks. Their diagnosis was that he was schizo-paranoid."

More delusions followed, most of them minor, all of them kept private. But after playing in the Westchester Classic in New York in the summer of '75, Bert left reality in the most public of places—an airport. "I had my son with me at Westchester, and Bert hollered at some marshals and acted kinda funny when he made some late bogeys in the fourth round," recalls Don January. "My son says, 'Golly, what went wrong with Mr. Yancey?' That afternoon, flying to Akron for the next tournament, that was the day he went zook-zook."

When they heard that security had detained Yancey when he attempted to get into the control tower at LaGuardia, it was clear to Bert's family and friends that the mania that had been dormant since his senior year at West Point had resurfaced. At Payne Whitney Hospital in New York, he was diagnosed, correctly, with manic-depression, also known as bipolar disorder. The implications were profound.

"As bipolar people have more and more manic episodes, there is actual damage to the DNA and RNA in the brain," says Dr. Ricardo Shack, a psychiatrist. "Picture a fraying rope."

So Yancey's first priority was to stop having manic attacks.

Lithium carbonate worked but its two main side effects could hardly have been worse for a professional golfer: muscle weakness and tremors. Thus the rest of Bert's life became a cat-and-mouse game with his medication and his disease. The stakes were high: The less lithium he took, the better his golf was—and the more likely he was to suffer another psychotic break. Complicating the situation was that lithium can take days or weeks to work, and that if the doses get too high, lithium toxicity can result, which is just as nasty as the disease the drug is intended to prevent.

Another complication compelled Yancey to approach the edge of the cliff: hypomania. Hypomania is the exhilarating mood just this side of madness, where the wittiest conversation lives and the best thinking and the greatest books and the most energy and the deepest truth. Ray Charles and Ernest Hemingway were bipolars who took advantage of the productive states preceding a mental crash. Ditto Robert Lowell, the manic-depressive American poet. To Charles Baudelaire, another poet, the ups and downs of his mental illness felt like "the wind of the wing of madness."

"When manic-depressives start to get the slightest bit high, that's the time to adjust the medication," says Yancey's ex-wife Linda [they divorced in 1977]. "But they don't want to because they're feeling so good."

Yancey returned to the tour in 1976, but his game had gone south: He missed cut after cut. "So he'd lower his dosage and play," his oldest son, Charles, told Bill Fields of *Golf World* in 2001. "And then he'd get a little high. Once he got a little high, he thought he didn't need to take it anymore and pretty soon he's back in the hospital. Then he'd have to receive higher doses to get him back to normal. Going on and off the medication, having to get the higher doses, can't be good. I think he killed himself over golf, really."

Bert often spoke to groups around the country to raise consciousness about and attempt to destigmatize his disease. Linda appreciates the irony: While telling these audiences that manic-depressive illness could be controlled with medication, he himself often ignored or finessed his doctor's orders.

He took club-pro jobs but, with his lithium-flattened personality, he couldn't be the upbeat guy in the shop that most golfers want. He gave lessons, he studied golf history, he hit thousands of balls, he solved calculus problems and he read medical texts for fun. A few more strands of the rope frayed. He turned fifty in 1988 and joined the Senior PGA Tour. He won fifty-one thousand dollars in 1991, but he had to play in thirty-one tournaments to do it. Deduct taxes and travel costs and he was just treading water.

Yancey collapsed on the practice tee before a Senior event at Park City, Utah, in 1994. Tom Weiskopf, his best friend, heard him hit the ground. Heart attack. A helicopter clattered down to fly him to the hospital, but it was too late. "I have to play," were Bert Yancey's last words.

CHAPTER TEN

NO QUIERO LA COPA

Time heals what reason cannot.

—SENECA

The two men who suffered the most in the infamous Masters miscount could eventually joke about it, if someone else wrote their lines. In 2000, De Vicenzo and Goalby made a commercial on behalf of Cobra, the golf equipment manufacturer. "It's unbelievable, Roberto," Bob says to start the thirty-second comedy. "You make one little scoring error and you never hear the end of it."

"This happen thirty-three years ago, Bob," Roberto replies. They're apparently standing on a first tee somewhere.

"Actually, it was thirty-two years ago, Roberto. But we've forgotten about it, right?"

"Right. I seventy-six year, I don't care anymore, Bob."

"But you're seventy-seven, Roberto."

"Ah, you right. Who care for this '69 Masters?"

"'Sixty-eight Masters." Goalby takes a Cobra club out of a bag. "OK, Roberto, let's settle this once and for all."

In the next frame, it appears that they've played their match;

we see a golf cart, with Goalby driving, rolling down a sunlit fairway. "Looks like we tied again," Goalby says.

Roberto: Let me check the scorecard.

Bob: It's correct.

Roberto: That's what they said the last time.

Roberto never really had a problem with numbers and Bob doesn't correct everyone's mistakes. But for a laugh and a paycheck, both men were willing to play to type. At last the scorecard incident had become worthy of satire. But as visits to Buenos Aires and Belleville revealed, neither man has forgotten any of it. Remembered pain is still pain. . . .

Cavallini takes a call on his cell as he drives south through the city toward Roberto's house. "Sí," Roberto's friend says. "Sí. Sí." The car stops at a light. A boy of about eight *años* stands between cars and juggles three scarred rubber balls, while an older man—perhaps his father—goes from car to car attempting to sell multicolored CD cases. With a sigh, Cavallini disconnects from his phone. He's just learned that a man who owes him eighty-five thousand dollars has moved to Spain. "I am not passing through my finest moments," the gray-haired former banker says.

The car moves slowly through Buenos Aires's odd mixture of classic architecture and hideous poured-concrete apartment buildings. A slim man in a tan suit and dark sunglasses sits motionless at a shady sidewalk café, the same man who'd sat like a mannequin at this same café all the previous morning. The street vendors seem dazed; no one is buying. Only the Popsicle man yells: "*Helado. Helado. Helado.*" *Aspartame Si Puedes—Catch Me If You Can*—is playing at the big movie theater on Avenida Nueve de Julio. At the Paseo La Plaza, it's the Broadway hit *Monologos de la Vagina*. It's the spring of 2003.

"Roberto has lived here fifty-five years," comments Cavallini an hour later, as his party reaches the outskirts of Ranelagh. Boys and men on bicycles crowd the street, and women pushing baby carriages, hungry-looking dogs, and walkers carrying plastic bags. "It's much better north of Buenos Aires. This is not exactly Beverly Hills. More like Beverly Downs."

The houses become bigger and the lawns greener and more expansive as the car approaches Ranelagh Golf Club. As Cavallini pulls in, he notices that Roberto's little black Audi is already in the lot in a corner under a tree. It's 11:00 A.M. and golf is scheduled for two o'clock. There's just enough time for lunch.

A week before, Roberto's presence in one of the public spaces at the Four Seasons Hotel in Buenos Aires caused employees and guests to mill around and whisper behind their hands—that's Roberto! I wonder what he's doing here? A few approached for autographs or to say I watched you win the Norpatagonico in '79. Like his North American counterpart, Arnold Palmer, he has remained patient over the years, even welcoming, with strangers who want to touch their hero. Afterward, he retreated to a guest room, where he sat in an upholstered chair and told amusing stories—about the on-course fistfight between Jerry Barber and Charlie Sifford, and the time Barber and J. C. Snead, who felt like murdering each other, used the third member of their threesome to communicate. "Tell the tall bastard he's away," Barber said to Roberto. "Tell the short son of a bitch to move his coin," said Snead.

"The biggest prize I ever won was in the second Hall of Fame tournament," De Vicenzo said. "My partner was Julie Inkster. She do everything. You know what I do? I get the ball out of the hole and say, 'Good shot.' "

He also told about the funny thing that happened the day he taped his commercial for Cobra with Goalby. He'd gone to the restaurant at the golf course for lunch and, finding it deserted, he took a seat at the bar. A customer was telling the bartender how well he'd played the day before. The customer, noticing Roberto, asked if he was a golfer.

"A pro," Roberto said. The man looked skeptical. "De Vicenzo. I won the British Open."

The man looked even more dubious and said, "Sorry, I've never heard of you."

De Vicenzo took off a ring that commemorated his win in some big tournament. No reaction from the man at the bar. Roberto put the ring back on and said, "I am the guy, the stupid guy, who signed the wrong card at the Masters."

"Oh!" the man said. "*Roberto!*"

The point of this story, Roberto explained, was that it had all worked out for him. He got far more recognition than if he'd won and earned far more money. "When I sign scorecard wrong, I cried," he said. "Later on, I have a nice feeling to do this mistake. So many good honors come my way in U.S., South America, England. If I no sign the scorecard wrong, I'd never be an honorary member at Saint Andrews. A green jacket, you can buy."

De Vicenzo is completely at ease at his club. Certain routines are in place: He sits at his regular table in his usual chair at the usual time. At noon, two liters of Quilmes Cristal Cerveza appear on his table—brewed in Argentina since 1890, according to the label—and plates of bread and butter. The conversation bounces everywhere and lands for a time on golfers who thank Jesus after winning. "They say '*Gracias a Dios*' and then they don't tip the caddie," Roberto says. "When you miss a putt like this"— he holds his hands two feet apart—"it doesn't matter how much religion you have."

He sips and looks out the window for a moment at the lush golf course. "Reality is what you do, not what you think," he says. "I could have been a philosopher."

After days spent with his guest at the golf course and the

house where he grew up, at the Argentina Golf Association museum, eating steak for lunch a couple of times, at his home, and now at his home course, De Vicenzo is ready to give his deepest thought on the story of April 15, 1968.

"I think Goalby makes a mistake in the presentation," he says. "Goalby says, 'I'm sorry for Roberto, but a rule is a rule.' If you put one hundred people in that position, one hundred would say the same thing. Goalby was *inteligente, pero no fue astuto*"—intelligent but not astute.

"You can't make a circus out of this, especially at Augusta. He can't refuse the tournament but what if he says"—and here, Roberto throws his car keys onto the center of the table—" '*No quiero la copa. Quiero jugar mañana.*' Only one in a million would do this. The committee would not have accepted. But everything would have gone better for him if he had said this."

I don't want the cup. I want to play tomorrow.

After lunch, you play nine holes with Roberto, Cavallini, and Roberto's student, an athletic young woman named Melissa Papucelli. You listen to his homespun wisdom—"He who thinks on the backswing makes himself harm. He who thinks about the follow-through, helps himself." You watch his sweet five-iron shot to the par-three sixth, see the birdie that results from it, and observe him casually hand ten-peso notes to two young spectators on the seventh tee. You notice that his picture is on the scorecard.

But what you think about is the thing that Goalby didn't say. How different things might have been if he had.

Cobra's ad agency produced six humorous TV commercials in 2000, including the spoof with Bob and Roberto. In another one, known internally as "Magnets," Goalby portrayed the only sane man in a locker room full of wackos. "When you've been playing golf as long as we have," Bob says, "you know it can be a really physical game. Right, Tom?" He walks past Tommy Bolt, who is about to eat a large mushroom and drink a bubbling witches brew. Goalby walks through the room, greeting George Bayer, Jack Fleck, and Doug Sanders, each of whom is going to great lengths to get a competitive edge. Sanders sits with his eyes closed, a pyramid of golf balls balanced on a board on his head. Fleck wears a big magnet on his back, on which are stuck a variety of iron and steel items, including knives, forks, and his car keys. Goalby leans into the camera with a knowing smile and says, "Magnets are big."

Only golf insiders of a certain age would have appreciated that, in the commercial, Goalby was doing what he'd always done. When the touring professionals declared their independence from the PGA of America in '68, Bob was the John Adams of the revolution. Again he was a pragmatic leader in the formation of the Senior PGA Tour and did the nuts-and-bolts work a third time in the establishment of a for-pay golf league called the Super Seniors, a group of remember-when guys like Doug Ford and Bolt and Al Besselink. Bob's skill at simplifying complex problems and his willingness to do the behind-the-scenes dirty work endeared him to his peers. He was their quarterback and their mechanic.

After a tournament or a round of fighting the good fight for his brother pros, Goalby always returned to Belleville. His love for his home town took a new shape in 1977, when he and Sarah bought a red-brick Civil War–era house on forty acres. "He liked it because he could hit a driver in the front yard," says Sarah, but it had to be more than that. Here was a house with roots in the land as deep as his own—although this is a spiritual thought he would never express and might not ac-knowledge. But the fact that the place also looked like a driving range waiting to happen was an appeal he talked about easily. They could put up some lights and build a tee and a little pro shop and Bob and sons Ky, Kel, and Kevin could work together right in their own backyard, the good life of a nineteenth-century flatland farm family. Sure, the house had some little problems. Of its fourteen rooms, none was a bathroom. No electrical wiring. No furnace. No air-conditioning. And no closets. In 1864, when the big brick box was built, they hung their clothes on hooks.

It would have been cheaper to push the thing over and build a new house, but the Goalbys persisted. They built bathrooms and Bob had urinals installed in each one, an avant-garde touch that Sarah didn't care for. They saved a bit on heating and cooling be-cause Bob was working for Amana then and got a good deal on three big units. But the house and driving-range project didn't go exactly as planned. The range was open to the public only for about three summers, after which it turned into a strictly private practice facility for friends and family. Bob was traveling heav-ily in the eighties for NBC, Nabisco, Amana, and the Senior PGA Tour; on one of these trips, Sarah had the telephone-pole-mounted range lights taken down. She thought they looked tacky. On another occasion, when her husband was out of town, she had a plumber remove a couple of the urinals. Made the place look like a locker room, she said.

After his TV deal ended in '89—there was a dispute over money—Goalby made a sad discovery. "I found out after I quit that it wasn't just me that made me in demand for speeches; it was the fact that I was on TV," he says. "I was busy as hell with other things—you follow me?—but if I had to do it over, I defi-nitely would have stayed [with NBC]."

In the fall of 2002, the old pro picks up a visitor at the St. Louis airport in his white Lincoln Town Car, a vehicle that, with ninety-six thousand miles on it, was a few years from the showroom yet seemed almost new. He works on it himself, of course. Goalby's own mileage is showing at the moment; his face is slightly swollen and he looks as if he's grimacing. But it isn't age. A few months earlier, while he was watching workmen swing sledgehammers on a patio he wanted to remove and rebuild, a random chip of concrete flew through the air and lodged itself in his right eye. The trauma and the acids in the concrete caused him to go blind in that eye, damn near, and necessitated five painful surgeries. He will eventually get most of his vision back with the help of a special contact lens, but his depth perception will never be the same. The bad eye changed him from a crack shot to a mediocre one, and he has to guard against hitting the golf ball fat.

From the airport, Goalby drives through East St. Louis, a hellhole with plywood on its windows and graffiti on the plywood. He expresses his complete disdain for those who won't take care of their own dwellings, and fears that these same don't-give-a-shit people on the banks of the Mississippi are doing what we're doing, which is going east, into Belleville.

Half an hour later he's pointing out some of the landmarks in his old neighborhood: the house where he grew up on South Seventy-seventh; the path through the trees to the golf course, a path he walked a thousand times about an hour before dark; and the coal mine.

Goalby goes in the front door of St. Clair Country Club these days, and his trophies are in a display case in the lobby of the clubhouse. From the waves and greetings from the members and the staff, it's plain that he isn't merely one of the guys at his club, he's The Guy. A plaque on the first tee states that this is the home course of the 1968 Masters champion. Bob at St. Clair looks a lot like Roberto at Ranelagh. They're two ex-caddies who brought glory to the clubs they served for modest wages so long ago. Now they're lions in winter, enjoying the view from the men's grille.

Because of the eye injury, he's not playing today, so after driving around the course in a cart he heads home. His magnificent house and grounds look like the place Abe Lincoln might have retired to if he'd made it back to Illinois. During a tour of the restored mansion, you notice that the urinals are back up. "There was no one reason we got divorced," Sarah Goalby says of their split in 1998. "Bob didn't drink too much or gamble or hit me, none of those things people get divorced over." But there was this one important issue: With the kids grown up, Sarah wanted to finally get out of Belleville and retire to someplace warm like Scottsdale or Palm Springs or South Carolina. But Bob simply loves his home town too much to leave.

"Know why the steaks are so good here?" Goalby asks. We're in a little restaurant in a little town on a crisp fall night that makes you think about high-school football, playing it or watching it. "It's because they come from the meat-packing plant right down the street."

Several men at the bar recognize the champ. In a scene from one of John Updike's Rabbit novels, one of them comes over to Goalby's table and shakes his hand. "I played ball for Collinsville," the man says. "Do you remember that pass you threw that beat us in the district game? That was a great pass." Bob says he remembers. "Okay, great, thanks for stopping by," Goalby says.

Over a man's meal of steak, baked potato, and Canadian whiskey, Goalby tells stories about the glory days and the glory guys. Snead, whom he loved. Byron Nelson, whom he disliked—a lot—for being the opposite of Snead. Hogan, whom he revered. Doug Ford, the best competitor he ever saw. His reflexive honesty compels him to say, no, he didn't much care for Weiskopf or Jacklin or Yancey. The younger guys didn't measure up to Sam and Ben, not by a long shot.

"The right decision was made, and it was good for golf, too," Goalby says without preamble of the event that gave him so much pride and pain. "It might have been different if they didn't go to Jones. For my sake, I'm glad he was there. It was funny how Roberto got to be a hero over it, almost. He played that 'poor me' role to the hilt for the rest of his life. And the press didn't understand what happened.

"I was kinda crucified for a long time. It wasn't very pleasant, let's say. Sometimes it was hard not to fire back.

"But I have the title and I have the jacket. I don't have an ax to grind."

The college boys who sat with Bobby Jones frequently had a party on Friday night, which always meant live music. The musicians invariably played Beach Music—the Tams and the Drifters—as well as Motown. The brothers of Sigma Chi were particularly fond of a rollicking song by the Swingin' Medallions called "Double Shot of My Baby's Love," partly because it was the signature tune of a band they often hired called The Medallions. Jimmy, the lead singer, was a member of the fraternity, and his band came cheap.

The girls were ADPs from Emory and AOPs from Georgia State. As the evening grew late, the Medallions—or whoever—would play slow songs from The Temptations or Marvin Gaye, something that gave you an excuse to hold your date in your arms. It was good to be young and a Sigma Chi brother in the spring of '68, when you had a little beer in your bloodstream and a whiff of perfume in your nose.

"Those parties made it hard to get someone to work on Friday nights," recalls John Lambert, one of the four or five student/athlete/fraternity men who sat with Mr. Jones every evening. "But then they hired Lilly as their live-in nurse. She was from Sweden, I think, and drop-dead gorgeous. And then we were fighting to go there."

Lilly lasted only a year with the Joneses, but Lambert endured. It took him a while to loosen up with the dying legend but, after a few weeks, he could talk easily about all the vitally unimportant news from the campus: how his classes were going, what the football team looked like, how the basketball team might do in the Atlantic Coast Conference. Jones gave John the fruit-and-nut basket that Bob and Dolores Hope always sent at Christmas. When he got something interesting in the mail, like a note from Richard Nixon or a get-well letter from a little girl addressed simply "Bobby Jones, Atlanta, GA," he shared it with Lambert. After their chat, John flipped on the TV. Mr. Jones would watch while sipping from the straws connected to the cups of water and bourbon.

On a Friday evening in the spring of '69, Lambert watched Jones's face light up when Pat Summerall wished him well in a televised Masters preview show. Insiders like the people at CBS knew that Bobby had attended the tournament for the last time. In fact, he'd attended everything for the last time. He wasn't strong enough to go to the doctor—his physicians came to him. His body had sunk and shrunk until it looked like a reliquary for his own bones.

Lambert recalls what may have been the last time Jones

left the house: "For the Homecoming game against Navy in '69, we came up with a particularly good entry in the Rambling Wreck contest. We [Sigma Chi] built a battleship that got tipped over by a moving torpedo. And there were bells and flashing lights and moving buoys. I told him about it. 'Could I come out and see this?' Mr. Jones said. 'I've got to go down to Tech one more time.' As weak as he was I knew it would take a Herculean effort.

"On the Saturday morning of the game, we saw this big blue Cadillac come slowly by. I got the guys who'd worked on the battleship to come out and meet him. He just grinned. Later, he told me over and over how much he enjoyed it."

Jones didn't leave his bed for the last four months of his life, Lambert says. Jones's biographer Dick Miller writes that it was the last eight months—but Mary Jones and Dr. Ralph Murphy asked the college boys to continue their visits. Dr. Murphy believed the contact had helped his patient live longer and more happily so Lambert continued to sit with the old man. He'd open up a *Reader's Digest* from time to time and ask Jones the quiz questions or the spelling words. "One I remember was 'name the three Shakespeare plays in which the two main characters are also the title,'" Lambert says. "The first two are easy—*Antony and Cleopatra* and *Romeo and Juliet*. No one ever gets the third—*Troilus and Cressida*—but Mr. Jones did. His mind stayed sharp right to the end."

Lambert was the last of the college kids to visit Jones. Mary Jones met him at the door that day in early December 1971 and asked John not to go to her husband's room. He doesn't want you to see him now, she said. You and the other boys should just remember him as he was. As usual, she pressed a five-dollar bill into the young man's hand as he left. "Mr. Jones is very weak," Mary said. "The end is near."

He died about two weeks later. He'd had a miserably long time to contemplate his own mortality and to review the peaks and valleys of his life. What did he think about at the end? If we know anything about Bobby Jones, we know that he was extraordinarily strict with himself. This is why he wasn't just polite, he was the perfect gentleman. He didn't just obey the Rules of Golf, he respected them "even beyond the letter," as he wrote in 1930. He couldn't just play golf. If golf was a thing worth doing, and it was, he'd do it better than anyone. He won the Grand Slam in 1930 and then retired, a burnout at age twenty-eight. He split a few infinitives in the half-million words he wrote for publication, but overall he was an excellent writer. He also cofounded the greatest-ever combination of golf course and golf tournament.

What occupied his mind as he lay dying? Religion, for one thing: To placate his wife, he converted to Roman Catholicism eight days before the end. "If I'd known how happy this would make Mary," he said over a postconversion drink with Monsignor McDonaugh, "I would have done it years ago."

If he reviewed his life, his knee-jerk humility would have focused his thoughts on the times he'd fallen short of perfection. He'd showed a blood-curdling temper for a while, which was regrettable, but forgivable, because he was only a teenager when he threw some clubs and broke others. Maybe he could have been a better parent. "Jones was a distant father," wrote Dick Miller in *Triumphant Journey.* "He had no great love for children. . . . Until they were almost teenagers, all the Jones children were raised by maids."

But Lambert never observed a depressed or even pensive man on his visits to the Jones home. *"Every single time* I saw him in those few years, he got this big grin on his face," recalls Lambert. "He was never sad, never moody, which is almost strange, because even healthy people have their moods. He accepted his disease and was happy until the end."

If Jones brooded in his final days—about the life he lost to syringomyelia or about the lost Masters of '68—no one noticed. "If this is all there is to it," he said three days before he died, on December 18, "it sure is peaceful."

Bobby Jones died with his secret thoughts secret.

ACKNOWLEDGMENTS

Special thanks to Roberto De Vicenzo and Bob Goalby

And to Judith Curr, publisher; Jim Cruise, editor; Jim Donovan, agent; and Tracy Behar and Wendy Walker

Also:

Atlanta: Charles Harrison, Robert T. Jones IV, Frank "Marble Eye" Stokes, Terry and Jan Stotts, Bruce Teilhaber

Argentina: Mariana Gonzalez Avalis and Claudia Mozzucco of Asociacion Argentina de Golf, Raul Cavallini, Eduardo "Achy" De Vicenzo, Soledad Gutierrez, Olivier Masson

Arizona: Sarah Goalby

Augusta: Danny and Nicole Fitzgerald, Macky Mulherin, Mike Rucker, Nick Skrine, Kathy Starrett, Sam Tyson, Colonel Tim Wright

Connecticut: Bill Fields, Guy Yocom

Golfers: Butch Baird, Al Balding, Miller Barber, Gay Brewer, Billy Casper, Bruce Devlin, Doug Ford, Vinnie Giles, Harold Henning, Don January, John Mahaffey, Ted Maude, Bob Rosburg

Illinois: Kevin Goalby

Los Angeles: Nonie Lann

Medical: Dr. Chris Gancarz, Howard E. "Butch" Morrette, Dr. Ricardo Shack

New Jersey: Arthur K. "Red" Hoffman

North Carolina: Carl Jackson, Ben Wright

Ohio: Kathy Dickerson, John Lambert, Bob and Ann Sampson

Oregon: Vern Tietjen

Philadelphia: Bill Earley, Bill Yancey

PGA Tour: Ward Clayton, Nelson Silverio

Readers: David Eger, John Strawn

Research: Jan Dowling

Texas: John and Clay Sampson, Mike Stafford

Uruguay: Soraya Barretta, Sebastian Isaza, Florencia Saliva, Randall and Pamela Thompson

USGA: Rand Jerris, Patty Moran

INDEX